Management Accounting

C000039179

Management Accounting

A spreadsheet approach

Neil Marriott and Roy Chandler
Cardiff Business School

PRENTICE HALL
New York • London • Toronto • Sydney • Tokyo • Singapore

First published 1993 by
Prentice Hall International (UK) Ltd
Campus 400, Maylands Avenue
Hemel Hempstead
Hertfordshire, HP2 7EZ
A division of
Simon & Schuster International Group

© Prentice Hall International (UK) Ltd, 1993

All rights reserved. No part of this publication may be
reproduced, stored in a retrieval system, or transmitted,
in any form, or by any means, electronic, mechanical,
photocopying, recording or otherwise, without the prior
permission, in writing, from the publisher.
For permission within the United States of America
contact Prentice Hall Inc., Englewood Cliffs, NJ 07632

Typeset in 10½/12 pt Times
by MHL Typesetting Ltd, Coventry

Printed in Great Britain by Redwood Books,
Trowbridge, Wiltshire

Library of Congress Cataloging-in-Publication Data

Marriott, Neil
    Management accounting : a spreadsheet approach / Neil Mariott and
Roy Chandler
        p.   cm.
    Includes index.
    ISBN 0-13-555152-8
    1. Managerial accounting — Data processing. 2. Electronic
spreadsheets. I. Chandler, Roy. II. Title.
HF5657.4.M37   1993
685.15'11'0285536--dc20   92-40486
                                                                        CIP

British Library Cataloguing in Publication Data

A catalogue record for this book is available
from the British Library

ISBN 0-13-555152-8 (pbk)

1 2 3 4 5   97 96 95 94 93

To Pru, Terryl, Hannah and Steven

Contents

Preface

The impact of information technology in the business world can be best described as revolutionary, with even the smallest firm now using the microcomputer for collecting and processing data. The information needs of some businesses may require custom-made computer systems to be purchased or developed. However, there are off-the-shelf packages which can be adapted to suit many needs.

The most commonly used is the spreadsheet package, which is both versatile and flexible. Its ability to reflect complex financial and other relationships makes it ideal for many business applications.

A companion text, *Financial Accounting: A spreadsheet approach*, by N. Marriott and J. Simon (Prentice Hall), develops an approach which uses the spreadsheet for dealing with bookkeeping and financial accounting problems.

Our primary aim in this text is to illustrate a spreadsheet modelling approach to *management* accounting. The level of the text and illustrations make it suitable for further education courses in specialist accounting degree (or similar) schemes, which increasingly call for integration of computer skills. However, the text may be used as a conventional introduction to management accounting since manually worked examples of typical problems are presented.

We also believe that the principles behind our approach may win converts among those who are already competent in both management accounting and spreadsheet use. Recent research has shown that many spreadsheet users are doing little more than constructing *ad hoc* solutions to daily problems. Few practitioners appear to be making the most of the full extent of the spreadsheet's capabilities and versatility.

The problem for both the novice and the time-constrained practitioner lies in discovering which of the many spreadsheet functions are most relevant to the solution of typical financial problems. The lengthy user manual which accompanies the typical spreadsheet package describes the entire range of its capabilities and is not specifically tailored to business applications.

We highlight those spreadsheet capabilities which are most relevant for business applications and demonstrate how to make the most of the flexibility of the spreadsheet. We repeatedly emphasize the advantage of the modelling approach. The ease with which our spreadsheet models can be adapted to solve different problems may appear rather too convenient. However, the principles of model construction, even at this introductory level, are equally applicable to more advanced situations.

We have organized the book to accommodate the needs of different readers. The main sections are as follows. Part I is a general introduction to the role and function of management accounting. Part II is concerned with basic computer and spreadsheet skills and provides an introduction to the concept of modelling. Part III deals with various aspects of costing. Part IV looks at different types of information essential for management control. Part V deals with the provision of information for decision-making purposes. For newcomers to the topics of management accounting and spreadsheets the whole text is relevant. Readers with some knowledge of management accounting should read first read Part II but may wish to pass over the manually worked examples in Chapters 5—14 and to turn straight to the sections headed 'The spreadsheet solution'.

Chapters begin with a summary of objectives in the development of both management accounting and spreadsheet skills. Where we have thought it valuable, we have included 'what if?' examples which require manipulation of either the input values or the structure of the model itself. Solutions to these examples are given in the text. Chapters 5—14 end with a few traditional questions, which should be attempted using the approach outlined in the text. A selection of answers are given in spreadsheet model format at the end of the text.

It has been suggested in academic circles that an 'algorithmic' approach is required to provide a better insight into the logic of computer processing. Such an approach involves development of logical mathematical relationships to solve accounting problems. Advocates of this approach claim that this is necessary in order better to use the capabilities of the computer. We considered adopting this approach throughout the text but decided against it since we feared that the large number of algebraic notations would tend to alienate more readers than it would attract. However, we recognize that there is much merit in the suggestion and in Chapter 12 we demonstrate how the approach could be applied to the cost—volume—profit relationship.

We also toyed with the idea adopted by some similar texts of including a disk with the text which would contain the ready-constructed spreadsheet models. For the reader these 'templates' are convenient and time-saving but we question the amount of expertise that may be gained merely from manipulation of figures in a pre-prepared model.

We think that more knowledge of both spreadsheets and management accounting is gained by readers constructing their own models. We have therefore gone to some lengths to describe the construction of each model as well as providing the sections of each spreadsheet (where necessary) in both numerical and formula format. We should caution the reader against slavishly following the exact cell references in an attempt to produce a perfect replica of our models. We have introduced certain spreadsheet labels such as headings and instructions for the purpose only of improving the appearance of spreadsheet solutions in the text.

Nevertheless, teachers adopting the text may wish to use the exact models for teaching purposes and a disk is available in Lotus 1—2—3 or Supercalc format. In addition, a teacher's manual is available which gives advice on using the modelling approach in the classroom environment and solutions to those end-of-chapter questions not answered in the text.

January 1993   NM & RC

Acknowledgements

We would like to record our thanks to the Association of Accounting Technicians, the Chartered Association of Certified Accountants, the Chartered Institute of Bankers and the Institute of Chartered Secretaries and Administrators, for their kind permission to reproduce questions from past examination papers. We are also indebted to some anonymous reviewers for their helpful comments on early drafts of the text and to Cathy Peck, the publisher, for her encouragement and support. Ultimately, however, we bear sole responsibility for any errors and omissions in the text.

Part I

Introduction

1 | The role and functions of management accounting

- to describe the purpose of accounting in its broadest sense within the information process;
- to explain the role and functions of management accounting within an organization;
- to compare and contrast management and financial accounting;
- to introduce the role of computers in accounting.

Introduction

There are many different types of organization involved in commmercial activities. These include public limited companies, private limited companies, partnerships and sole traders. Other organizations conduct economic transactions, though not with the aim of making a profit; examples of this second group include charities, trade unions, government and quasi-government bodies.

We will be concerned principally with organizations whose primary objective is to make a profit. In our examples and discussions we refer mainly to the form of organization known as a limited company. However, many of the principles discussed in the following pages could be applied to other forms of organization.

Whatever their nature, all organizations need to be managed and directed if they are to achieve the aims for which they were constituted. It would be impossible for management to control any organization without regular, detailed information. Accounting forms a vital part of the information process in any well-ordered organization.

Accounting can be said to involve:

- the collection and measurement of data, generally of a financial nature;
- the production of information by summarizing the mass of original data;
- the presentation of information in such a way that it is both adequate and meaningful, bearing in mind the needs of those entitled to receive the information.

The management of the organization is but one group with an interest in such information. Other parties with an interest in receiving information about a limited company include:

■ shareholders: the owners of the company;

■ creditors: those who provide the company with goods and services on credit;

■ lenders: those who provide the company with finance;

■ government departments: which are concerned with the regulation of an industry and levying taxes.

To meet the need for public accountability, it has become accepted that most organizations owe a duty to report publicly on their financial progress and financial position.

Employees, too, have a right to financial information concerning their employer. This may be needed to assist wage negotiations, profit-related bonus calculations or simply to assess the financial stability of the organization. With the recent trend in management buy-outs, privatizations and tax breaks, employees are now more likely also to have an ownership interest in their organization.

Financial versus management accounting

Financial accounting is the term used to refer to the reporting of information by the organization to outside interested parties, as described above. Typically this takes the form of financial statements prepared on an annual basis. For limited companies, the measurement, disclosure and presentation of financial information in the annual report are largely prescribed by legislation. Companies quoted on the International Stock Exchange in London have to comply with additional disclosure regulations as well as to provide summarized interim statements half-way through their financial year.

The purpose of management accounting is to provide the management of an organization with information to enable it to exercise control over its activities and to make decisions regarding its future direction.

These two aspects of accounting can be further distinguished as follows:

1. Frequency: management requires information on a much more frequent basis than others outside the organization.

2. Detail: the level of detail of the information prepared for management purposes is much greater than that used in the summarized financial statements presented to outsiders.

3. Non-standard format: while the format and measurement rules used in financial accounting are largely prescribed by statute, stock exchange requirements and accounting standards, the way in which management accounts are prepared and presented is left entirely to management.

4. Future orientation: financial accounts are mainly concerned with reporting the effects of past transactions and events; management accounting is as much concerned with looking to the future as to the past.

Despite these differences there is common ground between the two disciplines: both are concerned with converting raw financial data into useful information, relevant to the needs of users. In practice, it would be unusual for the management accounting and financial accounting functions to be completely separate. They would both have a concern that the initial capture of the raw data — the details of each and every transaction made by the company — should be complete. Thus in large companies there may be a common (computerized) data collection system which is accessible by both teams of management and financial accountants. The processes which are applied to the data, once captured, and the uses made of the resulting information, may be completely different but they have the same starting point.

The information process

The provision of information requires a complete process which may be presented diagrammatically as in Figure 1.1. We will not be concerned with the more mundane aspect of data capture or collection. The systems used in large companies which are involved in thousands of transactions every day, could not function without the support of massive computer facilities. These are worthy of independent study in themselves, but we will not concern ourselves with them here. We will simply assume that a good system exists to ensure completeness of the capture of all relevant data. This is not to denigrate the importance of the first stage of information production since unless some form of quality control is established at this stage no amount of subsequent manipulation can produce high-quality information. This is summed up in a typical piece of computer jargon: garbage in, garbage out.

The next stage of the process is concerned with the condensing of all the data after collection and validation. This will enable the company personnel to perform vital checks and controls, to update its accounting records, and the company itself to do business.

For example, a large manufacturing company will receive many purchase invoices from its suppliers each day. These will relate to the delivery of many different types of goods and services, materials used in the production process or stationery for the

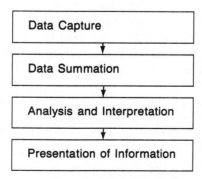

Figure 1.1 The process of information provision

general office, the servicing of transport vehicles or insurance of the premises. The invoices must be recorded and entered into the appropriate accounting records of the company. Different types of expenditure must be separated into different expense categories: it is useless for either management accounting or financial accounting purposes simply to be able to produce a total for the expenses incurred.

Before being processed for payment, the company must check that orders for the goods and services for which it is being charged were properly made by an authorized person and that the company did actually receive the benefit of the goods or services. Once these checks and controls have been carried out payment of the invoices may be authorized. If suppliers do not receive prompt payment they may choose to withhold further supplies, without which further production may be impossible.

Summarizing the raw financial data is an important part of the accounting process. Management cannot handle a mass of data. Summaries reduce the raw data to manageable proportions.

At this stage of the process, the management accountant or financial accountant may begin to see trends appearing which call for some initial enquiry: for example, expenditure in one department may appear significantly out of line with previous experience or expected levels. Enquiry at this stage may determine whether errors have been made at the stage of either data collection or data summary. On the other hand, there may be perfectly valid reasons for the particular trend. Whatever the cause, it is important that some explanation is found. The management accountant who does no more than deliver figures to a higher level with no knowledge of what the figures mean will not enjoy a lengthy employment.

The final stage is the presentation of the information, together with explanations to support the figures, to those who are entitled to receive it. In the case of the management accountant's information it will be to those in positions of authority within the organization. In this context, authority means the power to take some action or exercise some control over the activities within the company.

The use of computers and spreadsheets

Spreadsheets are now widely used in many aspects of accounting: in audit work for preparing working papers and in consultancy for financial modelling. Other typical applications are the preparation of projected cash flows, the consolidation of group financial statements and financial analysis of accounting numbers. In fact, any task in which a large number of calculations are routinely performed would lend itself to a spreadsheet application.

It is perhaps in management accounting that the power and versatility of the spreadsheet yield most benefits. Beyond routine record-keeping, management accounting is really a way of modelling the behaviour of the firm. Typical applications in management accounting include:

- initial budget preparation and updating;
- regular profit reporting;

- stock valuations;
- analysis for management decision-making;
- capital investment appraisal;
- detailed costing of products and services.

Conclusion

We have described in outline the nature of management accounting and the role that it plays in assisting the control of organizations. The use of computers and spreadsheets in particular is now a vital part of the provision of information for management needs.

In Part II we provide an introduction to computers, spreadsheet software and the concept of modelling. This section is essential reading for those not already familiar with personal computer technology.

In Parts III—V we describe a modelling approach to many of the typical management accounting applications. The scenarios we cover are necessarily rather simplistic, consistent with an introductory text. We would not claim to have produced the perfect models nor to have the last word in spreadsheet model design. However, the principles used in our designs are generally applicable and may be readily adapted to more complex, real-life situations.

Readers may wish to customize our models to deal with particular problems or to suit particular information needs. The only general advice we can give to the reader is: plan ahead, think logically, and be prepared to experiment.

Part II

Computers and spreadsheets

2 | Microcomputer basics

AIMS OF CHAPTER _____

- to introduce readers to some of the more commonly used computer terms and their meanings;
- specifically to examine the meaning of 'DOS' and the functions it performs;
- to learn how to manage computer disks, including formatting and checking disks, finding out the contents of a disk and creating sub-directories;
- to explain how to manage computer files, including copying, renaming and deleting.

A note on syntax

Keyboard keys are indicated by square brackets, for example [Enter] or [F4]. If you are asked to press the [Enter] key then you press this key once. *Do not type the word 'Enter' or the brackets*.

If you are asked to type anything then it will be contained within chevrons. For example, the instruction 'type ⟨ +A2⟩' means, type +A2. *Do not type the chevrons*.

All commands relate to Lotus 1−2−3 or similar software. While certain key combinations may differ, all spreadsheets will tend to offer the same facilities.

The first letters of some commands are in bold type to indicate that they are a menu option. Refer to your manual or help menus if you are not achieving the desired results.

Introduction

This chapter is included for readers who are not confident about using their microcomputer or who feel that their computer skills need a little refreshing. Consequently, this chapter, and the one that follows, are optional.

A note of caution: many PC users have developed their computer awareness in an an *ad hoc* manner, rather than following a structured training programme. This can lead to a chequered knowledge base with significant gaps or misapprehensions which remain undetected until some disaster or embarrassing moment occurs. Therefore, we would advise all readers to spend a few minutes reading through the next few pages. The worst that can happen is that you learn nothing new, but you may gain some useful revision!

Computer terminology

One of the first barriers PC novices encounter is the language used by computer technologists. The terminology may seem quite alien but with a little experience you will quickly see that most of it does make sense. We explain below some of the more commonly used terms.

Hardware

The starting point to the language of the computer user is the distinction between *hardware* and *software*.

Hardware is the equipment itself. The main components of the typical desktop PC are:

- the *keyboard*;
- the screen, usually referred to as the *monitor*;
- the box that the monitor sits on, the *system unit*.

The switch to turn the machine on or off is located either on the rear or on the side of the system unit. Its relative inaccessibility is designed to prevent accidental activation.

Constant advances in technology have led to smaller and more powerful machines, so there is now a family of personal computers ranging in size from desktop to laptop, notebook and even palm-sized. We will refer to desktop models, although the features described and used are present in all members of the microcomputer 'family'.

The keyboard and 'special' keys

The way to communicate with the computer is through the keyboard and/or a *mouse*. The mouse is the hand-held device that speeds up cursor movement on the screen for some programs, especially ones that use *icons*: symbols instead of words for access to menu options.

The computer keyboard has the 'qwerty' alphabetical and numerical layout, as found on a standard typewriter. Other keys are:

The *function* keys, [F1] to [F10] (or [F12]), which perform specific tasks depending on the program used.

The *cursor* keys, four keys that point left [←], right [→], up [↑] and down [↓].

[Home], [End], [PageUp] and [PageDown], keys which control the cursor for larger movements.

[Insert] and [Delete] keys to insert or delete text etc. in the position of the cursor.

The *numeric key pad*, on the right-hand side of the keyboard, has a dual role: one which allows numbers to be keyed in, the other which allows the same keys to be used for [Insert], [Delete] and cursor movements. This cluster of keys includes keys for [+] and [−] as well as the keys for divide [/], multiply [*] and [Enter]. A [NumLock] key 'toggles' the numeric key pad from numbers to cursor movement.

[Caps Lock] to type upper-case (capital) letters.

[Print Screen] which prints exactly what is on the screen.

[Scroll Lock] to 'freeze' the movement of text on the screen.

[Pause] which puts the program on hold.

The escape key [Esc], used extensively in many programs for cancelling a command and in most spreadsheets programs for menu backtracking.

The [Enter] key, often symbolized with a leftward pointing bent arrow.

Keys marked [Ctrl] for 'control' and [Alt] for 'alternative', the functions of which will depend on the software in use.

The [Insert] key, which may be used as a quick way of inputting data.

A left arrow [←———], the backspace key, above the [Enter] key, deletes the space to the left of the current cursor position.

Many newcomers to computers find the keyboard layout quite intimidating at first and often fear hitting the wrong key. All we can say is that whatever you do, whether intentionally or not, can always be undone. The very worst that can happen is that you have to reboot your PC!

Printers

The printer, which produces output on paper (*hard copy*), is known as a *peripheral* device. Each computer program to be used will require you to specify which make and model of printer is connected to your PC.

Printers come in three types:

- A *daisy wheel* printer has the character set on a plastic disk which physically strikes the paper. The daisy wheel is not able to print graphs.

- A *dot matrix* printer constructs each character or symbol using a series of dots. The definition of the printed output is determined by the number of dots per inch (dpi).

■ The most expensive type of printer is the *laser* printer. This produces a high-definition hard copy and works on a similar principle to a photocopier in that the image is produced on a drum. The laser printer offers the versatility of the dot matrix and the print quality of the daisy wheel, but is quieter in operation than both.

Software

The term *software* refers to the programs used which contain both instructions and means of handling data. Smaller programs can be run from floppy disks. Larger programs may need to be installed on the hard disk.

In the business world, computer software can be analyzed into the operating system and applications software. Accountants are not computer programmers. Although it can be argued that some knowledge of programming is useful for the accountant, it is not our intention to cover such material in this text.

Operating systems

Every PC requires a *disk operating system* (DOS) to perform functions and to run programs. There are different systems available. The market leader is IBM's PC DOS, although compatible alternatives can be found, such as MS DOS (MicroSoft Disk Operating System). Other operating systems are available which are not necessarily IBM-compatible, such as CP/M and UNIX.

Applications software

Applications software is a term that refers to programs written to perform specific functions. A spreadsheet is an example of applications software; other examples include databases and word processing; integrated packages are available which combine all three. Running applications packages is the most common usage of microcomputers in the business world.

Computer memory

The computer's ability to store and use information is referred to as its *memory*. It comes in two forms, random access memory (RAM) and read only memory (ROM).

The RAM is where the software is stored when it is in use. It is a temporary memory, empty until filled with the program you are about to use. Computer memory is measured in *bytes*. Each byte consists of eight *bits* — from which it derives its name ('by eight'). Modern RAM sizes of between 2 Mb and 4 Mb (Mb = megabyte: just over a million bytes) are now some eight times the 512 kb or 640 kb (kb = kilobytes: just over 1000 bytes) norm of a few years ago. The more sophisticated programs require more RAM.

ROM is in effect the computer's subconscious and need not concern us here.

Computer disks

Long-term or permanent memory is in the form of disks, either *floppy disks* or the *hard disk* in the system unit. The hard disk's storage capacity can vary from, say, 20 Mb to 200 Mb and beyond.

The system unit has at least one *disk drive*, the letterbox for the floppy disk. Storage capacity varies according to the physical size of the disk and its *density*. Disks, and the drive units which read them, come in two sizes, 3½ inch and 5¼ inch. The 5¼ inch disk is slightly bendy, hence the term 'floppy'. The 3½ inch disk is of more rigid construction with a metal cover over the magnetic read/write area. Disks of each size may be either high density (HD) or double density (DD). A high-density disk holds more information than a double-density disk. The storage capacities of each are as follows:

	HD	DD
3½ in.	1.44 Mb	720 kb
5¼ in.	1.2 Mb	640 kb

Before buying disks you must know the size and density of the drive in the machine which you intend to use. Although HD drives can read DD disks, a DD drive will not be able to read a HD disk.

The disks have to be inserted the right way up and the right way around for the disk drives to read them. On the left-hand side of each disk (as it sits in the drive) is a *write-protect* notch which can be covered to protect the information on the disk from being overwritten.

Installing DOS in the RAM

The installation of DOS is known as *booting up*. Once you switch your PC on, the ROM starts to search for the DOS. Specifically, it is searching for a file having the filename **COMMAND.COM**. Its search commences in the alphabetic order of the disk drives. Usually, the floppy drive is drive A, or if the PC has two floppy drives, A and B. The hard disk is drive C, although it can be 'configured' into drives C, D and E, etc.

Depending on the speed of the microchip, it takes only a few seconds to load the DOS in the RAM. Once this is done the 'prompt' on the screen will read:

C:\〉

This tells you that DOS is successfully installed and the current drive is the hard disk.

To change to a different drive, just type in the required drive letter followed by a colon [:], e.g. ⟨A:⟩ or ⟨B:⟩ and press [Enter].

Note that as DOS makes no distinction between upper- and lower-case letters, there is no need to type capitals. We use capitals in the DOS commands below only for the sake of the clarity of print.

Using DOS

Unlike the user-friendly applications packages, DOS is not a menu-driven system. DOS is used by typing in a command followed by the [Enter] key. To repeat a command just press the function key [F3] for the whole command or [F1] for one letter at a time.

We will examine the main uses of DOS, although this is only a brief summary. Your PC should come with a DOS system installed and a more extensive manual. Because the various options do not appear on screen, you must learn how to use the commands from scratch.

The VER command

There are many versions of DOS. The more up-to-date applications packages may have specific DOS requirements (DOS 2.2 or later). To find out which version of DOS you are using type ⟨VER⟩ and [Enter].

The DIR command

DIR is an abbreviation for 'directory'. Typing ⟨DIR⟩ followed by [Enter] produces a list of the contents of the current directory or disk drive. The list includes filenames (up to eight letters/numbers) and extensions (up to three letters/numbers), together with the number of bytes taken up by each file and the date it was saved. The file list will end with an indication of how many bytes are available on the disk.

If the disk in use contains a large number of files type either ⟨DIR/W⟩ which presents the file list in a series of columns, or ⟨DIR/P⟩ which produces the file list in screen-sized chunks.

The FORMAT command

Before you can use any new disk it must be *formatted*. This enables the DOS to store and retrieve files on the disk. To format a disk in the A drive, at the DOS prompt C:/⟩, type:

⟨FORMAT A:⟩

The space between the command 'FORMAT' and the drive indicator 'A:' is very important and this is a feature of rigid DOS syntax. Any mistake results in an unhelpful error message. A correct execution of the command results in the computer instructing you to insert the disk in the appropriate drive and pressing [Enter] to proceed.

The formatting process takes a few minutes, after which the message 'Format complete' appears, together with information on the storage capacity of the disk and the extent of any bad sectors on the disk.

Be prepared to discard disks with bad sectors, since they may cause problems at a later stage. A disk costs relatively little compared to the hours of work it can contain and which might be lost if the disk developed a malfunction at a most inconvenient time.

Great care must exercised when using the **FORMAT** command since formatting overwrites all the contents of the disk. For this reason *never* type ⟨FORMAT C:⟩ as this will erase everything on the hard disk.

One useful derivative is the **FORMAT/S** command, which not only formats a new disk, but also simultaneously copies the DOS system files should these be required, for instance, for use on another PC.

The CHKDSK command

This is the abbreviation for 'Check Disk'. This command produces more information about the status of the disk and the files it contains than the DIR command. It is a good habit to run the **CHKDSK** command on formatted disks as a check for any bad sectors.

One useful derivative of this command is **CHKDSK A:/F** to correct disk errors (in drive A) and to allow data lost in bad sectors to be retrieved.

Using directories

All disks can be subdivided into directories. A directory can be compared to the drawers of a filing cabinet. They are useful for collecting files of a similar nature in one place.

The first step is to create a directory. This is done using the **MD** (Make Directory) command followed by that important space (or you can type [\] instead of a space), with a directory name of up to eight letters. For example, to create a directory to hold your exercises on Chapter 5 on a floppy disk in drive A, type at the DOS prompt A:\⟩:

⟨MD CHAP5⟩

To use that directory you must change from the current directory. Do this by typing:

⟨CD CHAP5⟩

This results in the prompt now containing the directory name:

A:\CHAP5⟩

Directories can have any number of sub-directories made in the same way. To move back to the next highest level of directory you can type either of the following, at the DOS prompt A:\CHAP5⟩:

⟨CD..⟩

or

⟨CD\⟩

Directories can be removed using the **RD** (**R**emove **D**irectory) command followed by the directory name, provided that the directory to be removed is not the current directory and that it contains no files.

File management

Creating and naming files (for example, individual spreadsheets) will be performed using the spreadsheet package itself. But some aspects of file management may be more conveniently performed while in DOS.

The most often used commands affecting individual files are the **COPY** command, **REN** (rename) command and **DEL** (delete) command.

Copying

To copy a file requires you to identify both the source and the destination of the file to be copied. For example, after reading Chapter 5 you may wish to make a back-up copy on drive B of the spreadsheet saved on the disk in the A drive sub-directory **CHAP5** under the filename **HALKSWOR**. For a Lotus 1−2−3 spreadsheet file, the complete filename would include the extension **.WKS** or **.WK1**, which is inserted automatically by the spreadsheet package. To make the back-up copy, enter the following command at the DOS prompt, A:\CHAP5⟩:

⟨COPY HALKSWOR.WKS B:⟩

If the file has to be copied to a specific sub-directory on the disk in drive B, then this must be specified in the copy command, for example:

⟨COPY HALKSWOR.WKS B:\CHAP5⟩

The back-up copy may be saved under a different filename to distinguish it from the original. This is quite simple:

⟨COPY HALKSWOR.WKS B:\CHAP5\HALKSWOR.BAK⟩

The procedures for renaming and deleting files follow the same principles.

Renaming

For example, should you wish to rename a file, using the command REN, at the prompt, A:\CHAP5⟩ type:

⟨REN HALKSWOR.WKS CHAP5-1.WKS⟩

Deletion

Unwanted files can be deleted using the DEL command. Files which have been inadvertently deleted may be undeleted or restored, provided no new files have been saved to the disk. Consult your manual for instructions on this procedure.

Wildcards

To copy, rename or delete a number of files may become a somewhat tedious task but there are short-cuts through the use of *wildcards*. The [?] key can be used in place of a single character and the [∗] key can be used to represent any number of letters/numbers in the filename and file extension. So if you have a PC with twin drives, to back-up all your worksheets on Chapter 5, at the prompt A:\CHAP5⟩ type:

⟨COPY ∗.WKS B:\CHAP5\∗.BAK⟩

A quick way of erasing all files on a floppy disk (provided it has no sub-directories) is to type: ⟨DEL A:\∗.∗⟩ or ⟨B:\∗.∗⟩. This command will result in the prompt 'Are you sure (Y/N)?'. Before pressing ⟨Y⟩ (for Yes), take a second or two to consider whether the files to be deleted contain valuable data which it may not be possible to retrieve without considerable effort.

Exiting and rebooting

The correct exiting procedure should be used whichever type or package of applications software is being used. Most software menus are so user-friendly that it is obvious how to *exit* or *quit* the program. Following the prompted steps may have the added advantage of ensuring that you do not forget to save a file.

Simply turning off the computer will certainly get you out of the program but may cause problems on re-entering or may store the data which would have been lost in a temporary file, which is an unnecessary use of hard disk space.

If in using the program you encounter a problem such as where the program 'locks' or 'jams' disabling all the keys, try pressing simultaneously [Ctrl] and [Break]. If this does not work or if the proper exiting procedure cannot be followed, you will have to *reboot* the computer, by pressing [Ctrl], [Alt] and [Delete] at the same time. Do not turn off the machine and immediately turn it back on since this may cause serious damage.

Conclusion

Having completed this chapter you should be familiar with some of the more commonly used computer terms and their meanings. You should now have a clearer understanding of the meaning of 'DOS' and what it does.

You should be able to use DOS to handle computer disks, including formatting, checking, finding out the disk contents and dividing the disk into directories.

You should also be able to manipulate computer files, including copying, renaming and deleting.

3 || *Spreadsheet basics*

AIMS OF CHAPTER _____

- to discover the origins of the electronic 'worksheet';
- to explain the uses it was intended to serve and how it is used in business today;
- to identify the main features present in most popular spreadsheet packages;
- to explain the usefulness of the windows and titles facilities;
- to examine the 'classic' menu structure of Lotus 1−2−3, the most popular spreadsheet package which is emulated by many rivals;
- to present a few common pitfalls faced by novice users and how they can be avoided.

Introduction

The spreadsheet or, to give it its original generic name, the 'electronic worksheet', started life in the mind of an MBA student, Dan Bricklin, at Harvard Business School in the United States in the late 1970s. Bricklin was preparing forecast financial statements based on a company acquisition project with a group of his postgraduate colleagues.

The work required performing continual recalculations of the financial projections under different assumptions. The approach the researchers used was the same as that used by accountants and analysts in practice. This consisted of using large sheets of ruled paper divided into columns, a design which suited multiple calculations. However, with all the calculations being performed using a calculator, it was a tedious, time-consuming task prone to human error. In addition, the number of columns and rows available constituted severe physical limits on the number of calculations which could be performed. The manual worksheet was particularly poor at answering 'what if?' questions as the whole process of recalculation had to be performed again, and checked, before the results were known. Although computers might have helped, the programs needed too much manipulation to cope with changes in the basic assumptions.

21

As the saying goes, necessity is the mother of invention, and Bricklin, with Bob Frankston, came up with the idea of producing a computer program which used the same approach as the manual worksheet. The original role of the first electronic worksheet was to make it easier to answer the 'what if?' type of question.

In 1979 the first electronic worksheet was launched for use on the Apple II microcomputer under the name 'Visicalc'. It was affordable and sold extremely well. Competition, in the form of Supercalc, came in 1981, and in 1982 Lotus 1−2−3 was launched. Both packages offered features not present in Visicalc, such as graphs and database capabilities and would run on IBM PCs.

Since its earliest and crudest form, the computer spreadsheet has been refined and developed into a sophisticated piece of applications software. The refinements have produced what are called second, third and fourth generation software, with subsequent releases offering improvements on the preceding version.

Nowadays, there are many different products on the market, but the essential features of the spreadsheet are common to them all. The market leader is Lotus 1−2−3, currently on Version 3.0 which is a three-dimensional version of earlier spreadsheets. The three-dimensional spreadsheet appears on screen as a series of 'pages', one behind the other. This allows easy access to and linking of related spreadsheets.

Many software manufacturers offer 'add-ins', which are additions to the basic spreadsheet that increase its versatility even further. For example, 'Allways' is a desktop publishing add-in for Lotus.

Another development has been to link the spreadsheet to other common applications software such as a word processor and a database. These are called *integrated* packages. One example is Lotus Symphony, which was first launched in 1984.

Spreadsheet packages

The success of Lotus 1−2−3 and its main rival, Supercalc, has led to a large number of lookalike packages which offer better value for money. Lotus *compatibility* is a term that is used rather loosely in the advertising copy; despite the hype, the genuine Lotus 1−2−3 may reject spreadsheets created on other packages.

Although in the text we refer to the Lotus 1−2−3 menu structure, it is not essential to have this package. All the necessary calculations, formulae and models are presented in a way which can be readily adapted to *any* spreadsheet package.

The advances in software design and reductions in the relative price of hardware (and software) in the 1980s meant that more and more people were using spreadsheets, and not just to answer 'what if?' questions. While a spreadsheet can appear quite complex at first, the menus and commands are readily mastered and any task that would have required pen, paper and calculator is often performed far more quickly and with greater accuracy on a spreadsheet. Consequently, the spreadsheet has become one of the all-pervasive business tools of the late twentieth century, used in offices throughout the world.

Accountants use them to prepare financial projections, to analyze cash books, to prepare small business accounts, to analyze budget variances, to prepare cost statements and to calculate payslips.

However, like any application, spreadsheets have their limitations. In cases involving a large number of transactions a dedicated accounting package with in-built checks and controls would be preferred for routine bookkeeping.

Of course, it must always be borne in mind that while spreadsheet packages will not make a *programmed* error, they are far more vulnerable to *programmer* error in that their output is only as good as the person who prepared the spreadsheet.

The acquisition of adequate spreadsheet skills has never been more valuable. This stems from the fact that nearly all accounting offices and departments use some sort of spreadsheet. Although different spreadsheet packages are available, they have many similarities and the skill of using one package can easily be transferred to another package.

Spreadsheet *convergence*, then, has led people to talk of the ability to use a spreadsheet as a 'transferable skill'. Given the rate of computerization in organizations, this is a skill well worth developing, as for most accountants the spreadsheet is likely to form as much a part of their working life as the calculator was to the previous era of 'beancounters'.

However, student readers of this text are advised to develop their ability to use a calculator as they are not generally allowed to take a PC into the examination room!

Using a spreadsheet

With the computer turned on and the current directory changed to that containing the spreadsheet package files, the Lotus 1−2−3 spreadsheet is *loaded* by typing the command, ⟨123⟩ and [Enter].

If you are not using Lotus 1−2−3, find the command which will run your particular spreadsheet package by typing a ⟨DIR⟩ command at the DOS prompt for the relevant sub-directory or disk drive. Look for the file with the extension **.EXE**. To activate this executive file type the filename (without the extension) and [Enter].

Other packages may have batch files which allow the spreadsheet to mimic Lotus 1−2−3; for example, Quattro has a file called **Q123.BAT**. This is activated by typing ⟨Q123⟩ and [Enter].

On screen you will now see a blank matrix of columns, alphabetically labelled along the top, and rows, numbered on the left-hand side. The rows above the matrix are known as the *control panel* (see Figure 3.1). Indicators below the matrix show whether the [NumLock] key and other functions are toggled on.

The cursor is highlighted in the extreme top left *cell* of the matrix which is referred to by its *cell address* as A1 and which is shown on the first row of the control panel by the *cell indicator*.

Moving around the spreadsheet

At any given time all you are able to see is a screen-sized portion of the spreadsheet:

Worksheet	Range	Copy	Move	File	Print	Graph	Data	View	System	Quit

A 1 :

	A	B	C	D	E	F	G
1							
2							
3							
4							
5							
6							
7							
8							
9							
1 0							
1 1							
1 2							
1 3							
1 4							
1 5							
1 6							
1 7							
1 8							
1 9							
2 0							

SHEET1.WK1   NUM   READY

Figure 3.1   A typical spreadsheet top left-hand corner

6 columns and 20 rows. Many users are fooled into thinking that the spreadsheet 'exists' in some physical sense. But it is merely a set of data, stored electronically in the computer's RAM, and *presented* in a form which resembles the accountant's worksheet.

The cursor keys

By pressing the cursor keys you can move the cursor around the screen. If your keyboard has a numeric pad, make sure that the [Num Lock] key is toggled off before attempting to move the cursor.

If you move to the right enough times you will notice that the column letters change. Similarly, if you move down enough the row numbers will increase.

If you want the cursor to remain stationary while the spreadsheet moves press the [Scroll Lock] key and use the cursors. Notice that the indicator 'Scroll' has now appeared on the bottom of your screen. To stop scrolling press [Scroll Lock] again.

Quicker moves

To move more quickly you can use the [PageUp] and [PageDown] keys which move the cursor in a vertical axis in blocks of 20 rows, that is, in screen-sized chunks. Moving along the horizontal axis in this manner is achieved by holding [Ctrl] and pressing either the right or the left cursor key. Alternatively, press [Tab] to move one screen to the right and [Shift] and [Tab] to move one screen to the left.

To return quickly to cell A1, press the [Home] key.

To get to the final row of the spreadsheet press [End] and then the down arrow [↓]. You should now be in cell A8192. That's right: column A, row 8192! If your computer has less RAM then this may be a lower row number, but you will agree that it is still impressive. Notice that when [End] is pressed, an 'End' status indicator appears in the bottom right of the screen.

To move to the bottom right-hand corner press [End] and then the right arrow [→]. You should be in cell IV8192, depending on the package you are using. The alphabetical list of columns follows the sequence A to Z, then AA to AZ, then BA to BZ and so on. So column IV is the 256th column. In total there are over 2 million cells available.

To utilize every cell would require more RAM than most PCs possess and in any event a spreadsheet is probably not the right tool to perform such a large task.

Once you have constructed a spreadsheet model, you may wish to move to an extreme corner of the used portion of the spreadsheet. For example, should you want to move the cursor to the extreme right-hand corner of the used area, then press the [End] key followed by the [Home] key.

The various cursor 'jumps' are well worth learning as they are valuable time-savers, especially in the case of large models.

Another quick way of moving around the spreadsheet is the '**GoTo**' function, the [F5] key on Lotus-style packages. After pressing [F5], note the control panel prompting you for a cell address. So, for example, if you want to go to cell J10 then type ⟨J10⟩ as the cell address, press [Enter] and the cursor will move to J10, shown in the top left of the screen. Note that as the spreadsheet does not distinguish between upper- and lower-case letters, so there is no need to type capitals for a cell address.

Cell contents

The contents of a cell can be in the form of:

- numbers (or *values* in spreadsheet terminology);
- text (or *labels*); or
- formulae.

Values

Values can be numbers such as 198, 2346, 300000. When entering numbers do not punctuate with commas: for example, do *not* type ⟨300,000⟩. If commas are used then the spreadsheet will believe the contents of the cell to be a label which cannot be used for mathematical manipulation.

The spreadsheet also views what we would call formulae as values: for instance, $198 + 2346$, or $300000 - 2346$.

Labels

Labels are the pieces of text which are needed in most spreadsheets, for example as descriptions for items or column headings, such as 'Monday' or 'Total Expenses'. The first character in label must be a letter.

The label can be *aligned* to the left, right or centre of the cell. The label align indicators for Lotus-based packages are typed prior to the text itself and are

['] for left align;
["] for right align;
[ˆ] for centred labels.

The left align label indicator is automatically put in if you type a label without using any indicator. Notice that none of the indicators appear on the cell contents on the matrix itself.

If you want to type a label beginning with a number, for example ⟨25th June⟩ then you *must* prefix this with a label indicator otherwise the spreadsheet will prompt you that you have made an error entering a value.

There are two more indicators worth mentioning. The backslash ([\]) key is the repeat key. If you press [\] (in some packages [']) followed by text then the text is repeated for the length of that cell. This can be used to draw lines across the entire spreadsheet width or the width of the cell: ⟨\-⟩ produces lines of '---------' or ⟨__⟩ gives '_____' as desired. These lines may be used to improve the appearance of spreadsheets by separating a mass of numbers from column headings or to denote that a column of figures has been summed to produce a total figure.

Pressing the [¦] key when in the first cell of a row will suppress that row in printing out hard copy.

Formulae

A cell can also contain formulae. Formulae can best be described as mathematical expressions. They can contain arithmetical calculations, specialist functions, cell references or combinations of these elements.

For example, to show how formulae can perform mathematical manipulations of data with input values derived from other cells, enter ⟨100⟩ in cell A1 and ⟨500⟩ in cell A3 then in cell A5 type ⟨+A1+A3⟩. Cell A5 will display the solution 600 on screen. Note that the control panel will continue to show the formula, +A1+A3, for cell A5. To replace the formula with the value, press [F2] and [F9] when the cell indicator shows you are in the appropriate cell.

You can combine values and cell references in formulae. For example, in cell A3 you could have typed ⟨+A1+500⟩ the solution 600 would then have appeared in cell A3.

In creating formulae it is good practice to 'point' to cells rather than typing in the cell address. In the top right of the screen you will see a mode indicator which reads '**Ready**'. While in cell A5 type ⟨+⟩; the mode indicator changes to '**Point**'.

Now use the cursor key to move to cell A1; the cell contents automatically reproduce the current cell: +A1. Another ⟨+⟩ allows you to point to another cell, for instance A3. You can write formulae in this way until you press [Enter], which returns you to the cell A5.

In spreadsheet formulae, multiplication is performed using the [∗] key. Division requires the [/] key.

The spreadsheet performs the mathematical calculations in the order in which they appear in the formula, thus:

$$2+3*4 = 20$$

The use of brackets can transform this since the spreadsheet obeys the brackets first:

$$2+(3*4) = 14$$

When constructing formulae think carefully about the relationship between the elements of the calculation. If you are in any doubt about the order in which calculations are to be performed, use brackets. The spreadsheet will not object to unnecessary brackets although it will prompt you if you use brackets inappropriately or forget to put a closing bracket.

There are several other keys which perform special functions in spreadsheet formulae and these will be introduced at the appropriate stages.

Menu structure

The [/] key is known commonly as the 'slash' key. It is on the right of the keyboard with a '?' above it. By pressing [/] the first word 'Worksheet' is highlighted in the control panel. This is the first *option* in the main menu.

To select your menu choice either use the cursor keys until your selection is highlighted or press the first letter of the word of your choice. The menu is divided into sub-menus and sub-sub-menus. The location of various options is dependent upon the menu structure. In this and subsequent chapters we will consider a few important options that you are likely to use.

More help can be obtained immediately for the current menu or sub-menu by pressing [F1], the help function common to most spreadsheet packages.

To see the full range of capabilities, you are recommended to refer either to the manual which came with your spreadsheet or to one of the software guides published for popular packages.

⟨/Worksheet, Insert⟩

This menu sub-option allows you to insert either a row(s) or column(s) at the cursor location, or a specified location. This will not affect the rest of the spreadsheet as any cell references are automatically changed. Columns and rows may be deleted using the ⟨/Worksheet, Delete⟩ option.

⟨/Worksheet, Column, Set Width⟩

The width of columns can be increased or reduced from the standard default of 9 characters. You can either type in the new column width or use the left or right cursor keys until the desired width is achieved. If you find that a cell's contents are displayed as a string of asterisks then this indicates that the column is not wide enough.

⟨/Worksheet, Titles⟩

This is a handy option which allows you to retain rows (horizontal titles) or columns (vertical titles) or both in place while moving to another cell.

For example, a monthly expense account might require columns to be headed with the name of the month and the rows to be headed with the type of expenditure. In moving either down a column or across a row, the heading disappears from the screen. The ⟨/Worksheet, Titles⟩ option may be used to 'fix' the headings.

You can only move into the title area using the [F5] method. The titles can be cleared by using the same sub-menu.

⟨/Worksheet, Windows⟩

This option is used extensively in practice, due to the large scale of the spreadsheets often used. It enables two areas of a large spreadsheet to be viewed simultaneously by dividing the screen in two, either horizontally or vertically. The window can be Synchronized (the same rows or columns displayed in both windows), or Unsynchronized (any rows or columns displayed). You can move from one window to another by pressing [F6]. This facility also allows you to 'point' to cells in another window for formula construction.

Even in our simplified models we will make extensive use of the unsynchronized horizontal window.

⟨/Range, Format⟩

A *range* is any rectangular block of cells such as A1 to A10 or A1 to C45. A range is indicated by the cell addresses of the opposing corners of a block separated by two full stops: A1..A10 or A1..C45. A range may also consist of a single cell.

The ⟨/Range, Format⟩ option allows you to change the presentation of cell contents. The sub-options include selecting the number of decimal places required. The , (comma) option allows figures to be displayed punctuated with commas for financial presentations. The Text option displays cell formulae rather than their numeric answers.

The Percentage option displays a number or the result of a calculation as a percentage (including the % sign) rather than as a decimal. With a cell formatted to

Percentage a number to be keyed in must first be divided by 100. Thus for the cell to show 100% the value to be keyed in is 1; for the cell to show 10%, the value keyed in is .1 and so on.

〈/Range, Name〉

It is good practice to name commonly used blocks of cells, using 〈/**R**ange, **N**ame, **C**reate〉. Naming ranges makes for ease of printing and selection of other options. Instead of manually moving the cursor to highlight a particular range simply refer to it by name.

Pressing [F3] displays the list of created range names. You can also move quickly to ranges in this way by pressing [F5] (the '**Go To**' function) then [F3] to give a list of range names from which you can select the range required.

〈/Move〉

As the name implies, this allows you to move ranges of cells from one place to another. Cell references remain relative to their original references. For example, if cell A1 contained the value 100 and cell A3 the formula +A1*52, the range A1..A3 could be moved to column B without altering the model or its result. However, the cell contents of B3 would now read +B1*52.

〈/Copy〉

This works in the same way as the **Move** command, but repeats the cell contents. The same relative cell references are maintained in any formula, unless the cell reference is made absolute using [F4] or inserting a '$' in front of either the column or row reference or both. Absolute cell references do not change when moved or copied.

With both Move or Copy the first prompt gives you the current cell displayed as a range, for example A5..A5. The first A5 is 'anchored' and any cursor movement only affects the second reference. In this way ranges can be pointed to on screen.

If you wish to remove the anchor, then press [Delete] or [Esc] and move to the new position of the start of the range. A full stop then anchors the new cell and a new range can be pointed to.

〈/File, Save〉 and 〈/File, Retrieve〉

To save a spreadsheet which has been created requires the 〈/File, Save〉 menu choice. You need to specify precisely which disk drive and directory the file is to be saved to as well as giving the spreadsheet a filename. Remember the eight-letter limit.

For ease of later retrieval, it is best to devise a logical system for naming files. There is no need to specify the file extension which is inserted automatically by the package.

If you happen to have chosen the name of an existing file (or if you are saving a file after modifying it) you will be prompted that a file of that name already exists and you will be asked to choose whether to **Replace** the existing file, **Save** it as a back-up or **Cancel** the save command. Great care needs to be used here as you may risk losing a file by having it overwritten.

The ⟨/File, Retrieve⟩ command allows you to load a saved file to the screen. Again you will need to specify the exact location of the file. If it is held on a different disk drive or directory, use the ⟨/File, Directory⟩ to change the default setting to the appropriate drive or directory.

⟨/Print⟩

Before using the print option to produce hard-copy output, make sure that the spreadsheet package has been set up with the right type and model of printer specified. It is also worthwhile ensuring that the printer itself is correctly set up and connected to the PC. Most printers have an indicator to show that the connection is online and the printer is ready to print.

Always align the printer before each new printed range. Large print ranges must be printed on more than one piece of paper.

You can also 'print' the contents of the spreadsheet to a printer or to a file on disk which will automatically be given the extension **.PRN**.

⟨/Graph⟩

This menu is usually easy to follow and the settings can be customized until the right visual impression is achieved.

⟨/Data, Fill⟩

This allows a range of values to be inserted into a selected range of cells in any set increment. For example if a spreadsheet were to be used to calculate the total value of a batch of 300 invoices consecutively numbered from No. 101, these invoice numbers can be quickly entered in the appropriate column by using the ⟨/Data, Fill⟩ option. Specify the starting value, 101, the step value (increment), 1, and the end value, 400: the list is produced immediately. Of course, the invoice values themselves will need to be keyed in.

⟨/Data, Sort⟩

This allows the order of rows to be placed in alphabetical or numerical order, either ascending or descending.

⟨/Data, Regression⟩

This allows for linear regression, single or multiple, for up to 16 independent variables and presents other useful statistics such as *t*-values and the coefficient of correlation.

⟨/Data, Table⟩

This option is ideal for sensitivity analysis, which calculates the effect on the model of a change in one or two variables.

⟨/System⟩

This allows you temporarily to exit the spreadsheet and return to DOS, a facility particularly useful for formatting blank disks without having to quit the spreadsheet program completely. Once the disk is formatted, just type ⟨EXIT⟩, which returns you to the current spreadsheet at the point where you left it.

The function keys

The function keys (the F keys) at the top of the keyboard perform specialist functions, some of which are so useful that they are used with virtually every spreadsheet model. Others are quite specific.

[F1]   The help key provides instant guidance concerning the current menu choice. Pressing [Esc] returns you to the spreadsheet.

[F2]   The '**Edit**' key allows alterations to be made to cell contents.

[F3]   This key displays the range names created. A range is a block of cells. Selecting the required range name moves the cursor to that block of cells. If different sections of the spreadsheet have been given range names, the [F3] key can be used to speed movement between the different sections.

[F4]   This key is used to make the cell address to the left of the cursor an absolute cell reference. This means that its contents can be copied or moved to other cells without changing. Copying or moving a relative cell reference will change the contents.

[F5]   The '**GoTo**' key is a quick way of moving the cursor to a specific cell reference.

[F6]   This key moves the cursor between 'windows' when the screen has been split into separate windows.

[F7]   The '**Query**' key is used in relation to databases, which are not covered in this text.

[F8] The '**Macro**' key displays a list of created macros; selecting one runs that particular macro. A macro is a short-cut, performing a set sequence of key strokes.

[F9] The '**Calculation**' key commands the spreadsheet to perform the calculations in its formulae. This key is only used if the automatic calculation option has been turned off, in which case the 'CALC' indicator at the bottom of the screen will be shown.

[F10] The '**Graph**' key displays the current graph.

Some of these function keys can be used in combinations. For example, [F5] followed by [F3] produces a quick way of moving to a named range.

A few spreadsheet tips

Save your work at regular intervals rather than only at the end of the exercise as mistakes do happen and it could be time-consuming to reconstruct work which has been inadvertently lost.

Always take back-up copies of your important files, preferably on a different disk. Your back-up disks should be rotated so that old back-up files are overwritten when no longer required. This reduces the numbers of disks required and creates a good organizational discipline.

Use your printer to its best advantage: for example, where possible use compressed print modes. Your spreadsheet may have landscape (sideways) print utilities which are invaluable. If not, there are commercial add-in packages available that will print most files in landscape format and give you a selection of font sizes, page lengths, and print qualities.

A golden rule is to ensure that the spreadsheet is doing as much work for you as possible. There may be some minor features available that can make life easier such as the repeat key (['] or [\ ], depending on your spreadsheet package).

One important point concerns the development of good habits when working with computers. The common-sense care needed when using disks should be clear. They are not bits of paper; they can be damaged by magnetic fields, heat, damp, pressure, bending and finger prints.

Your computer is the tool that you will use to help you. Treat it with respect, it is a delicate piece of machinery. If you are using the facilities of an institute of learning, think of those students who will follow you and who will need to use the equipment. If something is not working, report it, it is not going to heal itself. Computers do not need breaks and do not smoke cigarettes or drink coffee. They react badly to both.

When you start a session of study make sure that you have a formatted disk with enough space on it to save your work to at the end or you will soon become frustrated. If you find a disk, do not be selfish and reformat it; it probably contains many hours of work of a fellow student and is worth far more to him or her than the blank is worth to you.

It also pays to put your name on the volume label so that you can identify a disk as being yours. Making the effort to enter the date and time during the DOS prompts can also avoid confusion later on, especially when using similar filenames. It can also be used to prove that the file is your work and not someone else's.

Further tips on spreadsheets in practice

In practice, great store is set on making spreadsheets usable by more than one person in the organization. Personnel changes mean that one colleague must continue work begun by another. A standard organizational style and layout is essential for continuity and helps supervisors/managers in reviewing the work of subordinates.

As figures produced on a spreadsheet appear to be formal and hence, by implication, correct, it is important that the output is reliable and that adequate controls are developed during model construction.

A layout map on paper is another useful feature for use with large spreadsheets.

Conclusion

This chapter is a form of overview. Many aspects of the spreadsheet have not been covered or have been dealt with very succinctly. Specific spreadsheet formulae and commands are explained more fully in the necessary chapters.

Nevertheless, after studying this chapter you should know how a spreadsheet works and why it was developed. You should have gleaned enough knowledge to use a spreadsheet to perform the tasks set in this book. If you find difficulty in applying our instructions on your particular spreadsheet then you may find it helpful to refer to the specialized program manual for your package.

Our approach in this book is one that concentrates on the construction of spreadsheet models. Our aim is to develop your spreadsheet skills in learning about and in applying management accounting principles.

4 | *The spreadsheet and model-building*

AIMS OF CHAPTER _____

- to introduce the concept of a model, including an understanding of the terms 'variable' and 'parameter';
- to indicate the possible stages of model design in general;
- to outline the uses of a spreadsheet and how it works;
- to present briefly the common features of spreadsheet packages;
- to demonstrate the construction of a basic spreadsheet model from first principles.

SPREADSHEET SKILLS ACQUIRED _____

- basic spreadsheet model structure;
- widening columns;
- using formulae and values in spreadsheet cells;
- formatting cells to show financial figures and decimal places.

Introduction

Models come in various forms: working models, models that merely represent an idea, and models that behave in different ways to reality. Models are used commercially to assist decision-making; it is as well to see the effects of various choices on a model prior to making a final commitment to a project.

Consider some familiar forms of models in general and how they are used. A model of a building may be used by architects to test weight stresses or it may just be used to give a three-dimensional representation of the appearance of the eventual building.

A model aeroplane is a scaled-down version of a real aircraft. Apart from being used in leisure activities, it could be used for testing the design of a prototype such as the Lockhead SR-71 Blackbird, which can fly at three times the speed of sound for up to nine hours. Production of the final aeroplane would have been preceded by many models examining the many facets of its design: for example, wind tunnel tests for aerodynamics, benchtests for engine design, and the effects of gravitational forces simulated in a large centrifuge.

In theoretical terms a model is the representation of an object in another medium. It does not have to be an exact representation of the real object, but it can pinpoint a particular area of reality in an attempt to clarify it. One feature common to all models is that they simplify real-world situations. The strength of a model is that it is removed from reality and experiments of the 'what happens if ... ?' kind can be performed. The effects of changes to the model can be analyzed with less risk and less cost than experimenting with the real thing.

In modelling terms, computers represent a further dimension. Information technology has revolutionized the design of new machines and buildings. The experimenter can now achieve quicker results using a computer model. It is now possible to model a new aircraft in numeric terms and perform many tests on a computer simulation without even constructing a proper three-dimensional model. Flight simulators are now commonplace, mimicking the entire aircraft's controls and the response to the pilot's manoeuvres. So modern-day test pilots are able to fly a prototype aircraft as if they were old hands.

Just as computers have had an enormous impact in the engineering profession, so they have had their effect on accounting, finance and economics.

The accountant's models

Accountants and economists attempt to model the way in which a business or industry behaves and use their model to predict reality. It is no good starting a new business venture if its demise can be predicted in advance. It is also clearly better to model the proposed new business and to find out its weaknesses and strengths than immediately to 'launch' the 'prototype'. Merely from the exercise of modelling the business, accountants and financial advisers gain knowledge of how the business will operate and are better placed to understand the reality of the situation.

It is prudent at this point to mention the caveat that business models are not completely analogous to engineering models in so far as reality and the model imitation can be quite different. With the tightly constructed laws of physics, predictive capacity can be very high. However, in a business model the equalities are not exact. In fact, the norm is for the model to be wrong.

The accountant's modelling clay is most often in the form of spreadsheet software, and this book shows how accountants model various aspects of businesses with which they are concerned.

Stages of model design

To assist in the understanding of this section, we will model the financial problem faced by a first-year student living on a fixed income (Y). To simplify reality we will assume that the student has only two spending options, accommodation (A) and entertainment (E), and that total expenditure cannot exceed income.

There are certain stages to be followed in model construction. The starting point is to decide what is the purpose of the model. It is only when the objective of the model is clear that successful model construction can begin. Let us assume that our student is a 'party animal' mainly concerned with how many nights' entertainment per term can be bought.

The next stage is to specify the assumptions made in designing the model. This leads us to identify the variables and parameters of the model. A *parameter* is something that is given and is completely exogenous to the model. In the example of a university fresher, the ten weeks in an academic term is a parameter which can be expressed as follows:

$$A = 10r$$

where r is the rent per week, and A is the total cost of accommodation per term. The '10' is a constant for all students and is fixed for this situation, but it could vary from problem to problem; for instance, if the term consisted of 12 weeks or if the problem were based on a year and not a term this constant or parameter would have to change.

A *variable* can be dependent or independent. The value of a *dependent* or output variable is determined by one or more other inputs to the model. An *independent* or input variable is often exogenous and cannot be determined by the operator, that is, the student. So in our fresher's model, A is the dependent variable in that it is dependent on the parameter of 10 weeks per term (a constant), and r is the price of the accommodation determined by the market and not by the student. The student can choose from a range of accommodation priced at different levels, so we say that this is a *controllable* variable. If the student, as a fresher, is required to live in halls of residence then the price of the accommodation becomes a non-controllable variable.

We can expand the model to take account of the other independent variable, spending on entertainment. Let us assume that for every evening out the fresher spends an average of £7.50. This becomes a parameter for this model although in reality it may be allowed to vary. Some simplification is required in order to develop a useful model.

We can therefore state that spending on entertainment is:

$$E = 7.5n$$

where E is the amount spent on entertainment per term, and n is the number of nights out.

Putting all we know together in one model, we have:

$$Y = A + E$$

where Y is total income per term, and A and E are as already given. Substituting for

A and *E*, we get:

$$Y = 10r + 7.5n$$

and this can be expressed as an *objective function*, how many nights out the fresher can have in the first term:

$$7.5n + 10r = Y$$
$$7.5n = Y - 10r$$
$$n = (Y - 10r)/7.5$$

This is an algebraic model which states that the number of nights the fresher can go out depends on the income *Y* and the price of accommodation per week, *r*.

Let us assume that income for the term is £1000 and the cost of accommodation chosen amounts to £40.00 per week. If we insert these values for our variables, we can solve the expression:

$$n = (1000 - (10 \times 40))/7.5$$
$$n = 80$$

In other words, our fortunate undergraduate can go out every single night of the term (7 days × 10 weeks) and still have money left over.

The usefulness of the model is that it can answer 'what if?' questions. What if the fresher's parents are not happy to see their offspring going out so much and cut their contributions to income by £225? Running this through the model gives $n = 50$, meaning that the student can only go out five times a week. What if the rent also goes up to £47.50? Now *n* becomes 40, so that the student can only go out four times a week. By running the model with revised values for the variables, we are able to predict what will happen in reality, that is, the outcome in terms of *n*, if the variables alter.

The accuracy of the model depends on the accuracy of the estimates of the variables. These may not always be measurable with precision. For example, it is unlikely that our student will spend £7.50 every night out. Even if all the variables and parameters did hold, it is unlikely that *n* would be as predicted because other factors will impinge in reality and invalidate the model. This is not to say that the model serves no purpose. The model may give a trend or a broad indication of the likely actual result, but it is not the product of an exact science.

The fact that a model attempts to predict the future means that the parameters and variables are forecasts, often based on observed historical data. These forecasts are likely to vary in reality because the set of circumstances pertaining when they were measured may no longer hold. It is prudent to keep an eye on changes in the environment which will lead to changes in parameters and variables. For example, the general price level may rise and the cost of a night out rises from £7.50 to £8.00. If this happens then our model needs to change because a parameter has changed.

The next section describes how to develop this model on a spreadsheet and demonstrates the ease with which the model can be run with changed values for variables.

Model construction using a spreadsheet

When preparing a spreadsheet model you must bear in mind the purpose of the model and the format in which the output is required.

To allow for insertion and deletion of rows and columns and changes of column width in sections without disrupting other sections, a diagonal layout, sometimes referred to as a *cascade*, is recommended, as shown in Figure 4.1. The sections of the spreadsheet are split into blocks of 20 rows, which is the amount visible on the screen at any one time. Each section can be given a range name to facilitate movement between sections. A reference system should be employed so that each section bears a reference in one corner to assist users in knowing where they are in the spreadsheet.

The control section gives broad details of the spreadsheet model, including a location table and a series of range names which will be created as we construct the model.

The input section contains all variables and parameters in absolute value terms, that is, you should key in the original numbers in this section.

The output section is made up of cell references that have their ultimate origins in the input section. The advantage of this approach is that it is easier to check the completeness and accuracy of input if it is in one place. It also means that all the data which can alter the results of the spreadsheet are visible in one place and can be changed without recoding formulae. The main modelling advantage is that new input variables can be added and the model amended without too much disruption.

Figure 4.1 The cascade approach

The fresher's model as a spreadsheet

The first spreadsheet solution we have prepared is the control section, which informs the user of the objectives of the model and its structure (see Spreadsheet Solution 4.1). The structure is given in a location table, complete with the names of ranges which will be created as we go along. Note that the section fits neatly onto one screen and that the user is told how to find the next section. If the explanation had to be more long-winded then two or three screen-sized chunks would be prepared.

Since we will only need two columns in this section we can expand columns A and B to fill the screen. In fact column A needs to be widened substantially whereas column B only needs to be widened by a few spaces. First widen column A with the command ⟨/Worksheet, Column, Set Width⟩, then set the width with the right arrow cursor key.

Spreadsheet solution 4.1 Control section

	A	B
1	Spreadsheet Solution 4-1: Control Section	
2		
3	The Fresher's Model	
4		
5	Model Description	
6		
7	This model examines the expenditure plans of a student.	
8	The student has only two expenditure choices, accommodation	
9	and evening entertainment.	
10		
11	The model's purpose is to find the maximum times the student	
12	can go out in one term given various parameters & variables.	
13		
14	Location Table	Range Name
15	--------------	-----------
16	Input Section	INPUT
17	Output Section	OUTPUT
18		
19		
20	For Input Section press F5 and select INPUT	

Now type in the brief description of the model as shown in Spreadsheet Solution 4.1. Note that the first line of text in cell A7 is longer than the width of column A, but will still appear on the screen once you press [Enter]. If you were to enter text or a value in cell B7 part of the text in cell A7 would not appear on screen. Spreadsheet packages are not word processors so each line of text has to be entered separately with a hard return [Enter] at the end of each line, that is to say, the spreadsheet will not automatically introduce a soft return once the line of text is long enough to fill the row on screen.

Leave the location table and the instruction on the last line for the moment. This will be completed once we have finished constructing the model.

The next section is the input section, which should be located beneath and to the right of the control section (see Spreadsheet Solution 4.2). Again column C needs to be widened to contain the labels (the row headings). To format cell D37, Nightly Entertainment Spend £, to show the amount to the nearest 10p, that is one decimal place, type ⟨/**R**ange, **F**ormat, ,(comma) **1**⟩, where the 1 refers to the number of decimal places in the amount. Once you have completed the input section, name the range using ⟨/**R**ange, **N**ame, **C**reate⟩, highlight with the cursor the range C22..D37 and [Enter], then type the range name ⟨INPUT⟩.

The final section, the output section (Spreadsheet Solution 4.3) is where the solution to the problem will appear. This illustrates the modelling approach and the continuation of the cascade layout. The output section is located at the bottom right-hand corner of the input section and the entire numeric output is achieved using cell references.

Having widened column F and entered the labels, examine the formula-based

Spreadsheet solution 4.2   Input section

	C	D
22	Spreadsheet Solution 4-2: Input Section	
23		
24	Variable Name	Value
25	-------------	------
26		
27	Income per Term £	1000
28		
29	Accommodation Charge per Week £	40
30		
31		
32	Parameters	
33	----------	
34		
35	Weeks per Term	10
36		
37	Nightly Entertainment Spend £	7.5
38		
39		
40		

Spreadsheet solution 4.3   Output section

	F	G
41	Spreadsheet Solution 4-3: Output Section	
42		
43	Total Accommodation Spend is	400
44		
45	Total Income is	1,000
46		
47	Available for Entertainment	600
48		
49	Number of Nights Out	80

Spreadsheet solution 4.4   Output section

	F	G
41	Spreadsheet Solution 4-4: Output Section	
42		
43	Total Accommodation Spend is	+D29*D35
44		
45	Total Income is	+D27
46		
47	Available for Entertainment	+G45-G43
48		
49	Number of Nights Out	+G47/D37

back-up of this section given in Spreadsheet Solution 4.4. Note that no numbers have been keyed in. Now enter the formulae shown in Spreadsheet Solution 4.4. To show the income per term as a figure punctuated with a comma (i.e. 1,000 not 1000) format this cell using ⟨/**Range**, **Format**, ,(comma) 0⟩, where the **0** refers to the number of decimal places in the figure. Then give the whole output section the range name ⟨OUTPUT⟩. Notice how the algebraic formulae developed earlier in the chapter have been converted into cell references. As an illustration of this point let us recall the formula for the total cost of accommodation, *A*:

$$A = 10r$$

where *r* is the rent per week. The rent per week is given in cell D29 and the number of weeks per term is given in D35 so the formula is:

⟨+D29 * D35⟩

which is the contents of cell G43.

The reason for the plus sign before the cell reference D29 is to distinguish it from a cell label beginning with the letter 'D'. The formula can be written either by typing the formula as above or by 'pointing to' the cells D29 and D35 after first typing the mathematical sign.

Also note that in the spreadsheet expression, the parameter for the number of weeks now takes the form of a variable. If we know that the number of weeks per term will not change then the formula for G43 could be:

⟨+D29 * 10⟩

Finally, return to the control section where the location table can be completed now that the two other sections of the spreadsheet have been given range names.

This model is very basic and is used to illustrate the main features of model design. Already we can use the model for 'what if?' purposes and we can also test the model to see if it works. Model testing is performed by inputting values for variables for which the output has been manually calculated. In this example this does not present a problem, but in complex models it is more difficult and can be done only by testing the change in output from varying one variable at a time.

To make use of the model and to see if it works, answer the following questions by changing the relevant values in the input section and seeing the effect on the output section. Attempt each question individually, that is, return the input variables to their original settings after attempting each question.

'What if?' questions

1. If the accommodation charge is £55 per week, how many nights out can our fresher afford?

2. If our student spends £15 per night out, what is the effect on the possible number of nights out?

3.   If the income per term is reduced by £225, how many nights does the student have to spend at home?

'What if?' solutions

1.   Change the cell in the input section which relates to the accommodation charge per week (D27) to £55. Look at the output section: the cell containing the number of nights out has changed to 60.

2.   Return the input section to the original values. Change cell D37 to 15 and monitor the output section. The number of nights out now becomes 40.

3.   Return the input section to the original values. Change the cell containing income per term to 775. The number of nights out becomes 50, that is, 20 nights at home.

Conclusion

We have outlined the modelling approach which we favour. The illustrative example has been kept relatively simple in order to demonstrate the principles of the approach. In the chapters which follow the models developed are more complex.

To become familiar with the modelling technique requires a certain dedication and study but this will pay dividends when the full extent of the spreadsheet's flexibility is appreciated.

Part III

Costing

5 | Cost behaviour and cost classification

AIMS OF CHAPTER _____

- to outline the various ways in which costs can be classified according to their behaviour;
- to use a spreadsheet model to graph cost functions for various levels of output;
- to introduce the topic of break-even analysis by combining cost and revenue functions.

SPREADSHEET SKILLS ACQUIRED _____

- centred labels;
- pointing to ranges;
- using the **Data F**ill function;
- using the **C**opy command;
- graphing;
- using the @**SUM** command;
- using relative and absolute cell references.

Introduction

Management accountants working for a company used to be known as 'cost and works' accountants. This title was replaced as it failed to describe the full complexities of the role played by these 'financial advisers' to management. However, the original title does emphasize the importance of 'cost' to the work of a management accountant, and this is the first of three chapters on the subject.

Information on costs is important to management as the basis for a wide range of decisions. Perhaps to state the obvious, the price of a product must exceed its cost if a profit is to be made. When the price charged for a product is determined by market forces (that is to say, is a given parameter in modelling terms), we say that the firm is a 'price-taker'. If management cannot influence the price charged for a product, the profitability of the company depends on managerial decisions affecting costs. If costs are not controlled, profit levels will be eroded.

In this chapter we will examine how costs react to changes in output levels which are determined by management decisions. In fact, choices regarding production levels represent some of the most important decisions made by a company's managers. Unless there is an understanding of the nature of the company's costs and their behaviour over a range of output, potentially disastrous decisions could be made.

Classification of costs

Variable costs

Different types of costs have different behaviour patterns. Costs which vary in direct proportion to changes in output levels are referred to as *variable* costs. Examples are easy to find in manufacturing processes, including raw material usage, piece-rate labour, power, and so on. In the selling and distribution of finished products, variable costs will include sales commissions, packaging and delivery charges. Both large and small businesses may analyze their costs in this way. For example, the fuel used by a taxi driver is a variable cost, as it will tend to vary according to output levels, that is, miles travelled.

Graphically, variable costs can be illustrated as shown in Figure 5.1. The linear relationship can be algebraically defined as:

$$y = bx$$

where y represents cost, b is a constant term, and x represents the output level. The value of b can be determined by various methods described in the next chapter, but it can be shown to be the slope of the line AA', that is the rate of change of y (costs) with respect to x, or

$$\frac{dy}{dx} = b$$

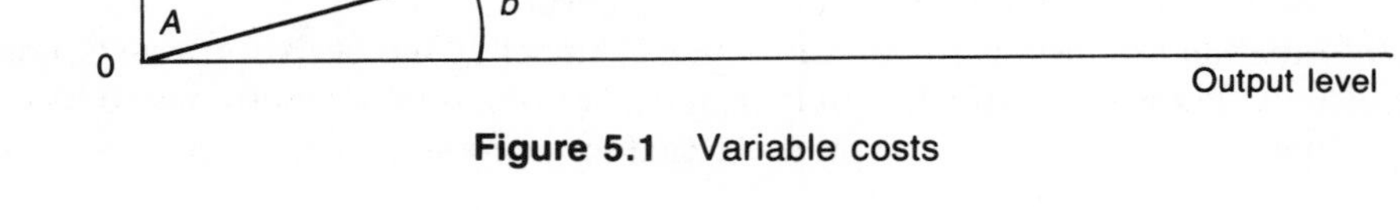

Figure 5.1   Variable costs

Fixed costs

Just as some costs vary directly with output levels, there are costs which do not vary. They are constant, irrespective of output, and are known as *fixed* costs. Examples of fixed costs are rent, salaries of the general administration staff, insurance premiums and lease payments. The fixed costs of the driver of a taxi would include the vehicle's licence, vehicle testing and insurance.

Figure 5.2 graphically portrays fixed costs. Here the algebraic representation does not contain any reference to output levels (x):

$$y = a$$

where y again represents cost and a is a constant. The BB' line has no slope ($b = 0$), and a is determined by factors other than output.

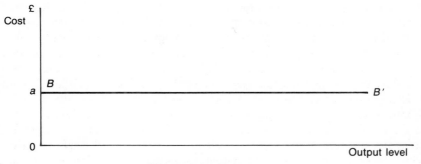

Figure 5.2 Fixed costs

Semi-variable costs

A third category of costs exhibits characteristics of both fixed and variable costs, referred to as *semi-variable* or *mixed* costs. The two components include an element which is incurred irrespective of output levels and an element which is totally dependent on output levels. Common examples include telephone and fax charges, electricity and gas bills, and any other cost which has a fixed rental component and a variable usage component.

Semi-variable costs are displayed by the line CC' in Figure 5.3. The relationship can be algebraically defined as:

$$y = a + bx$$

where x is output and y cost, as before; a is a constant representing fixed costs and b the rate of the variable component. The total cost line of a company also tends to take this form as fixed and variable costs are aggregated.

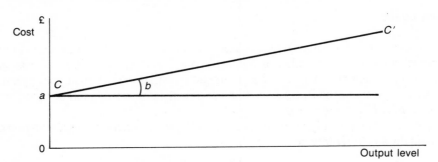

Figure 5.3   Semi-variable costs

Stepped costs

The term *stepped* costs is used to refer to costs which display the same characteristics as fixed costs until a given level of output is reached. Typically, stepped costs cannot be increased in small amounts and have to rise by predetermined steps. In all forms of industry an output level is reached which results in an increase in costs otherwise thought to be fixed. For example, in a production process which is already working to maximum capacity, in order to increase output beyond the existing level a company might be required to build new plant and employ a whole new shift.

Graphically, stepped costs are shown by the line *DD'* in Figure 5.4. Stepped costs are discontinuous functions and are not easy to model and even more difficult to express algebraically. If the 'steps' are shallow then these costs can be approximated to variable costs. Alternatively, if output levels can be predetermined then the appropriate step can be identified and treated as if it were a fixed cost.

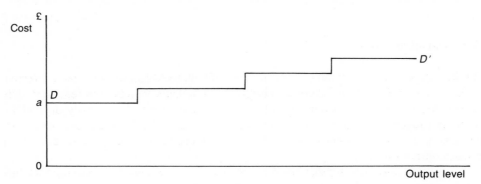

Figure 5.4   Stepped costs

Cost−volume−profit analysis

This topic is considered in more detail in Chapter 12, but we need briefly to mention the concept of *break-even* to place the analysis of costs into perspective.

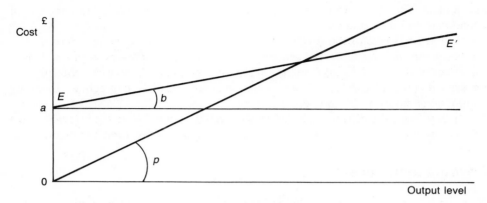

Figure 5.5 Break-even output level

One way of using the total cost line is to combine it with the revenue function to determine the output level required to cover costs incurred. Again, assumptions are made to simplify the model.

The main assumption is that the firm can sell all it produces at a given price. This may be an unrealistic assumption for firms operating in mature, saturated market conditions. For others adequate market research will usually make this assumption tenable. The total revenue line is therefore a straight line drawn from the origin and measuring the product of price (per unit) and quantity (of units).

Figure 5.5 illustrates the intersection of the total cost and total revenue lines which determines the break-even level of output.

This type of analysis may be complicated by the presence of stepped costs which can result in two or more break-even points. This is a sensitive situation for a management having to make decisions. The lowest point is obviously most significant, and management usually requires additional information such as the total profit for each level of output before deciding on courses of action.

The assumption of linearity and the relevant range

Modelling is a simplification of the real world which can enable decisions to be made and tested in a simulated environment. The more precise the simulation, the more difficult and more costly it is to model. In some cases precision is vital: for example, the design of a new component for the brakes of a car or flight simulators to train fighter pilots.

In a business context, is it worthwhile modelling the costs of a business from very small levels of output, which are known to be loss-making situations, to output levels which would require a dramatic increase in the firm's market share and asset base?

In management accounting we are only interested in the more likely levels of output which we say are within the *relevant range*.

Economic theorists postulate that the cost functions facing any business will be curvilinear. They point to the law of diminishing returns as well as to concepts of economies and diseconomies of scale.

The same is true of the revenue function. According to economic theory, sales increases can only be achieved, *ceteris paribus*, through decreases in price. This is the effect of the elasticity of demand. While the economist's theory of the firm can be argued quite plausibly, it complicates decision-making in practice. Linearity assumptions simplify this process.

In any event the difference between the models is small over the relevant range and the simplicity of the accountant's model means that it is favoured by practitioners.

Environmental costs

This section so far has only examined the financial costs faced by a business, but many output decisions will have wider consequences. Many production processes result in some form of pollution of the air, land or water and/or the production of noise. These are costs that are borne by society in general, but are caused by the managers of firms and their output decisions.

There is an environmentalist argument which states that firms should be forced to pay for the damage that they inflict in this indirect manner. Ideally, legislation would force all businesses to operate in an environment-friendly way and this would have an impact on costs. Harmful gas emissions may be reduced by filters which would have a fixed installation cost and variable or semi-variable running costs. Some products may be made more environmentally sensitive by the removal of certain ingredients which would reduce some variable costs. Governments may apply environmental taxes which may affect fixed or variable costs and hence increase break-even points or increase prices.

The analysis of cost behaviour is therefore not a redundant tool to the 'green' accountant. The implications of more environmentally sound production methods can be modelled in the same way and break-even output levels determined.

Ultimately, however, a company's profits are subject to market forces which reflect consumer demand. If consumers in sufficient numbers demand products that have been produced using processes kinder to the environment, companies will be forced to provide such products to maintain profit levels.

Modelling cost behaviour

In addition to its versatility in manipulating figures and formulae, the modern spreadsheet package has a graphics capability. This enables the user to chart numeric data on a graph with considerable scope for customizing the presentation to suit particular circumstances.

Example 5.1

Table 5.1 presents output and cost data relating to Halksworth Ltd, a manufacturing company making medical equipment. The above data can be converted into more

Table 5.1 *Halksworth Ltd cost data*

Output (in units)	Factory Overheads	Labour	Direct Materials
1,000	20,000	10,000	7,000
1,100	20,000	10,000	7,700
1,200	20,000	10,000	8,400
1,300	20,000	15,000	9,100
1,400	20,000	15,000	9,800
1,500	20,000	15,000	10,500
1,600	20,000	15,000	11,200
1,700	20,000	15,000	11,900
1,800	20,000	20,000	12,600
1,900	20,000	20,000	13,300
2,000	20,000	20,000	14,000

Halksworth sells its product for £30.33.

usable information in a number of ways:

- by graphing each of the cost components in turn, in order to classify these costs appropriately;
- by calculating the total cost and its behaviour;
- by producing a graph showing total revenue and total cost from which the break-even point can be determined.

The ease with which the spreadsheet can produce the information is described below.

The spreadsheet solution

Since there is only one section to this spreadsheet we will not need a control section. Go straight to inputting the data from Table 5.1 into your spreadsheet (see Spreadsheet Solution 5.1) by following the steps below.

The column headings are in the form of text (labels). Notice that some spill over into the next column and may partially disappear when the heading for the next column is keyed in. You will need to widen some columns, which you can do by typing ⟨/Worksheet, Column, Set Width⟩.

Centred labels

To improve the appearance of the spreadsheet, centre these labels by typing ⟨/Range, Label, Centre⟩, inserting the cell reference of the cell containing the label and then pressing [Enter]. Note how the label indicator in the control panel changes in this cell from ' ' ' to ' ^ '. This can be done individually for each cell in the column headings or by a quicker route, pointing to a range.

Spreadsheet solution 5.1   Halksworth Ltd

	A	B	C	D	E	F	G
1	Spreadsheet Solution 5-1 - Halksworth Ltd						
2							
3	This spreadsheet contains cost and output data for a company that						
4	manufactures medical equipment.						
5							
6	Price		30.33				
7							
8	Output	Factory	Labour	Direct	Total	Total	Profit\
9	(in Units)	Overheads		Materials	Cost	Revenue	Loss
10							
11	1000	20000	10000	7,000	37,000	30,330	6,670
12	1100	20000	10000	7,700	37,700	33,363	4,337
13	1200	20000	10000	8,400	38,400	36,396	2,004
14	1300	20000	15000	9,100	44,100	39,429	4,671
15	1400	20000	15000	9,800	44,800	42,462	2,338
16	1500	20000	15000	10,500	45,500	45,495	5
17	1600	20000	15000	11,200	46,200	48,528	(2,328)
18	1700	20000	15000	11,900	46,900	51,561	(4,661)
19	1800	20000	20000	12,600	52,600	54,594	(1,994)
20	1900	20000	20000	13,300	53,300	57,627	(4,327)
21	2000	20000	20000	14,000	54,000	60,660	(6,660)

Pointing to ranges

Instead of typing in a range, for example A8..G9, when asked for a range by the prompt line, you can use the cursor keys to 'point' to the cells desired. If you are already positioned over one of the corners of your range you can move immediately to the extreme opposite corner of the range using the cursor keys and the range is shaded on the screen.

If you are not positioned at the desired point, press [Esc], move to one of the corners of the desired range, anchor the cursor by pressing [.], and move the cursor to the diagonally opposite corner of the range. When you have shaded in the required area, just press [Enter] and this becomes the accepted range.

This may seem long-winded, but pointing can be very quick (especially if you use a mouse), and the screen shading acts as a visual aid to ensure the correct cells are included.

Using the Data Fill option

The output levels in Table 5.1 are in increments of 100 starting at 1000 and ending at 2000. These can be input quickly using the **Data Fill** option.

Position the cursor over the first cell to contain the output values: in Spreadsheet

Solution 5.1 this is cell A11. Select ⟨**/D**ata, **F**ill, A11..A21⟩. An alternative to typing ⟨A11..A21⟩ is to point to this range on screen.

Once the range is input you are prompted to insert a start value; type ⟨1000⟩. The next prompt is for the step value, that is, the increment; type ⟨100⟩.

The last prompt is for a stop value. The stop value default is 8192, the maximum number of rows available. Provided you have correctly specified your output range, there is no need to type ⟨2000⟩, since the Data Fill will not go beyond the specified range. Simply press [Enter] and column A, Output (in Units), is automatically created.

The figures for the categories of cost must be keyed in. Remember not to punctuate the figures with commas but to format the relevant cells to display punctuated figures with 0 decimal places, ⟨**/R**ange, **F**ormat, **,**(comma), **0**, [Enter]⟩. However the **Copy** command can provide a short-cut.

Copying values

The factory overheads remain unchanged irrespective of output, so enter the original value ⟨20000⟩ in cell B11, then copy *from* B11 *to* the remaining cells in column B using the **Copy** command. With the cursor on B11, type ⟨**/C**opy, B11, B12..B21, [Enter]⟩. Once again make use of the pointing facility to highlight the range B12..B21 when you reach the 'Copy to' prompt.

The **Copy** command can also be used in smaller ranges for the labour costs. For example, type ⟨10000⟩ in cell C11 and copy it to C12..C13, then in C14 type ⟨15000⟩ and copy it to C15..C18, and repeat the procedure to input ⟨20000⟩ in cells C19..C21.

Direct materials costs increase by £700 for each increase of 100 units of output. Use the **Data Fill** command to complete column D with a start value of 7000 and a step value of 700. Remember that you must either specify the fill range or replace the default stop value with 14000.

Graphing data

Using the spreadsheet's graphing capabilities is one of the easiest and most rewarding tasks to perform. To graph the various cost functions, select ⟨**/G**raph⟩ to access the graph menu structure. The first option is **Type**. Selecting ⟨Type⟩ produces the graph types available. We want a **Line** graph so [Enter] this option.

The X range refers to the horizontal axis which will be the output levels. This option requires a range to be input, by either typing the cell addresses, ⟨A11..A21⟩, or by pointing to (highlighting) the range.

The letters A through to F refer to the number of data series that can be graphed at any one time. Let us make series A refer to the factory overheads, ⟨B11..B21⟩.

Using [End] and arrow keys to point

A quick way to point to a range of values is to anchor the start cell (B11) at the range prompt and then press [End] and then [↓], which will move the cursor to the last value it comes to before a blank cell.

To view your graph at this stage press ⟨View⟩ or [F10]. The result is not very impressive! We need to use the **Graph** options to improve the presentation.

The options sub-menu starts with **Legend**. This is the key to the lines plotted on the graph. It allows you to enter a text description of the line, for instance ⟨Overheads⟩. A main title and a secondary title for the graph as a whole can be inserted in the same as well as titles for the X and Y axis.

If the necessary text is already in a cell you can use a cell reference rather than reinputting the text. For example, a quick way of labelling the X axis 'Output' is to type ⟨\A8⟩, (cell A8 contains the heading 'Output'), at the appropriate prompt.

The other problem with our graph is the default setting for scaling, which is set on automatic. This allows for the extremities of the data. In our case the only value for overheads is £20,000 and that is the first point on the Y axis. This is clearly unsatisfactory and we need to replace it with a zero. While in the graph menu, type ⟨Options, Scale, Y-Scale, Manual, 60000⟩ to set manually the upper limit on the Y axis to £60,000.

Once you have completed your **Graph** options, the **View**ed graph should look like Figure 5.6. Replace the A series with the other costs individually to produce Figures 5.7 and 5.8.

Using graphing techniques clearly illustrates the behaviour of different costs. However, the spreadsheet cannot readily reproduce the graph shown in Figure 5.4. The stepped labour costs are produced as a continuous function in Figure 5.7 with smooth lines joining the points where the step appears. These could be replaced by vertical lines if the X axis were more precise, that is, plotted from 1 to 2000 in increments of 1.

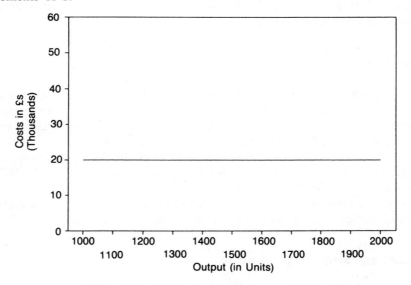

Figure 5.6   Halksworth Ltd: factory overheads

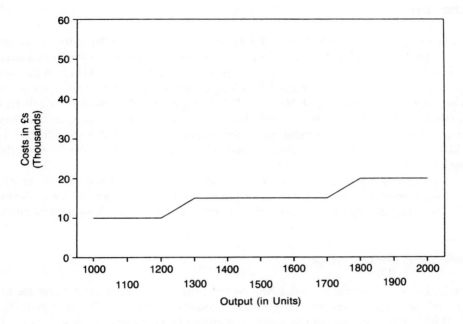

Figure 5.7 Halksworth Ltd: labour costs

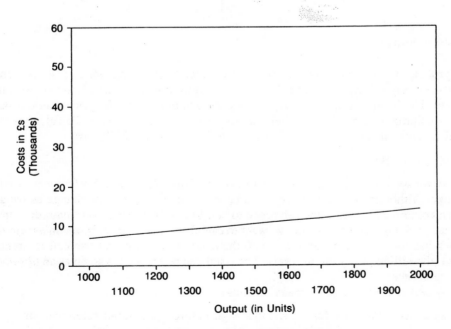

Figure 5.8 Halksworth Ltd: direct materials costs

Total costs

In cells E8 and E9 enter ⟨Total⟩ and ⟨Cost⟩, respectively, to form the column heading. In column E to calculate the total cost for each level of output we could add each of the cells in a given row, for example in cell E11, ⟨+B11+C11+D11⟩. A quicker way is to use the @**SUM** command which adds the contents of the cells in a given range. In cell E11 type ⟨@SUM(B11..D11)⟩. Now copy the contents of cell E11 to cells E12..E21. Notice how the cell references in the formula change so that they remain relative to the particular row; for example, the formula in cell E21 is @SUM(B21..D21). The movement of total cost is graphed in Figure 5.9, using the range E11..E21 as the series values.

An alternative presentation of the information uses the ⟨/Graph, **Type**, **Area**⟩, with each type of cost being used as series values, A−C. The result is shown as Figure 5.10. Note that the top line of this graph is identical to Figure 5.9 showing total costs.

Saving and printing graphs

Graphs are saved within a spreadsheet by 'naming' them under the **Graph** menu. 'Saving' the graph under the **Graph** menu produces a **.PIC** file for later printing.

With some computer set-ups it may sometimes be necessary to use a Printgraph facility, external to the main spreadsheet. This is a technical problem for which you may need to consult the user manuals for your spreadsheet package and printer.

Total revenue

To produce a graph showing total revenue we need to insert the selling price per unit into a cell, say cell B6, which has been formatted to show the contents to two decimal places. The formula required will multiply the output level by the price. Let us open a new column, column F, and label it appropriately, Total Revenue. To calculate the total revenue at the first level of output, the formula in cell F11 is:

⟨+A11*B6⟩

If we were to copy this formula to cells F12 to F21, the cell references would change. Although we want the cell reference to the output level to change as we go down column F, we want the reference to cell B6, selling price, to remain the same for each level of output. That is, we want to calculate total revenue by using a formula which has one cell reference *relative* to the level of outcome and one cell reference fixed (the selling price) for all levels. The fixed cell reference is known as an *absolute* cell reference.

A cell reference can be made absolute:

■ as to its column by typing a dollar sign before the column reference; or

■ as to its row by typing a dollar sign before the row reference; or

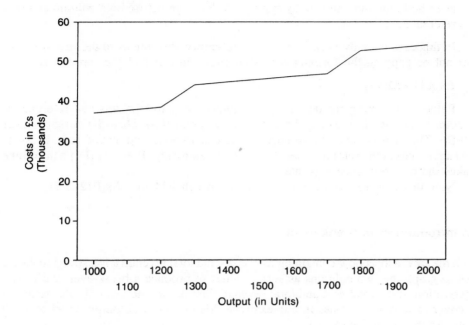

Figure 5.9   Halksworth Ltd: total costs

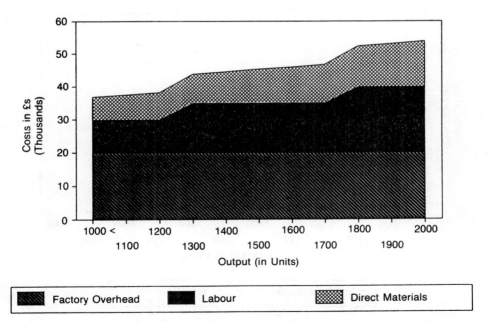

Figure 5.10   Halksworth Ltd: aggregation of costs

■ as to both column and row by typing a dollar sign before both column and row reference.

In this case we only need to make the reference absolute as to the row since we will not be copying the formula across columns. In cell F11 the formula is:

⟨ +A11 * $B$6 ⟩

Rather than typing the dollar sign, a quicker way to 'fix' this cell reference is to point to cell B6 in creating the formula and press [F4] when the cursor is over cell B6. This makes the cell reference absolute as to both column and row. Pressing [F4] again makes the reference absolute as to column only. Pressing [F4] a third time makes the row reference absolute.

Now this new formula can be copied from cell F11 to cells F12..F21.

An introduction to break-even

With the spreadsheet now containing total costs and total revenue it is a straightforward task to graph the two columns as series values to produce a break-even chart. The intersection of the total cost and total revenue lines shows the level of sales required to cover exactly total costs. In our example this occurs at an output level of 1500 units, as shown in Figure 5.11.

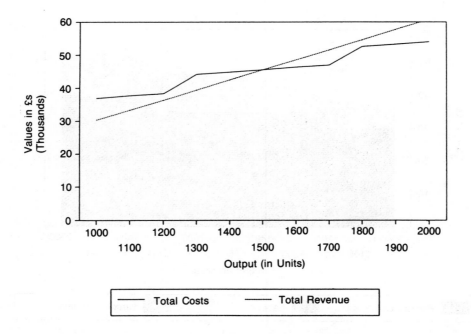

Figure 5.11 Halksworth Ltd: total revenues and costs

Spreadsheet solution 5.2   Halksworth Ltd

	A	B	C	D	E	F	G
1	Spreadsheet Solution 5-2 - Halksworth Ltd						
2							
3	This spreadsheet contains cost and output data for a company that						
4	manufactures medical equipment.						
5							
6	Price	30.33					
7							
8	Output	Factory	Labour	Direct	Total	Total	Profit\
9	(in Units)	Overheads		Materials	Cost	Revenue	Loss
10							
11	1000	20000	10000	7000	@SUM(B11..D11)	+A11*$B$6	+E11-F11
12	1100	20000	10000	7700	@SUM(B12..D12)	+A12*$B$6	+E12-F12
13	1200	20000	10000	8400	@SUM(B13..D13)	+A13*$B$6	+E13-F13
14	1300	20000	15000	9100	@SUM(B14..D14)	+A14*$B$6	+E14-F14
15	1400	20000	15000	9800	@SUM(B15..D15)	+A15*$B$6	+E15-F15
16	1500	20000	15000	10500	@SUM(B16..D16)	+A16*$B$6	+E16-F16
17	1600	20000	15000	11200	@SUM(B17..D17)	+A17*$B$6	+E17-F17
18	1700	20000	15000	11900	@SUM(B18..D18)	+A18*$B$6	+E18-F18
19	1800	20000	20000	12600	@SUM(B19..D19)	+A19*$B$6	+E19-F19
20	1900	20000	20000	13300	@SUM(B20..D20)	+A20*$B$6	+E20-F20
21	2000	20000	20000	14000	@SUM(B21..D21)	+A21*$B$6	+E21-F21

For the sake of completeness let us create a final column to calculate the profit or loss at each level of output. The profit or loss is calculated simply by deducting total cost from total revenue, column F − column E. Spreadsheet Solution 5.2 shows the formula of the completed spreadsheet.

The following examples demonstrate the usefulness of the spreadsheet model in providing solutions to 'what if?' types of questions.

'What if?' questions

1. What is the new break-even point if the price charged is forced down to £28? Change cell B6 and read off the new break-even point from the graph.

2. If the government gives the company a choice of either facing a one-off 'industry' tax of £5000 per annum or paying a levy of £2 per unit produced, which option should the company take?
    First restore the price to its original level of £30.33. To find the solution increase fixed costs and determine the break-even point. Restore fixed costs and increase the variable costs and determine the break-even point.

'What if?' solutions

1. Approximately 2000 units. The break-even point rises as the slope of the revenue function has fallen, i.e. selling price has decreased.

2. Option 1: the industry tax results in a break-even point of around 2000 units.

Option 2: the output tax results in a break-even point lying between 1600 and 1700 units and a break-even point between 1800 and 1900 units.

The company should accept option 2.

Conclusion

We have considered different patterns of cost behaviour. It is important for management to have information on cost behaviour for without this it would be difficult to predict financial consequences of vital decisions.

In the next chapter we discuss different methods of measuring the relationship between costs and output levels and in subsequent chapters we explain how the information produced can be used as the basis for management decision-making.

Exercises

Question 5.1

(a) Explain what you understand by the term 'cost behaviour', why it is important in the context of cost and management accounting, and what behaviour patterns may be encountered.

(b) What factors influence the behaviour of costs in response to changes in an organization's level of activity?

No answer provided   *(ACCA)*

Question 5.2

You are required to show, by means of a sketch, a separate graph of cost behaviour patterns for each of the listed items of expense. You should indicate the axis of each clearly.

(a) Electricity bill: a standing charge for each period plus a charge for each unit of electricity consumed.

(b) Supervisory labour.

(c) Production bonus, which is payable when output in a period exceeds 10,000 units. The bonus amounts in total to £20,000 plus £50 per unit for additional output above 10,000 units.

No answer provided   *(ACCA)*

6 | *Cost estimation*

AIMS OF CHAPTER _____

- to indicate the importance of accurate methods of cost estimation;
- to consider the various methods of cost estimation, along with their usefulness and limitations;
- to develop spreadsheet models that enable each method to be compared, based on the same sample of cost data.

SPREADSHEET SKILLS ACQUIRED _____

- **Data Sort**;
- more graphing;
- @**MAX** and @**MIN** functions;
- @**VLOOKUP** function.

Introduction

Cost information is used for many decisions, not just in break-even analysis as discussed in the last chapter. Various financial reports that are crucial for the control of the business will use cost data. We will see later how various budget reports are prepared and used for this purpose. We will also examine the term *standard cost* and how *variance analysis* is used to highlight problem areas in large and complex organizations. As cost information is so pervasive, it is important that the method used for estimating costs is an accurate one. Mistakes at this stage can have wide-ranging implications throughout the firm.

Past and future decisions

We have already discovered that some costs will behave differently to others and should be appropriately classified. In the example of Halksworth in the previous chapter we estimated the behaviour of costs on the basis of a number of output levels, but this may not have been very accurate. The essential feature of the information was that it related to the *past* and was the consequence of previous managerial decisions. In making decisions managers can only influence the *future* and they require information on how future costs will behave.

Because managers cannot be totally accurate in their forecasts, the term *cost estimation* is used to indicate the potential inaccuracy of the information produced. Managers can reduce this inaccuracy by carefully selecting the best method of cost estimation from the range available. This chapter examines the main methods used and develops the respective spreadsheet models.

Engineering method

A prerequisite for using past information is that the firm's environment has not changed, that is, it uses the same production methods as before. If this is not the case, the only reasonably accurate method of cost estimation is the *engineering method*.

This method relies on the analysis of the technical relationships between inputs and outputs. From time and motion studies, sampling and product specifications, engineers will determine the likely relationships that apply. Using these techniques, production engineers can estimate, for example, how much raw material is used per unit and how many units can be produced on the assembly line.

It is possible to use the spreadsheet to produce a cost model that incorporates the range of parameters and variables that engineering methods produce.

This form of cost estimation can be very complex and take into account economies and diseconomies of scale, learning curves (the rate at which workers become used to the new tasks) and even result in the redesign of work processes to more ergonomically sound methods.

To achieve any degree of accuracy, specialist operations management personnel may have to be used and, given the complexity of many production processes, this method of cost estimation can work out expensive.

It is also inappropriate to use this method for indirect costs as often there are no observable and measurable relationships between changes in such costs and changes in output levels.

Given the disadvantages involved, the engineering method is only used if past cost data are unavailable or inappropriate. We now consider the methods that use past cost data to estimate costs.

Visual inspection method

The easiest method of estimating costs is little more than an attempt to 'eyeball' the figures to ascertain how costs vary with output.

Example 6.1

Table 6.1 presents data relating to output and costs for Palmer Ltd. The first point to notice is that the information is in the order in which it was collected. In order to model the cost behaviour, we must first determine what is the independent variable. As we are dealing with total costs we would expect to discover the relationship $y = a + bx$, with y being the dependent variable (total costs) and x the independent variable (output level). This relationship was first introduced in Chapter 5. Time, in months, is also an independent variable, but we would not expect costs to vary directly with time except in highly seasonal businesses.

We are using past data based on historic cost principles. Adjustments may be required to allow for the effects of inflation and any other changes in external factors. For the purposes of simplicity we will assume that inflation is negligible.

Table 6.1   *Palmer Ltd output and costs data*

Month	Output Level (units)	Total Costs (£)
1	2,800	16,100
2	2,500	15,100
3	2,700	16,000
4	2,900	16,700
5	3,000	16,900
6	2,600	15,600
7	3,100	17,400
8	2,300	13,100
9	2,400	14,500
10	3,200	17,700
11	3,400	19,100
12	3,300	19,000

The spreadsheet solution

For this model we will not use a control section so the first section of the spreadsheet is the input section. Enter the data from Table 6.1 into the input section of your spreadsheet. After allowing for column headings the numerical data should fill the range A7..C18, with column A containing the number of the month, column B the output levels and column C total costs. We will use the same data for all the methods of cost estimation, and, to facilitate subsequent manipulation of the data, create range names for the various ranges. The command for this is ⟨/Range, Name, Create⟩. After selecting the **Create** option, at the prompt 'Enter name to create/modify' enter ⟨LEVELS⟩, then at the next prompt 'Enter range' point to the range ⟨B7..B18⟩. Repeat this procedure to create a range name ⟨COSTS⟩ for the range ⟨B7..C18⟩, the range which includes both output levels and costs. We will make use of these range names later.

Data Sort

Our first task is to arrange the data in ascending order of output level. To arrange the data we use the command ⟨/Data, Sort, Data Range⟩. Having selected the option **Data Range**, at the prompt 'Enter Data range' type ⟨A7...C18⟩. The spreadsheet will only adjust the columns and rows that are in this range and will leave all other parts of the spreadsheet unaffected.

Once this range has been selected you need to decide on your ⟨**Primary Key**⟩. In our case this is the column containing the output levels. You need only select the first cell of the output column which contains a number, that is, B7.

The **Sort Order** to be selected is ⟨Ascending⟩; then select ⟨**Go**⟩.

The data should now be arranged as shown in Table 6.2. Using the graphing skills developed in the last chapter, graph the data using the output level as the X series and total costs as series A. The graph produced is not a complete picture since the output levels are confined to a small band, from 2300 to 3400 units. To get a fuller picture we need to take output levels down to zero.

Table 6.2   *Input section for Example 6.1*

Month	Output Level (units)	Total Costs (£)
8	2,300	13,100
9	2,400	14,500
2	2,500	15,100
6	2,600	15,600
3	2,700	16,000
1	2,800	16,100
4	2,900	16,700
5	3,000	16,900
7	3,100	17,400
10	3,200	17,700
12	3,300	19,000
11	3,400	19,100

Using ⟨/**Worksheet**, **Insert**, **Row** command⟩, insert 23 additional rows for the missing X-values (0 to 2200 in increments of 100) above the existing output levels and associated costs, that is, perform the insert command with the cursor on A7, highlight the column down to A29, then [Enter]. Your input section should now appear as in Spreadsheet Solution 6.1.

Displaying a graph with markers

Using the **Options** command in the **Graph** sub-menu, **Format** either the graph or series A to display Symbols. Your graph should resemble Figure 6.1, with the heavy blocks representing the observations in Table 6.2. This is known as a *scatter graph* or *scatter plot*.

The line of 'best fit' which disects the points has to be manually drawn. In our

Spreadsheet solution 6.1 Input section

	A	B	C
1	Spreadsheet Solution 6-1		
2			
3	Input Section		
4			
5		Output	Total
6		Level	Costs
7		0	
8		100	
9		200	
10		300	
11		400	
12		500	
13		600	
14		700	
15		800	
16		900	
17		1,000	
18		1,100	
19		1,200	
20		1,300	
21		1,400	
22		1,500	
23		1,600	
24		1,700	
25		1,800	
26		1,900	
27		2,000	
28		2,100	
29		2,200	
30	8	2,300	13,100
31	9	2,400	14,500
32	2	2,500	15,100
33	6	2,600	15,600
34	3	2,700	16,000
35	1	2,800	16,100
36	4	2,900	16,700
37	5	3,000	16,900
38	7	3,100	17,400
39	10	3,200	17,700
40	12	3,300	19,000
41	11	3,400	19,100

example this intersects the Y axis at about £6000. This gives us the *a*-value. To find the *b*-value pick a point on the line, for instance, with coordinates of 3200 units on the X axis and, on the Y axis, costs of £17,700. We know that our fixed costs are estimated at £6000 so our *total* variable costs are £17,700 — £6000 = £11,700; taking this value, £11,700, and dividing by 3200, gives us a *b*-coefficient of £3.66.

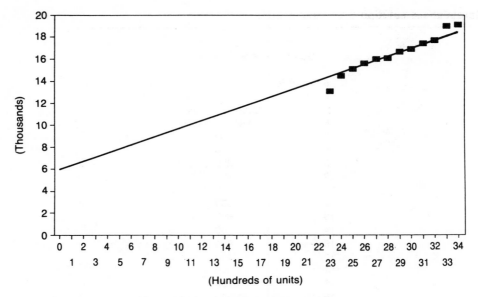

Figure 6.1 Visual inspection method

Our estimate of total costs is therefore:

$$y = 6000 + 3.66x$$

This is manually input into output section 1 (cells D42..G47) of the spreadsheet model (see Spreadsheet Solution 6.2) which we will use later when comparing the results of the different methods of cost estimation.

Spreadsheet solution 6.2 Output section 1 — Visual inspection

	D	E	F	G
42	Spreadsheet Solution 6-2			
43				
44	Output Section 1 - Visual Inspection			
45				
46	a =	6,000		
47	b =	3.66		

The visual inspection method has the advantage that it is quick and easy and produces a result which is intuitively acceptable. However, its accuracy is questionable and rests on the estimator's subjective judgement, which may be unduly swayed by 'outliers' (extreme and unrepresentative observations).

High—low method

This is a straightforward method of cost estimation that limits its analysis to two observations which represent the highest and lowest output values. While this is fairly easy to do manually we will take the opportunity to introduce some spreadsheet functions that can be used for more complex modelling later.

@MAX and @MIN

These @ functions, when placed in a cell formula, examine a range of figures and find the maximum or minimum values within that range. Unlike the visual inspection method, the data need not be arranged in a particular order.

Create a heading for output section 2 (which will occupy cells H48..K58). In cell I52 type the formula ⟨@MAX(LEVEL)⟩. Note: at the open parenthesis type [F3] and when the choice of range names appear, select ⟨LEVEL⟩ and close the parenthesis. Edit this formula using [F2] and move the cursor within the formula to the start of the range name in parentheses, then press [F4] to make the range absolute.

This formula can then be copied to cell I53 and edited to change the **@MAX** function to the **@MIN** function so that the minimum level of output will appear in this cell. The answers which should appear are 3400 and 2300 respectively (see Spreadsheet Solution 6.3).

Spreadsheet solution 6.3   Output section 2 — high—low method

	H	I	J	K
48	Spreadsheet Solution 6-3			
49				
50	Output Section 2 - High-Low Method			
51				
52	Maximum Value	3,400	Associated Cost	19,100
53	Minimum Value	2,300	Associated Cost	13,100
54		----------------		----------------
55		1,100		6,000
56				
57	b =	5.45		
58	a =	554.55		

@VLOOKUP

This function is very powerful and can be used in a wide variety of ways. It is often ignored by many spreadsheet users as it appears complicated, but in fact it is very easy to learn.

We need to find the total costs associated with the two extreme (highest and lowest) output levels we have isolated. We can perform this manually by inspecting the list of output levels, finding the maximum and minimum output levels and reading the corresponding total costs which are in the column offset to the right. By breaking down our own thought process in this way we can see how the **@VLOOKUP** function works. The form the function takes is as follows:

@VLOOKUP(selector cell, range, +offset)

To find the total cost associated with the maximum output level, in cell K52 type ⟨@VLOOKUP(I52, COSTS, +1)⟩. What does this mean? What are we looking up? We are trying to find the cost associated with the maximum output level within the range named 'COSTS'. (Note that the range COSTS includes both output levels and associated costs.) The maximum value of output units is 3400, given to us in cell I52. This is known as the selector cell. The +1 refers to the location of the solution we are seeking, that is, the cost associated with the maximum output will be found one column to the right of the selector cell. This tells the spreadsheet which value to look up and return it to cell K52.

After editing the formula to make the range name 'COSTS' an absolute reference, this formula can be copied to find the total cost associated with the minimum output level.

(The 'V' in @VLOOKUP refers to a vertical table. A similar expression can be used for horizontal tables, @HLOOKUP.)

To solve for b just take the difference between the two values (£19,100 − £13,100 = £6000) and divide it by the difference between the two output levels (3400 − 2300 = 1100). This gives a b-coefficient of 5.45. This can be substituted in either of the observations to find the constant a:

$$19,100 = a + 3400(5.45)$$
or
$$13,100 = a + 2300(5.45)$$

Both result in a-values of £555 (to the nearest £). The formulae for this output section are given in Spreadsheet Solution 6.4.

So our cost estimation model is:

$$y = 555 + 5.45x$$

We can see that this result differs significantly from the visual inspection method. What we have done is produce a line that connects the two extreme points, which

Spreadsheet solution 6.4   Output section 2 — High−low method

	H	I	J	K
48	Spreadsheet Solution 6-4			
49				
50	Output Section 2 -	High-Low Method		
51				
52	Maximum Value	@MAX(LEVEL)	Associated Cost	@VLOOKUP(+I52,$COSTS,+1)
53	Minimum Value	@MIN(LEVEL)	Associated Cost	@VLOOKUP(+I53,$COSTS,+1)
54		--------------------------------		---
55		+I52-I53		+K52-K53
56				
57	b =	+K55/I55		
58	a =	+K52-($I$57*I52)		

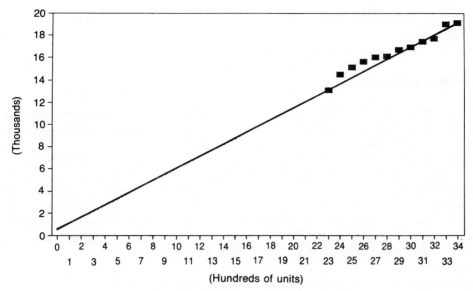

Figure 6.2 High–low method

is not necessarily representative of normal levels of activity. This is graphed in Figure 6.2.

However, there are more sophisticated methods of cost estimation which can be easily performed on a spreadsheet and which may give more reliable results.

Linear regression method

One of these more sophisticated methods is called *linear regression analysis*. It comes in two forms, *simple* and *multiple regression*. The simple form assumes that there is just one independent variable: in our example, units of output, x. Multiple regression is used to solve the problem when there are two or more independent variables x_1 to x_n.

To an extent we have been attempting less complex forms of linear regression in the lines of best fit produced under the previous cost estimation methods. These methods lacked accuracy either because they were subjective or because they failed to take account of all of the observations. However, it is possible mathematically to produce a line of best fit using a method called *ordinary least squares*.

This technique works by producing a line of best fit which minimizes the deviations of the observations from the line. As deviations can be above or below this 'line of best fit', they are squared in the resulting algorithm to produce a line which cannot be drawn any better, hence the term 'best fit'.

Manually to produce this line the following simultaneous equations need to be solved to find a and b:

$$\Sigma Y = na + b\Sigma x$$

$$\Sigma xy = a\Sigma x + b$$

Simple regression

This is a long-winded, repetitive calculation which is loathed by students in examinations as it is easy to make an arithmetic error. However, the spreadsheet model can produce the output very quickly by using ⟨/**Data**, **Regress**⟩.

At the regression sub-menu you will need to select the X (independent variable) range, then at the following prompt type ⟨LEVEL⟩ and [Enter]. For the Y (dependent variable) range, you will need to point to the range C30..C41. The third menu selection is an output range for the solution. Select a cell below and to the right of output section 2. You need only select the cell which will be the top left-hand corner of the output. In our example we chose cell L59. On typing ⟨**Go**⟩, the output of the regression will appear. The output appears as in Spreadsheet Solution 6.5.

Spreadsheet solution 6.5   Output section 3 — Linear regression

	L	M	N	O
59	Spreadsheet Solution 6-5			
60				
61	Output Section 3 - Linear Regression			
62				
63		Regression Output:		
64	Constant			2,781
65	Std Err of Y Est			365
66	R Squared			0.96
67	No. of Observations			12
68	Degrees of Freedom			10
69				
70	X Coefficient(s)		4.79	
71	Std Err of Coef.		0.31	

The term 'constant' refers to the a-value, in this case 2781, whereas the b-coefficient is labelled 'X Coefficient(s)', in this case 4.79. So the result of our third method of cost estimation gives us the total cost model:

$$y = 2781 + 4.79x$$

This is graphed in Figure 6.3.

Notice that the output range gives far more information other than the line of best fit. It also produces a statistic called 'R **Squared**', more usually written as r^2. This is known as the *coefficient of determination*; r is the *coefficient of correlation*, calculated using the formula:

$$r = \frac{n(\Sigma xy) - (\Sigma x)(\Sigma y)}{\sqrt{[n(\Sigma x^2) - (\Sigma x)^2]}\sqrt{[n(\Sigma y^2) - (\Sigma y)^2]}}$$

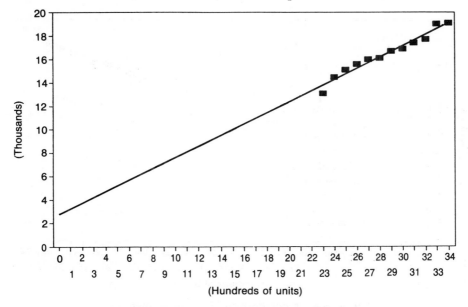

Figure 6.3   Linear regression method

It gives an indication of how good the fit is — the closer to 1 the better. A 'loose' fit produces *r*-values closer to 0.

The predictive ability of the model is indicated by stating how much of the change in total costs can be accounted for by changes in output. In our example, 96% of the change in costs is due to changes in output levels, which is a very good fit.

The other statistics refer to standard errors which can be used with the *t*-distribution to produce confidence intervals. As this is only an introductory text, a discussion of these techniques is not considered appropriate.

Multiple regression

In our example, we only had one independent variable, output. In practice, there may be more than one explanatory variable which may be able to predict costs. The coefficient of determination can be improved if more predictors are included in the model. This is called multiple regression.

The spreadsheet can cope with up to 16 independent variables. One problem with this method is that the predictors themselves may be correlated. This phenomenon is known as *multi-collinearity*. The spreadsheet package will test for this and reject the output with the message 'Cannot invert matrix'.

The three methods compared

The three methods have all produced different results as follows:

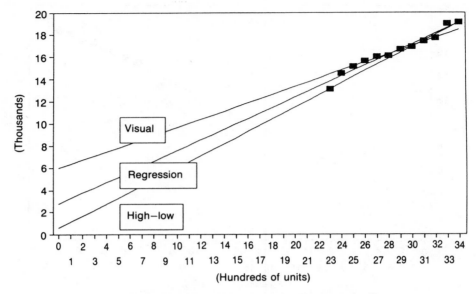

Figure 6.4　A comparison of the three methods

Visual	$y = 6000 + 3.66x$
High−low	$y = \quad 555 + 5.45x$
Regression	$y = 2781 + 4.79x$

These different results can be used to produce different estimates of costs across the complete range of output levels from 0 to 3400 (or beyond if necessary), as shown in Spreadsheet Solutions 6.6 and 6.7. Note that for each method of estimation only cell references are used to estimate costs based on the expression $y = a + bx$ but using the different values for a and b produced by each method. The results can be graphed as in Figure 6.4.

If output levels are within the production limits encountered in the past then let us see which method produces the closest result. Say production is set at 2500, which produced an observable total cost of £15,100. Using the results of the three methods to predict costs associated with an output of 2500 units gives us:

Visual	$y = 6000 + 3.66(2500) = 15,150$
High−low	$y = \quad 555 + 5.45(2500) = 14,180$
Regression	$y = 2781 + 4.79(2500) = 14,756$

Which method is best depends upon the intended use. In this case the visual method is closest, but none of the methods is more than about 6% away. This can be regarded as a satisfactory level of accuracy.

Merely looking at the scatter graph would imply that there is some form of stepped cost function. The lowest output takes place in month 8. If this is August then the factory could have been partially shut down, or closed completely for a week or two,

Spreadsheet solution 6.6   Output section 4

	P	Q	R	S	T	U
	Spreadsheet Solution 6-6					
72						
73						
74	Output Section 4					
75						
76		Output	Total	Visual		
77	Months	Level	Costs	Inspection	High Low	Regression
78		0		6,000	555	2,781
79		100		6,366	1,100	3,260
80		200		6,732	1,645	3,739
81		300		7,098	2,191	4,218
82		400		7,464	2,736	4,697
83		500		7,830	3,282	5,176
84		600		8,196	3,827	5,655
85		700		8,562	4,373	6,134
86		800		8,928	4,918	6,613
87		900		9,294	5,464	7,092
88		1,000		9,660	6,009	7,571
89		1,100		10,026	6,555	8,050
90		1,200		10,392	7,100	8,529
91		1,300		10,758	7,645	9,009
92		1,400		11,124	8,191	9,488
93		1,500		11,490	8,736	9,967
94		1,600		11,856	9,282	10,446
95		1,700		12,222	9,827	10,925
96		1,800		12,588	10,373	11,404
97		1,900		12,954	10,918	11,883
98		2,000		13,320	11,464	12,362
99		2,100		13,686	12,009	12,841
100		2,200		14,052	12,555	13,320
101	8	2,300	13,100	14,418	13,100	13,799
102	9	2,400	14,500	14,784	13,645	14,278
103	2	2,500	15,100	15,150	14,191	14,757
104	6	2,600	15,600	15,516	14,736	15,236
105	3	2,700	16,000	15,882	15,282	15,715
106	1	2,800	16,100	16,248	15,827	16,194
107	4	2,900	16,700	16,614	16,373	16,673
108	5	3,000	16,900	16,980	16,918	17,152
109	7	3,100	17,400	17,346	17,464	17,631
110	10	3,200	17,700	17,712	18,009	18,110
111	12	3,300	19,000	18,078	18,555	18,589
112	11	3,400	19,100	18,444	19,100	19,068

as many workers took their holidays. The largest output level occurs in month 11, just before Christmas. There may have been a rush of orders at this time, with resulting overtime payments or materials being bought in at above normal price. The relevant range excludes these extreme values.

Spreadsheet solution 6.7   Output section 4

	P	Q	R	S	T	U
				Visual		
	Months	Output Level	Total Costs	Inspection	High Low	Regression
72	Spreadsheet Solution 6-7					
73						
74	Output Section 4					
75						
78		0		(Q78*$E$47)+$E$46	+$I$58+($I$57*Q78)	+$O$64+(+$N$70*Q78)
79		100		(Q79*$E$47)+$E$46	+$I$58+($I$57*Q79)	+$O$64+(+$N$70*Q79)
80		200		(Q80*$E$47)+$E$46	+$I$58+($I$57*Q80)	+$O$64+(+$N$70*Q80)
81		300		(Q81*$E$47)+$E$46	+$I$58+($I$57*Q81)	+$O$64+(+$N$70*Q81)
82		400		(Q82*$E$47)+$E$46	+$I$58+($I$57*Q82)	+$O$64+(+$N$70*Q82)
83		500		(Q83*$E$47)+$E$46	+$I$58+($I$57*Q83)	+$O$64+(+$N$70*Q83)
84		600		(Q84*$E$47)+$E$46	+$I$58+($I$57*Q84)	+$O$64+(+$N$70*Q84)
85		700		(Q85*$E$47)+$E$46	+$I$58+($I$57*Q85)	+$O$64+(+$N$70*Q85)
86		800		(Q86*$E$47)+$E$46	+$I$58+($I$57*Q86)	+$O$64+(+$N$70*Q86)
87		900		(Q87*$E$47)+$E$46	+$I$58+($I$57*Q87)	+$O$64+(+$N$70*Q87)
88		1,000		(Q88*$E$47)+$E$46	+$I$58+($I$57*Q88)	+$O$64+(+$N$70*Q88)
89		1,100		(Q89*$E$47)+$E$46	+$I$58+($I$57*Q89)	+$O$64+(+$N$70*Q89)
90		1,200		(Q90*$E$47)+$E$46	+$I$58+($I$57*Q90)	+$O$64+(+$N$70*Q90)
91		1,300		(Q91*$E$47)+$E$46	+$I$58+($I$57*Q91)	+$O$64+(+$N$70*Q91)
92		1,400		(Q92*$E$47)+$E$46	+$I$58+($I$57*Q92)	+$O$64+(+$N$70*Q92)
93		1,500		(Q93*$E$47)+$E$46	+$I$58+($I$57*Q93)	+$O$64+(+$N$70*Q93)
94		1,600		(Q94*$E$47)+$E$46	+$I$58+($I$57*Q94)	+$O$64+(+$N$70*Q94)
95		1,700		(Q95*$E$47)+$E$46	+$I$58+($I$57*Q95)	+$O$64+(+$N$70*Q95)
96		1,800		(Q96*$E$47)+$E$46	+$I$58+($I$57*Q96)	+$O$64+(+$N$70*Q96)
97		1,900		(Q97*$E$47)+$E$46	+$I$58+($I$57*Q97)	+$O$64+(+$N$70*Q97)
98		2,000		(Q98*$E$47)+$E$46	+$I$58+($I$57*Q98)	+$O$64+(+$N$70*Q98)
99		2,100		(Q99*$E$47)+$E$46	+$I$58+($I$57*Q99)	+$O$64+(+$N$70*Q99)
100		2,200		(Q100*$E$47)+$E$46	+$I$58+($I$57*Q100)	+$O$64+(+$N$70*Q100)
101	8	2,300	13,100	(Q101*$E$47)+$E$46	+$I$58+($I$57*Q101)	+$O$64+(+$N$70*Q101)
102	9	2,400	14,500	(Q102*$E$47)+$E$46	+$I$58+($I$57*Q102)	+$O$64+(+$N$70*Q102)
103	2	2,500	15,100	(Q103*$E$47)+$E$46	+$I$58+($I$57*Q103)	+$O$64+(+$N$70*Q103)
104	6	2,600	15,600	(Q104*$E$47)+$E$46	+$I$58+($I$57*Q104)	+$O$64+(+$N$70*Q104)
105	3	2,700	16,000	(Q105*$E$47)+$E$46	+$I$58+($I$57*Q105)	+$O$64+(+$N$70*Q105)
106	1	2,800	16,100	(Q106*$E$47)+$E$46	+$I$58+($I$57*Q106)	+$O$64+(+$N$70*Q106)
107	4	2,900	16,700	(Q107*$E$47)+$E$46	+$I$58+($I$57*Q107)	+$O$64+(+$N$70*Q107)
108	5	3,000	16,900	(Q108*$E$47)+$E$46	+$I$58+($I$57*Q108)	+$O$64+(+$N$70*Q108)
109	7	3,100	17,400	(Q109*$E$47)+$E$46	+$I$58+($I$57*Q109)	+$O$64+(+$N$70*Q109)
110	10	3,200	17,700	(Q110*$E$47)+$E$46	+$I$58+($I$57*Q110)	+$O$64+(+$N$70*Q110)
111	12	3,300	19,000	(Q111*$E$47)+$E$46	+$I$58+($I$57*Q111)	+$O$64+(+$N$70*Q111)
112	11	3,400	19,100	(Q112*$E$47)+$E$46	+$I$58+($I$57*Q112)	+$O$64+(+$N$70*Q112)

'What if?' questions

1. (a) Excluding the extreme values of months 8, 11 and 12 from the analysis, produce cost estimates from the 9 remaining values, using the three methods described.

    (b) What happens to r^2 and the standard errors? Explain your observations.

2. If management decided to use new technology to double production to 7000

units, what would total costs be and which would be the best method to estimate them?

'What if?' solutions

1. (a) Assume no significant change in the visual inspection method. The high–low method produces the following results:

Output Area 2 — High–Low Method

Maximum Value	3200	Associated Cost	17,700
Minimum Value	2400	Associated Cost	14,500
	800		3,200

$b =$ 4
$a =$ 4900

The linear regression output is as follows:

Output Area 3 — Linear Regression

Constant	5488.889
Std Err of Y Est	130.3232
R Squared	0.986695
No. of Observations	9
Degrees of Freedom	7
X Coefficient(s)	3.833333
Std Err of Coef.	0.168246

The three methods give the following cost estimation models:

Visual	$y = 6000 + 3.66x$
High–low	$y = 4900 + 4.00x$
Regression	$y = 5489 + 3.83x$

For example, assuming the 2500 output level is produced, then the cost estimates are as follows:

Visual	$y = 6000 + 3.66(2500) = 15150$
High–low	$y = 4900 + 4.00(2500) = 14900$
Regression	$y = 5489 + 3.83(2500) = 15064$

So removing 'outliers' results in fewer deviations in the estimates produced. This may mean that the problem for management accountants is not in their choice of method, but in the careful scrutiny of the data.

(b) The r^2 increases to 99% and the standard errors all decrease, implying that there is greater confidence in the results and in the explanatory power of the new regression line.

2. If management decided to adopt new technology then all past data would be irrelevant. The only method which can be used is the engineering method.

Conclusion

After completing this chapter you should:

- be able to recognize the need for accuracy in estimating costs;
- be able to use three main methods of cost estimation in your spreadsheet;
- be aware of the advantages and drawbacks of each method.

Exercises

Question 6.1

You have been provided with the following information:

Month	Machine Hours	Total Costs (£000's)	Labour Hours
July	34	640	1,390
August	30	620	1,340
September	34	620	1,300
October	39	590	1,270
November	42	500	1,100
December	32	530	1,090
January	25	500	1,040
February	26	500	1,080
March	31	530	1,040
April	35	550	1,100
May	43	580	1,300
June	48	680	1,590

Using the high−low and regression techniques discussed in the chapter, prepare a brief report on observed cost behaviour for the management of this business.

Refer to any limitations of your methods or of the results of your analysis.

Answer on page 261

7 | *Costing methods*

AIMS OF CHAPTER

- to show different methods of tracing costs to different types of product or service;
- to explain the ways in which costs associated with joint and by-products are calculated and accounted for;
- to demonstrate the construction of spreadsheet models to perform the various costing calculations.

SPREADSHEET SKILLS ACQUIRED

- formatting cells to display percentages and formulae;
- protecting cells;
- data tables or 'what if' tables.

Introduction

We have already seen how different costs behave in different ways over a range of output levels. We now consider how the costs involved in producing products or services are measured and allocated to those products or services. The information produced is needed for management control purposes, inventory valuation and possibly pricing.

The method to be used for the measurement and allocation of costs will depend on the nature of the product or service produced. For example, a company that customizes luxury cars according to the individual specifications of its customers will need to keep track of the costs associated with each individual order. The nature of such cost record-keeping will be quite different from the case of the ordinary car manufacturer which produces lines of identical cars. Both these examples will be different again from the oil or chemical producer whose products may appear at different stages of the refining process.

The management accounting system involved in each case must be tailored not only to the particular needs of management but also to the nature of the product or service produced. We cover below the basic principles of the main types of cost measurement. The complexity of actual businesses means that in practice management accounting and costing systems involve an incredible degree of sophistication, a description of which would be beyond the scope of a book such as this. Nevertheless, systems encountered in practice are merely an elaborate application of the principles described below.

Job costing

Job costing is the name given to the costing system used in businesses which produce products or services tailored to meet the needs of individual customers. Examples of such products include precision engineered components, customized luxury and sports cars, and non-standard double glazing units. Professionals, such as accountants, lawyers, surveyors and architects, all require job costing systems since, by the nature of their work, the services rendered to each of their clients will be unique.

Job costing requires a separate record to be kept for each job or each client. This record will track all the direct costs, labour and materials, which have been expended on that particular job or for that particular client. In addition, of course, there must be some element of the company's overheads to be recovered from each job. The company will need therefore to devise a method by which this charge is computed. For example, the overhead recovery rate may be expressed as a percentage of the direct labour cost or the prime cost (direct labour plus direct materials) of the job.

Example 7.1

Jackler Coachworks Ltd offers a customizing service for all makes of car. Typical jobs include upgrading standards of comfort as well as conversion of standard models of cars into estate cars or stretch-limousines. Mr Jones has a standard BMW which he wishes to upgrade to include a new paint job and additional luxury items. He delivers the car to Jackler's premises with specifications of his requirements. The accounts staff at Jackler assign the contract job number 121 and open a costing record to keep track of all the costs which will be incurred in completing the contract. Workers are required to complete a time-sheet at the end of each week to record the amount of time that they spend on each job. From these time-sheets the accounts staff can compute the labour costs to be charged to each job. Any materials and bought-in components used on each job are recorded on requisition sheets from which the costing record is updated by the accounts staff. The established policy of the company is to recover overheads at the rate of 100% of labour cost.

The costing record will therefore comprise a list of individual components and categories of labour expended on the particular job. A summary of the costing record for job no. 121 might appear as follows:

	£	£
Labour		
Coachwork 20 hours @ £12.50	250.00	
Electrical 5 hours @ £15.00	75.00	
Bodywork 3 hours @ £7.50	22.50	
		347.50
Materials		
Upholstery 15 m^2 @ £25.00	375.00	
Electrical components	550.00	
Paint	50.00	
		975.00
Overheads		347.50
Total cost		1670.00

The difference between the total cost for the job and the price charged to the customer (probably agreed in advance) represents the profit to the company.

It should be noted that these costing records are for internal purposes only. The record would not normally be shown to the customer since businesses are typically reluctant to allow outsiders to see how much profit is made on particular transactions. The customer nevertheless has a right to expect a detailed bill showing the cost of labour and materials consumed. However, the labour charge on the bill which the customer sees usually includes a mark-up to cover both overhead recovery and profit.

The spreadsheet solution

A brief description of the model appears in the control section of the spreadsheet (see Spreadsheet Solution 7.1).

We now move downwards and to the right to set up the input section. Here we enter all the data relating to job no. 121. For the labour costs, we need to set up columns for both hours spent on the job and the relevant rates for each category of labour.

Similarly, the materials for upholstery require both an amount consumed and a price for each unit of input (in this case square metres). The costs of bought-in electrical components and paint are entered as single figures.

Finally, the percentage rate at which overheads are to be recovered is entered. Use the ⟨/Range, Format, Percentage⟩ command to format cell E40 to display the contents as a percentage. To display the amount 100%, simply enter ⟨1⟩. See Spreadsheet Solution 7.2 for the completed input section.

We can now construct the output section to represent the costing of the various items expended on job no. 121, with sub-totals produced for labour, materials and overheads. As always, all the figures in the output section should be calculated by formulae with references back to the input section. This makes efficient use of the spreadsheet and is ideal for repetitive tasks such as maintaining job costing records.

Spreadsheet solution 7.1   Control section

	A	B
1	Spreadsheet Solution 7-1: Control Section	
2		
3	Example 7.1: Jackler Coachworks Ltd.	
4		
5	This model calculates the cost of particular	
6	jobs based on the job costing method.	
7		
8	Job No. 121 for customer Mr. Jones.	
9		
10		
11		
12		
13	Location Table	Range Name
14	--	--------------------
15	Input Section	INPUT
16	Output Section 1 - Job 121	OUTPUT1
17	Output Section 2 - 'What If?' Table	OUTPUT2
18		
19	For Input Section Press F5 and type Input	

Spreadsheet solution 7.2   Input section

	C	D	E
20	Spreadsheet Solution 7-2: Input Section		
21			
22	Job No.	121	
23	--	----------------	
24	Labour:	Hours	Rates
25			£
26	Coachwork	20.00	12.50
27			
28	Electrical	5.00	15.00
29			
30	Bodywork	3.00	7.50
31			
32	Materials:		
33			
34	Upholstery	15.00	25.00
35			
36	Electrical		550.00
37			
38	Paint		50.00
39			
40	Overheads Recovery Rate		100%
41			
42	Press F5 and type Output		

Spreadsheet solution 7.3   Output section 1

		F	G	H
44	Spreadsheet Solution 7-3: Output Section 1			
45				
46	Job No.		121	
47	--- -------------			
48	Labour:			
49				
50	Coachwork		250.00	
51				
52	Electrical		75.00	
53				
54	Bodywork		22.50	
55			-------------	347.50
56	Materials:			
57				
58	Upholstery		375.00	
59				
60	Electrical		550.00	
61				
62	Paint		50.00	
63			-------------	975.00
64				
65	Overheads			347.50
66				------------------
67	Total Cost			1,670.00
68				======

See Spreadsheet Solution 7.3 for the completed section and Spreadsheet Solution 7.4 for the formulae behind the figures.

'What if?' questions

1. What is the effect on the cost of job no. 121 if:

    (a) 40 hours are spent on coachwork?

    (b) the rate of pay for electrical work is £13.75 per hour?

    (c) the rate of overhead recovery is 75% of total labour cost?

2. Save the spreadsheet you have constructed for job no. 121 using ⟨/File, **Save**, filename⟩, since we will return to it later. Now, on the basis of the spreadsheet for job no. 121, we will set up another spreadsheet file for job no. 122. This job uses the same labour categories as job no. 121 but there is an additional category of labour, 'mechanical', with a rate per hour of £10.00. The labour hours spent on job no. 122 are:

Spreadsheet solution 7.4 Output section 1

	F	G	H
44	Spreadsheet Solution 7-4: Output Section 1		
45			
46	Job No.	121	
47	---	------------------	
48	Labour:		
49			
50	Coachwork	+D26*E26	
51			
52	Electrical	+D28*E28	
53			
54	Bodywork	+D30*E30	
55		----------------- @SUM(G50..G54)	
56	Materials:		
57			
58	Upholstery	+D34*E34	
59			
60	Electrical	+E36	
61			
62	Paint	+E38	
63		----------------- @SUM(G58..G62)	
64			
65	Overheads		+H55*E40
66			-----------------------------
67	Total Cost		@SUM(H55..H65)
68			==========

Coachwork	40
Electrical	15
Bodywork	10
Mechanical	15

Materials and overhead recovery rate remain exactly the same as for job no. 121. Calculate the cost of job no. 122.

'What if?' solutions

1. (a) The total cost increases to £2170, an increase of £250 on coachwork labour plus the same amount of overheads.

    (b) The total cost is £1657.50. To obtain this answer to two decimal places, make the appropriate change to the format of cell H67.

    (c) The total cost is £1583.13.

2. To answer this problem, you need to change the values in the input section as follows:

Coachwork (D26)   40
Electrical (D28)   15
Bodywork (D30)   10

You will also need to insert a row for the 'Mechanical' category. To insert a row, position the cursor on the row you wish to insert and type ⟨/**W**orksheet, **I**nsert, **R**ow⟩. You can insert more than one row at a time by indicating the range that you require at the final prompt. The solution is presented in Spreadsheet Solution 7.5.

Spreadsheet solution 7.5   Job no. 122

	F	G	H
46	Spreadsheet Solution 7-5: Job No. 122		
47			
48	Job No.	122	
49	--	-----------------	
50	Labour:		
51			
52	Coachwork	500.00	
53			
54	Electrical	225.00	
55			
56	Mechanical	150.00	
57			
58	Bodywork	75.00	
59		-----------------	950.00
60	Materials:		
61			
62	Upholstery	375.00	
63			
64	Electrical	550.00	
65			
66	Paint	50.00	
67		-----------------	975.00
68			
69	Overheads		950.00
70			-----------------
71	Total Cost		2,875.00
72			======

Protecting a range

Once a standard spreadsheet has been set up it can be used as the basis for all job costing records. The figures for each new job are simply keyed into the input section and the costing is automatically produced. Areas of the spreadsheet which are not likely to change (e.g. labour rates) may be *protected* to avoid inadvertent alteration and corruption of the costings.

To protect the cells containing the wage rates, for example, first turn on the protection capability with the command ⟨/**W**orksheet, **G**lobal, **P**rotection, **E**nable⟩. This protects the whole of the spreadsheet so that no further changes can be made. To protect only the cells containing the wage rates we need to unprotect all the other cells. Do this using ⟨/**R**ange, **P**rotection⟩ then highlight all the ranges which do *not* require protection.

Setting up a data table or 'what if?' table

The effect of changing one variable in the model can be quickly calculated by the use of the data table or 'what if?' table. For example, suppose we wanted to find out the effect on the total cost of job no. 121 of different overhead recovery rates, say, from 50% to 150%.

First return the spreadsheet for job no. 121 to the screen by typing ⟨/**F**ile, **R**etrieve, Filename⟩. Now prepare a second output section with two columns headed 'Overhead Recovery Rate' and 'Cost of Job 121'. In the column headed 'Overhead Recovery Rate' insert a range of values from 50% to 150%. These will form the *substitute values* for the variable to be altered in the data table. In the empty cell above and to the right of the range of substitute values (below the column heading 'Cost of Job 121'), insert the cell reference ⟨+H67⟩ and format the cell to Text so that the address +H67 appears on screen in cell J75. This cell gives the result of the model, total cost.

Using the ⟨/**D**ata, **T**able⟩ menu select ⟨**1**⟩ variable and point to the range that includes all the substitute values and the formula cell ⟨I75..J86⟩. Next you are prompted for the input cell which contains the original value to be substituted; in our example this is ⟨E40⟩, the existing overhead recovery rate. The data table is automatically

Spreadsheet solution 7.6   'What if?' table

	I	J	K	L
70	Spreadsheet Solution 7-6: 'What If?' Table			
71				
72	Overhead	Cost of		
73	recovery rate	Job 121		
74				
75		+H67		
76	50%	1,496.25		
77	60%	1,531.00		
78	70%	1,565.75		
79	80%	1,600.50		
80	90%	1,635.25		
81	100%	1,670.00		
82	110%	1,704.75		
83	120%	1,739.50		
84	130%	1,774.25		
85	140%	1,809.00		
86	150%	1,843.75		

produced giving the range of costs for job no. 121 using overhead recovery rates from 50% to 150%. The solution is presented in Spreadsheet Solution 7.6.

Batch costing

Some products are not produced individually but in batches. For example, building bricks are moulded and fired in a kiln in batches of hundreds or thousands; similarly, foodstuffs such as pies and cakes may be mixed and cooked not as a continuous process but in batches. The costing system used in such processes involves tracing the costs associated with separate batches rather than the individual units in the batch. Of course, the unit costs can be calculated if necessary by dividing the cost of the batch by the number of units in the batch.

Information on the costs of batches may be of use to management in a number of ways. Where the batches have been made to match the needs of individual customers, the costs must be determined for the purposes of profit measurement and to assist in pricing decisions. Where similar-sized batches of identical items are produced routinely, changes in the costs incurred from one batch to the next may give management essential information regarding the efficiency of the production process.

Process costing

Many industrial processes are more or less continuous in their production runs. What is being produced is not so much a large number of individual units as a continuous product from which individual units are extracted and passed on to customers. The industrial processes involving the production of liquids, for example, the chemical or petrochemical industries, are most commonly used to illustrate the nature of the problem. However, other industries which may use process costing include those in the timber and textile trades, where the product passes through a common production process, although further processing at later stages may convert the partly finished materials to quite different end-products.

In some ways the application of process costing may prove easier than job costing since it is the process itself which attracts the recording of costs rather than the individual units produced. That is, from a record-keeping point of view, all that is required is for costs associated with the process to be charged to that cost centre. The production workers are not required to keep track of their time for costing purposes since their time will be wholly taken up in the running of the process. The cost of materials which are used in the process will be charged exclusively to the process rather than identified separately with the units produced, which in many cases would be an impossible and unnecessary task.

However, there are certain problems associated with process costing which are not shared by other costing methods. The first of these is caused by the continuous nature of the process itself. For (both internal and external) reporting purposes, the quantity of stock and work-in-progress in hand at the year end has to be measured and valued. If it is technically not feasible, or commercially not viable, to halt the production process at the year end to allow the stock to be counted then alternative procedures for estimating the amount of continuously moving materials are needed. In practice, this can become a very complex matter and some tolerance for error is unavoidable.

Example 7.2

Chemace Industries Ltd operates a chemical plant which in the last period incurred the following production costs:

	£
Direct materials	166,625
Direct labour	22,550
Overheads	78,750
Total costs	267,925

For the sake of simplicity let us assume that it is possible to establish, with some degree of accuracy, the year-end stock in hand. Through established procedures it has been determined that during the period 10,000 gallons of the company's product have completely passed through the process and remain unsold at the period end. In addition, there are 1000 gallons still in the process. This is called *work-in-progress* to denote the fact that the units are only partly complete: the product could not be sold in this unfinished state.

The problem is how to value these incomplete units. We first need to assess the degree to which they are complete. In chemical processes it is often the case that most of the raw materials or ingredients enter the process in the early stages, with relatively little additional material added later. The process may become more labour intensive at these later stages. Chemace Industries has assessed the stages of its process at which the different costs are incurred and has determined that the 1000 gallons in work-in-progress are at the following stages of completion:

Direct materials	75%
Direct labour	25%
Overheads	50%

These estimates are used to value the partly completed units, by converting the cost components of the work-in-progress into equivalent complete units; for example, for materials 1000 gallons 75% complete are equivalent to 750 completely finished gallons:

	Equiv. Units, W-I-P	Complete Units	Total Units	Total Cost £	Av. Cost £
Materials	750	10,000	10,750	166,625	15.50
Labour	250	10,000	10,250	22,550	2.20
Overheads	500	10,000	10,500	78,750	7.50
				267,925	25.20

By dividing total costs by the total units (complete units plus equivalent units) we can calculate the average cost per unit for each cost component and arrive at total average cost per unit. This will be used to value the completed units; it also forms the basis for the valuation of 1000 gallons in work-in-progress:

Valuation of work-in-progress:

Materials	1000 × 75% × £15.50 =	11,625
Labour	1000 × 25% × £2.20 =	550
Overheads	1000 × 50% × £7.50 =	3,750
		15,925

Valuation of complete units:

	10,000 gallons × £25.20 =	252,000
Total		£267,925

The spreadsheet solution

The control section is presented in Spreadsheet Solution 7.7. The input section needs to contain a description of each of the cost categories and amounts incurred in the production process. We also need to key the number of completed and partially completed units and, in the rows in column F, the degree of completion of the work-in-progress relevant to each cost category. These latter cells should be formatted in percentage terms (see Spreadsheet Solution 7.8).

The output section (Spreadsheet Solution 7.9) starts with labels for the cost categories and cell references for the costs of each category, cells G40–H44. In column I we calculate the total equivalent units, complete units plus the equivalent complete units of the work-in-progress. For example, for materials in cell I40, the formula is ⟨E$24+(F$24*F28)⟩; note that the use of the absolute cell references allows this formula to be copied to the cells for labour and overheads (cells I42 and I44). Column J calculates the average cost by dividing total cost for each cost category by the total equivalent units for that category.

We can then move on to perform the inventory valuation for both completed units and work-in-progress. For clarity the number of completed and partially completed units are repeated in the Valuation of Inventory section, cells H52 and H54. The

Spreadsheet solution 7.7 Control section

	A	B
1	Spreadsheet Solution 7-7: Control Section	
2		
3	Example 7.2: Chemace Industries Ltd.	
4		
5	This model calculates the cost of production,	
6	cost of sales and the cost of work-in-progress	
7	according to the process costing method.	
8		
9		
10		
11		
12		
13		
14		
15	Location Table	Range Name
16	---	----------------------
17	Input Section	INPUT
18	Output Section	OUTPUT
19	For Input Section Press F5 and type Input	

Spreadsheet solution 7.8 Input section

	C	D	E	F
20	Spreadsheet Solution 7-8: Input Section			
21				
22			Complete	W-I-P &
23				% complete
24	Units Produced		10,000	1,000
25				
26	Production costs:	£		
27				
28	Materials	166,625		75%
29				
30	Labour	22,550		25%
31				
32	Overheads	78,750		50%
33		----------------		
34		267,925		
35		=====		

valuation of the completed units is relatively straightforward, being the product of the number of completed units in stock multiplied by the average cost per unit: in cell J52 the formula is $\langle +H52*J46 \rangle$.

The valuation of the work-in-progress involves first calculating the equivalent complete units for each cost category and then applying the average cost for that category. For example, for labour, cell H58 contains the formula $\langle F\$24*F30 \rangle$. The valuation, column I, then applies the average cost per unit for labour to the number

Spreadsheet solution 7.9 Output section

	G	H	I	J
36	Spreadsheet Solution 7-9: Output Section			
37		Costs	Total Equiv.	Average
38			Units	Cost
39		£		£
40	Materials	166,625	10,750	15.50
41				
42	Labour	22,550	10,250	2.20
43				
44	Overheads	78,750	10,500	7.50
45				------------
46				25.20
47				====
48				
49	Valuation of Inventory			
50		Units		Value
51				£
52	Complete	10,000		252,000
53				
54	W-I-P:	1,000		
55		-------------------		
56	Materials	750	11,625	
57				
58	Labour	250	550	
59				
60	Overheads	500	3,750	
61			----------------------	
62	Total W-I-P			15,925
63				-------------
64	Total Inventory			267,925
65				====

of equivalent units in work-in-progress, so that in cell I58 the formula is ⟨+H58∗J42⟩.

For the complete set of formulae see Spreadsheet Solution 7.10.

'What if?' questions

Observe the effects on the valuation of completed units and work-in-progress of each of the changes to the model for Example 7.2. Return to the original values before attempting each question.

1. Change the number of units of work-in-progress to 2000 units (cell F24).

2. Change the degree of completion for overheads to 75% (cell F32).

3. Change the materials cost incurred to £200,000 (cell D28).

Spreadsheet solution 7.10   Output section

	G	H	I	J
36	Spreadsheet Solution 7-10: Output Section			
37		Costs	Total Equiv.	Average
38			Units	Cost
39		£		£
40	Materials	+D28	+E$24+(F$24*F28)	+H40/I40
41				
42	Labour	+D30	+E$24+(F$24*F30)	+H42/I42
43				
44	Overheads	+D32	+E$24+(F$24*F32)	+H44/I44
45				----------------------------
46				@SUM(J40..J44)
47				=========
48				
49	Valuation of Inventory			
50		Units		Value
51			£	£
52	Complete	+E24		+H52*J46
53				
54	W-I-P:	+F24		
55		----------------------		
56	Materials	+F$24*F28	+H56*J40	
57				
58	Labour	+F$24*F30	+H58*J42	
59				
60	Overheads	+F$24*F32	+H60*J44	
61			----------------------------	
62	Total W-I-P			@SUM(I56..I60)
63				----------------------------
64	Total Inventory			@SUM(J52..J62)
65				=========

'What if?' solutions

1. Work-in-progress, £29,967; completed units, £237,958.

2. Work-in-progress, £17,669; completed units, £250,256.

3. Work-in-progress, £18,253; completed units, £283,047.

Joint and by-product costing

One feature of certain production processes is that more than one product may be produced as a result of the production process. For example, in the chemical industry the mixing of various chemicals may produce not one resulting compound but two (or more) simultaneously. Thus it may not be possible to create the desired product without inevitably producing another at the same time. If both products are marketable and both have significant market values, then they are regarded as *joint products*.

By-products are those which are inevitably produced as a result of the production process but which have minimal or insignificant market value relative to the value of the main product(s). It is not considered to be worthwhile to account separately for the costs of such products. Instead, any sales revenue generated by the sale of by-products simply goes to reduce the cost of production of the main product(s).

The problem for the management accountant is how to apportion the costs of production between the two joint products. This needs to be done for the purposes of inventory valuation and profit measurement rather than management control. Since the process must produce both products, there is little that management can do about the costs incurred in producing one or the other product.

There are two possible methods for assigning the costs of production between the two joint products: the first is a fairly logical allocation of the costs on the basis of the physical quantity of each joint product at the point of separation.

Example 7.3

Products A and B are formed as a result of passing through a particular chemical process. The production costs for the period under review total £240,000. Eighty thousand kilograms of product A and 40,000 kg of product B were produced. The selling prices per kilogram of A and B are £6.00 and £4.00, respectively. At the end of the period there remained in stock 8000 kg of product A and 10,000 kg of product B. The costing would be set out as follows:

	Product A	Product B	Ratio
Kilos produced	80,000	40,000	2:1
Joint costs allocated	£160,000	£80,000	2:1
Cost per kg	£2	£2	
Kilos in closing stock	8,000	10,000	
Valuation of closing stock	£16,000	£20,000	

Assuming that all the units which are not on hand at the end of the period have been sold at the regular price, the income statement (at least to the point of gross profit) would be as shown at the top of page 92.

The profitability of product A appears substantially higher than that of product B. This result has been produced by the higher price obtained from sales of product A while the allocated cost per unit is the same for both product A and B.

It might be argued that using the relative market values of the two products would produce a better and fairer allocation of the joint processing costs.

	Product A	Product B
Sales		
A 72,000 kg @ £6.00	432,000	
B 30,000 kg @ £4.00		120,000
Joint costs	160,000	80,000
Less: closing stock	(16,000)	(20,000)
Cost of sales		
A 72,000 kg @ £2.00	144,000	
B 30,000 kg @ £2.00		60,000
Gross profit	288,000	60,000
Mark-up on cost	200%	100%

Under this acceptable alternative method, the costing would appear as follows:

	Product A	Product B	Ratio
Kilos produced	80,000	40,000	2:1
Kilos produced valued at selling price	£480,000	£160,000	3:1
Joint costs allocated	£180,000	£60,000	3:1
Cost per kg	£2.25	£1.50	
Kilos in closing stock	8,000	10,000	
Valuation of closing stock:	£18,000	£15,000	

The income statement would look like this:

	Product A £	Product B £
Sales 72,000 kg @ £6.00	432,000	
30,000 kg @ £4.00		120,000
Joint costs	180,000	60,000
Less: closing stock	(18,000)	(15,000)
Cost of sales		
A 72,000 kg @ £2.25	162,000	
B 30,000 kg @ £1.50		45,000
Gross profit	270,000	75,000
Mark-up on cost	167%	167%

Thus on this basis the two joint products appear to be equally profitable, the joint costs having been allocated between the two products after allowing for their relative quantities and market values.

The fact that there is more than one way to calculate these joint costs should give you the necessary hint that, as with the allocation of overheads, the matter is an entirely subjective one. It would therefore not be wise to place too much reliance on the figures for decision-making purposes (see Part V, Chapter 13).

The spreadsheet solution

The control section is shown as Spreadsheet Solution 7.11. Construct the input section with columns for the two joint products and rows for the units produced, the units in inventory, the sales value per unit and the total production costs (see Spreadsheet Solution 7.12).

Set up output section 1 to calculate the cost per unit on the physical quantity basis. This is the total production costs divided by the sum of units of A and B produced, so cell G33 contains the formula ⟨D30/(D24+E24)⟩. The valuation of the closing stocks of A and B can now be performed by multiplying the number of units in stock by the joint cost per unit; for product A, this is done in cell G37 using the formula ⟨D26 * $G$33⟩ (see Spreadsheet Solution 7.13).

Now we can construct the income statement in output section 2 with the sales revenue calculated by multiplying the difference between units produced and units in hand by the selling price (see Spreadsheet Solution 7.14). The formulae for this spreadsheet are discussed below.

The allocation of joint production costs is based on the number of units of each product produced multiplied by the cost per unit. So for product B, for example, cell K47 contains the formula ⟨E24 * $G$33⟩.

Spreadsheet solution 7.11   Control section

	A	B
1	Spreadsheet Solution 7-11: Control Section	
2		
3	Example 7.3	
4		
5	This model calculates the joint cost of production	
6	of Products A and B, using alternative bases.	
7		
8		
9		
10		
11		
12		
13	Location Table	Range Name
14	--	--------------------------
15	Input Section	INPUT
16	Output Section 1	OUTPUT1
17	Output Section 2	OUTPUT2
18		
19	For Input Section Press F5 and type Input	

Spreadsheet solution 7.12 Input section

	C	D	E
20	Spreadsheet Solution 7-12: Input Section		
21			
22		Product A	Product B
23		------------------	------------------
24	Units Produced:	80,000	40,000
25			
26	Units in Inventory	8,000	10,000
27			
28	Sales Value per unit	6.00	4.00
29			
30	Joint Production costs:	240,000	

Spreadsheet solution 7.13 Physical quantity basis

	F	G	H
31	Spreadsheet Solution 7-13: Physical Quantity Basis		
32			
33	Cost per unit	2.00	
34			
35		Product A	Product B
36		----------------------	--------------------------
37	Valuation of Closing Stock:	16,000	20,000

Spreadsheet solution 7.14 Income statement

	I	J	K
39	Spreadsheet Solution 7-14: Income Statement		
40			
41	Income statement		
42		Product A	Product B
43			
44	Sales	432,000	120,000
45		--------------------------	--------------------------
46			
47	Joint production costs	160,000	80,000
48			
49	Less closing stock	(16,000)	(20,000)
50		--------------------------	--------------------------
51	Cost of sales	144,000	60,000
52		--------------------------	--------------------------
53	Gross Profit	288,000	60,000
54		=========	=========
55			
56	Mark-up on cost	200%	100%

The closing stock valuation is taken by reference to the relevant cell in output section 1, though this should be a negative reference since closing stock is deducted from production costs to arrive at cost of sales. So for product A cell J49 contains the formula ⟨ −G37⟩.

The cost of sales (cells J51 and K51) is calculated by the sum of production costs and the (negative) closing stock, as always using only cell references. So for product B we have either ⟨ +K47+K49⟩ or ⟨@SUM(K47..K49)⟩.

Gross profit (cells J53 and K53) is calculated by deducting cost of sales from sales revenue: the formula for product A in cell J53 is thus ⟨ +J44−J51⟩. This can be expressed as a percentage of the cost of sales, (the mark-up), by dividing gross profit by cost of sales (see Spreadsheet Solution 7.15) with cells formatted to **Percentage**.

Spreadsheet solution 7.15   Income statement

	I	J	K
39	Spreadsheet Solution 7-15: Income Statement		
40			
41	Income statement		
42		Product A	Product B
43			
44	Sales	(+D24-D26)*D28	(+E24-E26)*E28
45		------------------------	------------------------
46			
47	Joint production costs	+D24*$G$33	+E24*$G$33
48			
49	Less closing stock	-G37	-H37
50		------------------------	------------------------
51	Cost of sales	@SUM(J47..J49)	@SUM(K47..K49)
52		------------------------	------------------------
53	Gross Profit	+J44-J51	+K44-K51
54		=========	=========
55			
56	Mark-up on cost	+J53/J51	+K53/K51

'What if?' questions

Calculate the effect of management adopting the alternative (market value) basis for apportioning joint costs. Use the same modelling approach as for the physical quantity basis, but construct output sections 3 and 4 to contain the solution.

'What if?' solutions

The solutions for the market value basis are presented in Spreadsheet Solutions 7.16 and 7.17 with formulae back-up given in Spreadsheet Solutions 7.18 and 7.19.

Spreadsheet solution 7.16   Market value basis

	L	M	N
58	Spreadsheet Solution 7-16: Market Value Basis		
59		Product A	Product B
60		----------------------	-----------------
61	Joint costs allocated	180,000	60,000
62			
63	Cost per unit	2.25	1.50
64			
65	Valuation of closing stock	18,000	15,000

Spreadsheet solution 7.17   Income statement

	O	P	Q
66	Spreadsheet Solution 7-17: Income Statement		
67			
68	Income statement		
69		Product A	Product B
70			
71	Sales	432,000	120,000
72		------------------	---------------
73			
74	Joint production costs	180,000	60,000
75			
76	Less closing stock	(18,000)	(15,000)
77		------------------	---------------
78	Cost of sales	162,000	45,000
79		------------------	---------------
80	Gross Profit	270,000	75,000
81		======	=====

Spreadsheet solution 7.18   Market value basis

	L	M	N
58	Spreadsheet Solution 7-18: Market Value Basis		
59		Product A	Product B
60		--	---
61	Joint costs allocated	(+D24*D28/((D24*D28)+E24*E28))*D30	(+E24*E28/((E24*E28)+D24*D28))*D30
62			
63	Cost per unit	+M61/D24	+N61/E24
64			
65	Valuation of closing stock	+D26*M63	+E26*N63

Spreadsheet solution 7.19   Income statement

	O	P	Q
66	Spreadsheet Solution 7-19: Income Statement		
67			
68	Income statement		
69		Product A	Product B
70			
71	Sales	(+D24-D26)*D28	(+E24-E26)*E28
72		------------------------------	--------------------------
73			
74	Joint production costs	+M61	+N61
75			
76	Less closing stock	-M65	-N65
77		------------------------------	--------------------------
78	Cost of sales	@SUM(P74..P76)	@SUM(Q74..Q76)
79		------------------------------	--------------------------
80	Gross Profit	+P71-P78	+Q71-Q78
81		============	==========

Conclusion

Management needs information regarding costs to ascertain the profitability of various products, to determine where costs are being incurred and to measure the performance of different divisions. We have reviewed the different methods of arriving at the cost of products or services. Which method is most appropriate will depend on the nature of the company's production process.

Having studied this chapter you should be familiar with the different costing techniques and should be able to tackle examination questions on the subject. You should also be able to construct spreadsheet models to perform the calculations. Studying the effects of changes to the variables will reinforce your understanding of the concepts.

Exercises

Question 7.1

The following information is available for job no. 1234, produced to a customer's specifications:

	Dept X	Dept Y	Dept Z
Materials	£5000	£1500	£1000
Labour hours	250	175	325
Labour rates	£2.50	£4.25	£5.25

In addition, the company recovers indirect costs on the following bases:

Fixed production overhead	£4.00 per labour hour
Fixed administration overhead	75% on total production cost
Profit margin	25% on selling price

Calculate the total cost and selling price of job no. 1234.

Answer on page 263

Question 7.2

The marketing director of your company has expressed concern about product X, which for some time has shown a loss, and has stated that some action will have to be taken.

Product X is produced from material A, which is one of two raw materials jointly produced by passing chemicals through a process. Representative data for the process are as follows:

Output:	Material A	10,000 kg
	Material B	30,000 kg
Process costs:	Raw materials	£83,600
	Conversion costs	£58,000

Joint costs are apportioned to the raw materials according to the weight of output.

Production costs incurred in converting material A into product X are £1.80 per kilo of material A used. A yield of 90% is achieved. Product X is sold for £5.60 per kilo. Material B is sold without further processing for £6.00 per kilo.

You are required to:

(a) Calculate the profit/(loss) per kilo of product X and material B, respectively.

(b) Comment upon the marketing director's concern, advising him whether you consider any action should be taken.

(c) Demonstrate for product X, and comment briefly upon, an alternative method of cost apportionment.

Answer on page 266   *(ACCA)*

Part IV

Information for management control

8 | Budgetary planning and control

AIMS OF CHAPTER _____

- to examine the concept of budgeting, including why budgets are prepared;
- to analyze the role of budgets as part of the planning process;
- to examine the basis on which budgets are constructed, including short-term and long-term budgets, rolling/continuous budgets, incremental budgeting and zero-based budgeting;
- to emphasize the importance of updating and amending forecasts upon which budgets may be based;
- to consider the use of budgets in organizational control through the reporting of variances using feedback loops, and how the variance reporting system can use managers' time effectively through management-by-exception techniques;
- to determine the importance of responsibility accounting through the use of cost and profit centres, and how flexible budgeting and a good system of variance reporting are important;
- to see how budgets affect managerial motivation, why some 'slack' is necessary and how participation is the key to successful standard-setting;
- to develop a spreadsheet model to illustrate the preparation of budgets, including the functional budgets and the master budget.

SPREADSHEET SKILLS ACQUIRED _____

- the use of unsynchronized windows;
- developing a fully integrated model from input variables to forecast financial statements.

Introduction

This chapter is in two parts. The first part discusses the underlying concept of budgeting and the second part is a practical illustration of budget preparation using a large spreadsheet model. This model uses an extensive cascade layout and relies heavily on the variables found in the input section. You will discover the importance of the window facility and the flexibility of a large model constructed almost totally on cell referencing.

Budgeting

In this part of the chapter we will examine the purpose of budgeting, particularly in a large organization. We will specifically consider the role of budgets in planning and control and how they are used to motivate managers and workers.

Purpose

Budgeting is very useful in a large organization where decision-making is decentralized. In a very small firm one person, usually called the entrepreneur, is the owner and the managing director. This person is able to monitor the firm's activities and to ensure that objectives are achieved. As a firm grows, this coordinating managerial function becomes too much for one person and so decision-making is delegated to other managers. The way in which large companies are organized varies, but usually takes one of two main forms.

The first form is *functional* delegation, with the appointment of functional managers, such as the sales manager, production manager, individual factory managers, and financial managers. These are responsible for the operation of their function and report to the managing director on a routine basis.

The second form is *decentralized* in autonomous divisions, based on products and/or geographic territory. These divisions are headed by divisional managers, who may have functional delegation within their division.

The functions within a firm may seem to be run independently, but this is only an impression. The sales department can only sell goods that the production department has made. Similarly, the production department must not produce goods when the sales department cannot find customers for the product. Changes in sales and production levels have implications for other departments in the company: raw materials need to be purchased, labour redeployed/employed and finance raised.

The departments need to be kept in line, with all of them following the same detailed plan. This plan is stated in financial terms and is called a *budget*. The role of the budget is to help coordinate the interrelated functions within the organization.

Without coordination there is a risk that a phenomenon known as *sub-optimality* may result. This occurs where each of the functions attempts to maximize its own goals or objectives without realizing that the overall impact on the firm may be less beneficial. For example, the sales manager may try to maximize sales of the product with the highest revenue without recognizing that other products may contribute a greater profit margin. Similarly, the production department may aim to maximize output of the product which is easiest to make, without regard for the level of orders received from customers. The term used to describe such behaviour is *dysfunctional*. Dysfunctional behaviour may occur at any level in an organization.

The *budgetary process* is the term given to the coordinating role played by budgets. In the second part of the chapter we examine how the effects of the functional budgets (targets set by senior management for individual managers to meet) are brought together to form the master budget, which is the overall plan for the firm for the next financial period.

Planning using budgets

An organization will have a number of plans or goals that its senior management hopes to achieve. These are arranged according to the time-scale associated with their realization: short-term, medium-term and long-term. Military descriptions are often used to describe these plans: short-term plans are 'operational', medium-term plans are 'tactical' and long-term plans are 'strategic'. The principles involved in budgeting at these various levels are similar in each case. We shall illustrate these principles in relation to short-term budgets, the most commonly found form.

The basis on which budgets may be set include: rolling/continuous, incremental and zero-based. The *rolling/continuous* budget is a 12-month budget that is reviewed periodically, say every quarter, to update the original forecasts based on more recent and more accurate data. In addition, the original budgets and forecasts will have been based upon assumptions relating to the business environment. Unforeseen changes in this environment may require revisions to the assumptions underlying the original budgets and forecasts, for example tax changes following the government's annual Budget, increases in unemployment levels, changes in interest, inflation or exchange rates. Maintaining rolling budgets imposes an extra administrative effort but this may be offset by the improved accuracy of the continuing budget information and hence greater management control.

Incremental budgeting refers to the preparation of the coming year's budget on the basis of past data after making certain allowances for factors which are known to have changed, such as the effects of inflation and pay awards. This method of budgeting has the advantage of being relatively cheap to administer and easy for non-financial managers to understand. Its principal disadvantage is that current budget slack or inefficiency is perpetuated.

Zero-based budgeting (ZBB) seeks to avoid the disadvantage of incremental budgeting by requiring the existing level of expenditure to be justified before inclusion in the budget. Though this is a relatively more expensive form of system to administer, it can produce savings by eliminating built-up slack.

Whichever method of budgeting is used, the system should be formalized and the main target or objective of the budget stated in quantitative terms, for example to achieve a 10% increase in sales volume of product X at a price of £40 per unit.

The administration of the budgetary process may be the role of a single individual, the budget officer, or a budget committee with representation from different levels in the organization. This committee will set overall budget levels and budget policy, for example what level of variance is to be reported to senior managers.

Control using budgets

Budgets represent the organization's plan in financial terms. Without planning the future direction of the organization, its management cannot hope to be able to keep it on course in the future.

To take a non-financial analogy, the purpose of planning a long journey is to ensure that the desired destination is reached. The efficient achievement of that objective involves planning the best route and, while *en route*, taking bearings from landmarks passed. In this way any deviations from the planned route can be quickly detected and corrections made to bring the journey back on course.

In a business setting, one role of the accounting system is to produce information on actual expenditure which can be compared with planned or budgeted expenditure (and income). The differences between actual and planned outcomes are known as *variances* and these are reported to management. In information terms, the process is known as *feedback* and its purpose is to allow management to control the direction of the business (see Figure 8.1).

An approach known as *management by exception* concentrates management's attention on those areas which are not performing as planned. Areas, departments or divisions which turn in results in line with the plan are less likely to receive management attention. Management by exception results in greater efficiency in controlling the organization.

Further improvements can be obtained by stratifying variance reports so that only really significant variances are reported at a senior lower level of management, with relatively minor variances being dealt with lower down the organizational chain of command.

Figure 8.1 Feedback loop

Features of a good system of budgetary control

In establishing a system of budgetary control it is worth considering the aspects that are considered to be 'best practice'. If these features are not present then there is a strong likelihood that managers will reject the system. They may follow the rules and regulations set out by the system, but the system will be a 'stick' and not a 'carrot'. Ideally, managers should see the budget as a goal that *they* want to achieve, that is to say, they should *internalize* the budgetary objective.

One way of enhancing internalization is to operate a system of *responsibility accounting*. This means acknowledging the limitations of the manager's span of control and recognizing the areas of the firm's performance that can be laid at the manager's door.

Managers of *cost centres* are only accountable for expenditure within their department. Matters relating to income derived from the department are the responsibility of another manager, possibly within the sales department. This is a typical situation in functionally divided companies where the delegation of authority for decision-making is limited.

In decentralized companies managers are responsible for *profit centres*. In such companies, senior managers of divisions have control over income as well as expenditure. They are involved in decisions regarding marketing of the product and even the product mix itself. In the case of larger divisions, they may well have cost-centre managers reporting to them.

Very large firms have managers in control of *investment centres*, which implies delegation to divisional management of authority not only for income and expenditure but also for strategic planning involving capital investment.

The first rule of responsibility accounting is to place in a manager's budget only those items which can be controlled by that manager. A major problem is with the allocation of fixed overheads or the spreading of the costs of other departments, such as administration. While these may appear on the budget statement of the production manager, no variance should be attributed to the department. Many firms operate systems of 'standard costing' which carefully attribute variances to the appropriate person.

Flexible budgeting

A budget is based on forecasts. These may not be realized in the fullness of time. If the level of production has been lower than anticipated then one would expect the costs associated with that production level to be lower. Table 8.1 provides an illustration of a report which takes no account of changes in production levels.

From the unflexed budget in Table 8.1 the production manager is credited with a number of favourable variances, indicated by the 'F' next to the individual variances. It is clearly not right to give the production manager credit for these apparent cost savings, which have only been achieved because the level of the company's activity is 20% down from the expected level.

To produce meaningful information the budget is therefore adjusted to reflect the

Table 8.1 *Unflexed budget*

	Budgeted Production (10,000 units)	Actual Production (8,000 units)	Variance
Labour (£2/unit)	20,000	19,500	500 F
Materials (£1/unit)	10,000	9,250	750 F
Variable Overheads (£0.5/unit)	5,000	4,000	1,000 F
Fixed Overheads (£0.7/unit)	7,000	7,000	—
	42,000	38,350	2,250 F

Table 8.2 *Flexed budget*

	Budgeted Production (8,000 units)	Actual Production (8,000 units)	Variance
Labour (£2/unit)	16,000	19,500	3,500 U
Materials (£1/unit)	8,000	9,250	1,250 U
Variable Overheads (£0.5/unit)	4,000	4,000	—
Fixed Overheads (£0.7/unit)	5,600	7,000	1,400 U
	33,600	39,750	6,150 U

actual volume of activity. This method of adjustment is known as *flexible budgeting* and involves revising the variables in the original budget. Table 8.2 shows the effect of this flexing. The flexed budget indicates that the production manager has overspent the budget on labour and materials, producing an unfavourable variance, denoted by the suffix 'U', (or alternatively, 'A' for adverse).

One problem is how to account for the fixed costs, which remain the same regardless of the production level. The absorption-costing approach requires these costs to be apportioned on some basis. In the above example we have used a per-unit basis. As a result of the underproduction of 2000 units, overheads have been underrecovered to the extent of £1400 (2000 × £0.70). Whether this is charged to the production department depends on the company's policy and the cause of the underproduction. It would hardly be fair to charge the production department with the underrecovery if production had been reduced because of lack of demand for the product.

If the underrecovery of overheads were not to be charged to the production manager's budget the total unfavourable variance would be £4750 (the unfavourable variances on the labour and materials).

Other features of budget reporting

One feature of a good system of budgetary control is that it produces and reports variances on a 'timely' basis. The budget report must reach the responsible manager quickly enough to enable action to be taken before the next reporting cycle. For example, if the variances indicate that there is a problem with the quality of components, then the supplier can be contacted and the problem resolved before another order is placed.

The information must also be accurate. Flaws in the system can result in expenditure not being reported in the correct period or incorrect allocation of expenditure. This can have a demotivating effect on managers whose performance is measured by these budget statements. Even with the use of computers, mistakes can be made, especially on inputting data, and the result can be a loss of confidence in the whole system of budgetary control.

The manager must understand the report. Financially trained personnel are often accused of being insensitive to the needs of functionally trained staff. The budgets must be produced in a format with which the recipient is comfortable, rather than in the way which is most convenient for the management accountant.

Motivational aspects of budgeting

Exercising control in an organization is about managing people, and budgets should be seen in the context of how they influence people's behaviour. The main use of budgets is to monitor managerial performance, and they can reflect badly on some managers. If this happens routinely, managers may reject the budget as they never seem able to attain it. They will ignore the targets set as they are unable to meet them and perform to a level they are happy with, regardless of the wider impact on the company.

Take the above example of a production manager who is asked to produce 10,000 units a month, but is only ever able to produce 8000. In attempting to increase production, the manager may ask the workforce to work overtime at enhanced rates of pay. Even with a flexed budget, this is likely to produce adverse labour variances as the standard is based on normal rates of pay. The workers may find themselves under pressure and mistakes will increase. This will lead to wastage in production and to adverse materials variances. Meanwhile, the sales department has assumed that 10,000 units are forthcoming and will have to disappoint some customers who may now find alternative suppliers. The blame for all these problems is placed on the production manager, who is only trying to meet the target. Pretty soon both manager and workforce will become very disillusioned and demotivated.

The cause of the problem was the setting of too high a standard. Ten thousand units may have been the 'ideal standard' representing the maximum level of efficiency which would not take account of breakdowns of equipment, absenteeism due to sickness or loss of production due to material stock-outs. The 'currently attainable standard' is 8000, which may be less than perfect, but which is more representative of what can reasonably be achieved. To act as a motivating force, the budget should be set at a level just above 8000. The manager knows that the workforce can produce 8000 units most of the time but only occasionally produces 8200 units. If 8200 units are set as the target, this may have a motivational impact on both manager and workforce. However, the sales department should only expect 8000 units as the higher level of 8200 may not be achieved.

Usually the person best placed to decide the budget standard is the manager who is being controlled by the budget. Participation is vital if internalization of the budget is to be achieved. It may seem somewhat perverse to allow managers to decide their own budget level, but that is exactly what is recommended.

The risk is that participation can lead to bias and 'slack' being introduced, with managers setting budgets which are easily achieved. The production manager in our example may like the production budget to be set at 7500 units, but this might easily be achieved without expending any effort towards cost efficiency and effectiveness. Careful examination of previous records by budget officers may reduce the likelihood of such bias. Furthermore, if the reward system (for example, paying managers and workers a bonus for reaching peak performance) is structured appropriately the budget can be set at a relatively high level without loss of motivation.

Since every manager has individual attitudes and motivations, the behavioural implications of budgeting cannot be reduced to a simple set of rules. Some managers may be more money-motivated than others. It is best to adopt a contingency approach to each case.

To some extent slack must be tolerated in setting budgets as this may reduce conflict between different departments. However, the accountant needs to be wary of 'empire building' (overstaffing) and overstated expenses which allow slack to build up to unjustifiable levels.

New technology and Japanese-style methods of production have focused on slack reduction with great effect. However, this is part of a much wider debate on operations management and industrial relations.

Practical illustration of budget preparation

This part of the chapter illustrates how a spreadsheet can be used to prepare many organizational budgets from the same input data. Within the input range certain assumptions are made regarding sales levels, selling prices and expected production costs. The exact data required will, of course, vary from firm to firm, but it is important to include any *limiting factors* such as the maximum number of labour hours or material availability. The main limiting factor is usually sales volume at the given selling price.

Example 8.1

Our company commences with the existing actual balance sheet as at 1 April 19X7, as shown in Table 8.3. We cannot alter these figures and they therefore form part of the parameters contained in the input section of the spreadsheet.

Apart from the starting position, we are also given further data to be included in our input section. The company produces two products (X and Y), which require two types of materials (A and B) and two processes (machining and assembly). Apart from direct costs, factory and administration overheads need to be recovered. The complete section of input variables is presented in Table 8.4.

Having constructed the control section as shown in Spreadsheet Solution 8.1, we

Table 8.3 *Opening balance sheet*

Balance Sheet as at 1 April 19X7

	Cost £	Depn £	NBV £
Fixed Assets			
Land & Buildings	65,000	0	65,000
Plant & Equipment	295,000	95,000	200,000
	360,000	95,000	265,000
Current Assets			
Stock			
Raw Materials	11,500		
Finished Goods	25,100	36,600	
Debtors		7,300	
Cash		64,200	
		108,100	
Current Liabilities			
Creditors	7,600		
Taxation	15,500	23,100	85,000
			350,000
Financed by:			
Share Capital			250,000
Retained Profit			100,000
			350,000

can complete the input section containing the data from Table 8.4 and the opening balances as shown in Spreadsheet Solution 8.2.

The sales budget

As sales is our limiting factor we need to start our model with the plan for the Sales Department. This is based on forecast demand and price levels. These should be realistic aspirations agreed with the appropriate sales staff.

Various statistical analyses of past trends and seasonal factors may produce figures that are 95% 'accurate', but unless these are internalized by the sales managers they can prove to be dysfunctional. The sales staff are often more aware of the current business climate and are often able to predict sales very accurately. The agreed sales budget then becomes the target against which the performance of the sales department is monitored. The budget may be analyzed over months or quarters to take account of seasonal factors.

In our budget model, the sales variables will be cell referenced to the other budgets so any changes in forecasts or 'what if?' scenarios can be input and the resulting change

Table 8.4 *Input variables*

	X	Y
Sales Forecasts (units)	5,500	6,000
Selling Price (£)	40	52
Finished Goods:		
Closing Stock (units)	600	1400
Opening Stock (units)	500	400
Unit Cost of Opening Stock (£)	23	34
Plant Capacity: Machining (mins)	21	36
Plant Capacity: Assembly (mins)	15	24
Material A Content (kg)	2.0	1.0
Material B Content (kg)	2.5	4.5
Direct Labour (hours)	4	6
Direct Labour Cost per Hour (£)	4.75	4.75
Raw Materials:	Material A	Material B
Closing Stock (kg)	800	1,200
Opening Stock (kg)	1,300	5,500
Cost of Raw Materials (£)	2.50	1.50
Factory Overhead:	Machining	Assembly
	£	£
Supervisors' Salaries	25,000	10,550
Power	7,500	2,000
Maintenance & Running Costs	1,500	1,500
Consumables	2,350	1,500
General Expenses	19,410	6,950
Plant Used	100,000	195,000
Depreciation Rate	10%	10%
Proposed Acquisition (month 1)	40,000	
Selling & Administration Expenses:		£
Sales Commissions and Salaries		7,600
Travelling and Distribution		4,500
Office Salaries		9,790
General Administration Expenses		1,750
		23,640

Note. The new plant becomes operational in month 6.

in outcome for other budget holders and for the overall budget can be analyzed. The sales budget given in Spreadsheet Solution 8.3 is a straightforward annual target, (with formulae back-up shown in Spreadsheet Solution 8.4).

The production budget

The level of production planned for the coming period must take account of the existing level of opening stock of finished goods, the desired level of closing stock as well as the level of sales predicted for the period. The desired level of closing stock may be determined by the firm's need to keep certain stock levels as a 'buffer' against

Spreadsheet solution 8.1   Control section

	A	B	C	D
1	Spreadsheet Solution 8-1: Control Section			
2				
3	Example 8.1			
4				
5	This spreadsheet presents a fully integrated budgeting model			
6	based on a manufacturing company producing two products, X & Y.			
7				
8	Each product requires direct labour, raw materials and needs to			
9	pass through two processes, Machining and Assembly.			
10				
11	Location Table		Range Name	
12	---		------------------	
13	Input Section		INPUT	
14	Sales Budget		OUTPUT1	
15	Production Budget		OUTPUT2	
16	Plant Utilization Budget		OUTPUT3	
17	Materials Usage Budget		OUTPUT4	
18	Direct Labour Budget		OUTPUT5	
19	Factory Overhead Budget		OUTPUT6	
20	Cost of Finished Goods Budget		OUTPUT7	
21	Raw Materials Purchasing Budget		OUTPUT8	
22	Cost of Goods Sold Budget		OUTPUT9	
23	Budgeted Profit & Loss Account		OUTPUT10	
24	Budgeted Balance Sheet		OUTPUT11	
25	Cash Budget		OUTPUT12	

Spreadsheet solution 8.2   Input section

	E	F	G	H
26	Spreadsheet Solution 8-2: Input Section			
27				
28	Balance Sheet as at 1 April 19X7			
29		Cost	Depn	NBV
30	Fixed Assets	£	£	£
31	Land & Buildings	65,000	0	65,000
32	Plant & Equipment	295,000	95,000	200,000
33		-------------	-------------	-------------
34		360,000	95,000	265,000
35	Current Assets			
36	Stock			
37	Raw Materials	11,500		
38	Finished Goods	25,100	36,600	
39	Debtors		7,300	
40	Cash		64,200	
41			-------------	
42			108,100	
43	Current Liabilities			
44	Creditors	7,600		
45	Taxation	15,500		
46		-------------	23,100	
47		-------------		85,000
48				-------------
49				350,000
50				======
51	Financed by:			
52	Share Capital			250,000
53	Retained Profit			100,000
54				-------------
55				350,000
56				======
57				
58				
59			X	Y
60	Sales Forecasts (units)		5,500	6,000
61	Selling Price (£)		40	52
62				

63	Finished Goods:		
64	Closing Stock (units)	600	1400
65	Opening Stock (units)	500	400
66	Unit Cost of opening stock (£)	23	34
67			
68	Plant Capacity: Machining (mins)	21	36
69	Plant Capacity: Assembly (mins)	15	24
70			
71	Material A Content (kg)	2.0	1.0
72	Material B Content (kg)	2.5	4.5
73			
74	Direct Labour (hours)	4	6
75	Direct Labour cost per hour (£)	4.75	4.75
76			
77	Raw Materials:	Material A	Material B
78	Closing Stock (kg)	800	1,200
79	Opening Stock (kg)	1,300	5,500
80	Cost of Raw Materials (£)	2.50	1.50
81			
82	Factory Overhead:	Machining	Assembly
83		£	£
84	Supervisors' Salaries	25,000	10,550
85	Power	7,500	2,000
86	Maintenance & running costs	1,500	1,500
87	Consumables	2,350	1,500
88	General Expenses	19,410	6,950
89			
90	Plant Used	100,000	195,000
91	Depreciation Rate	10%	10%
92	Proposed Acquisition	40000	
93			
94	Selling & Administration Expenses:		£
95	Sales commissions and salaries		7,600
96	Travelling and distribution		4,500
97	Office Salaries		9,790
98	General administration expenses		1,750
99			-------------
100			23,640

Spreadsheet solution 8.3   Sales budget

	I	J	K	L
101	Spreadsheet Solution 8-3: Sales Budget			
102				
103		Demand	Price	Value
104		units	£	£
105	X	5,500	40	220,000
106	Y	6,000	52	312,000
107				----------------------
108				532,000

Spreadsheet solution 8.4   Sales budget

	I	J	K	L
101	Spreadsheet Solution 8-4: Sales Budget			
102				
103		Demand	Price	Value
104		units	£	£
105	X	+G60	+G61	+K105*J105
106	Y	+H60	+H61	+K106*J106
107				----------------------
108				+L106+L105

disruptions in production, either caused by material shortages, industrial disputes or other unforeseen disasters, and to act as a reserve to meet unexpected orders. This can result in winning new customers or keeping old customers happy. However, the firm should guard against holding excessive levels of stock since this may tie up working capital without earning any immediate profit.

The costs of production form part of the production budget, the various aspects of which we will consider in individual sections.

The production budget is given in Spreadsheet Solution 8.5 (with formulae back-up in Spreadsheet Solution 8.6). Notice that this is just the plan of production for the two products expressed in terms of physical units, and that no costs have been attached as yet.

Spreadsheet solution 8.5   Production budget

	M	N	O
109	Spreadsheet Solution 8-5: Production Budget		
110			
111		X	Y
112	Sales	5,500	6,000
113	Add Closing Stock	600	1,400
114	Less Opening Stock	(500)	(400)
115		--------------------	--------------------
116		5,600	7,000

Spreadsheet solution 8.6 Production budget

	M	N	O
109	Spreadsheet Solution 8-6: Production Budget		
110			
111		X	Y
112	Sales	+G60	+H60
113	Add Closing Stock	+G64	+H64
114	Less Opening Stock	-G65	-H65
115		------------------------------	------------------------------
116		@SUM(N112..N114)	@SUM(O112..O114)

The plant utilization budget

From the input data, standard production times for each unit in each department can be derived. These are used to provide an indication of the total time that the plant needs to be running and the mix of products to be produced.

Spreadsheet Solutions 8.7 and 8.8 give the plant utilization budget in figures and formulae, respectively.

The target for the production department generated by the plant utilization budget is used later in determining overhead recovery rates.

The materials usage budget

The materials usage budget, based on assumptions of the standard usage of materials,

Spreadsheet solution 8.7 Plant utilization budget

	P	Q	R	S	T	U
117	Spreadsheet Solution 8-7: Plant Utilization Budget					
118						
119			Machining	Machining	Assembly	Assembly
120		Units	Time (hrs)	Total (hrs)	Time (hrs)	Total (hrs)
121	X	5,600	0.35	1,960	0.25	1,400
122	Y	7,000	0.60	4,200	0.40	2,800
123				--------------------		--------------------
124				6,160		4,200

Spreadsheet solution 8.8 Plant utilization budget

	P	Q	R	S	T	U
117	Spreadsheet Solution 8-8: Plant Utilization Budget					
118						
119			Machining	Machining	Assembly	Assembly
120		Units	Time (hrs)	Total (hrs)	Time (hrs)	Total (hrs)
121	X	+N116	+G68/60	+R121*Q121	+G69/60	+Q121*T121
122	Y	+O116	+H68/60	+R122*Q122	+H69/60	+Q122*T122
123				--------------------		--------------------
124				+S121+S122		+U121+U12

is used to determine the amount and cost of the raw materials consumed in the production process. This contains assumptions on standard material usage. Variances from the budget are often caused by the purchase of poor-quality materials which may result in increased waste. Waste can also be the result of poorly trained labour.

The section of the spreadsheet model covering the materials usage budget is shown in Spreadsheet Solution 8.9 with the formulae given in Spreadsheet Solution 8.10.

Spreadsheet solution 8.9   Materials usage budget

	V	W	X
125	Spreadsheet Solution 8-9: Materials Usage		
126			
127		Material A	Material B
128	X	11,200	14,000
129	Y	7,000	31,500
130		----------------------	--------------------
131		18,200	45,500
132	Cost/Kg	2.50	1.50
133			
134	Cost of Materials Use	45,500	68,250

Spreadsheet solution 8.10   Materials usage budget

	V	W	X
125	Spreadsheet Solution 8-10: Materials Usage		
126			
127		Material A	Material B
128	X	+$N$116*G71	+$N$116*G72
129	Y	+$O$116*H71	+$O$116*H72
130		----------------------	----------------------
131		+W128+W129	+X128+X129
132	Cost/Kg	+G80	+H80
133			
134	Cost of Materials Use	+W131*W132	+X131*X132

The direct labour budget

The direct labour budget indicates the amount of hours needed to be worked and the price paid per hour. In practice, there may be many categories of direct labour and while the spreadsheet can cope with greater sophistication, there is little to be gained from the illustration by making it more complex. Variances can be caused by overtime working at enhanced rates of pay or by 'idle time' when workers cannot produce due to machine breakdown. Routine maintenance and 'natural' work breaks should be accounted for when determining the standard times. Inaccurate standards, especially those that are too tight, can be very demotivating.

Spreadsheet Solutions 8.11 and 8.12 give the figures and formulae, respectively, for the direct labour budget.

Spreadsheet solution 8.11 Direct labour budget

	Y	Z	AA	AB	AC	AD
135	Spreadsheet Solution 8-11: Direct Labour Budget					
136						
137		Units	Hours	Total hrs	Cost	Total £
138	X	5,600	4	22,400	4.75	106,400
139	Y	7,000	6	42,000	4.75	199,500
140						---------------
141						305,900

Spreadsheet solution 8.12 Direct labour budget

	Y	Z	AA	AB	AC	AD
135	Spreadsheet Solution 8-12: Direct Labour Budget					
136						
137		Units	Hours	Total hrs	Cost	Total £
138	X	+N116	+G74	+AA138*Z138	+G75	+AC138*AB138
139	Y	+O116	+H74	+AA139*Z139	+H75	+AC139*AB139
140						-------------------------
141		–				+AD138+AD139

The factory overhead budget

Modern production methods often involve numerous production departments. In our example there are just two departments, but this level of detail is sufficient to illustrate the main features of the budgeting process. Some costs have been allocated and apportioned and these are picked up from the input data. Most overheads by nature are fixed, although their inclusion as variables in the input section means that their level can be varied as required.

The amount of the depreciation charge is likely to alter in the next year due to the proposed acquisition of plant. The machine hours are picked up from the plant utilization budget. The complete figures and formulae for the factory overhead budget are presented in Spreadsheet Solutions 8.13 and 8.14, respectively.

The cost of finished goods budget

Part of the information produced is a unit cost statement that recovers fixed costs, that is to say, it gives the full cost of each product. This is useful for planning purposes and can give immediate access to standard variable/fixed cost data for the purposes of short-term decisions.

For the figures and formulae relating to the cost of finished goods budget see Spreadsheet Solutions 8.15 and 8.16.

The raw materials purchasing budget

Sometimes referred to as the *raw materials budget*, this provides the purchasing manager with the information required to prepare ordering schedules for the coming

Spreadsheet solution 8.13   Factory overhead budget

	AE	AF	AG
142	Spreadsheet Solution 8-13: Factory Overhead Budget		
143			
144		Machining	Assembly
145		£	£
146	Allocated & Apportioned	55,760	22,500
147			
148	Existing Depreciation	10,000	19,500
149	Proposed Depreciation	2,000	
150		----------------	----------------
151	Total Factory Overhead	67,760	42,000
152			
153	Machine Hours	6,160	4,200
154			
155	Absorption Rate per hour	11.00	10.00

Spreadsheet solution 8.14   Factory overhead budget

	AE	AF	AG
142	Spreadsheet Solution 8-14: Factory Overhead Budget		
143			
144		Machining	Assembly
145		£	£
146	Allocated & Apportioned	@SUM(G84..G88)	@SUM(H84..H88)
147			
148	Existing Depreciation	+G90*G91	+H90*H91
149	Proposed Depreciation	+G91*G92/2	
150		----------------------------------	----------------------------------
151	Total Factory Overhead	@SUM(AF146..AF149)	@SUM(AG146..AG149)
152			
153	Machine Hours	+S124	+U124
154			
155	Absorption Rate per hour	+AF151/AF153	+AG151/AG153

Spreadsheet solution 8.15   Cost of finished goods budget

	AH	AI	AJ
156	Spreadsheet Solution 8-15:		
157	Cost of Finished Goods Budget		
158		X	Y
159	Material A	5.00	2.50
160	Material B	3.75	6.75
161	Direct Labour	19.00	28.50
162	Machinery Overhead	3.85	6.60
163	Assembly Overhead	2.50	4.00
164		------------	----------------
165	Factory Cost per unit	34.10	48.35

Spreadsheet solution 8.16 Cost of finished goods budget

	AH	AI	AJ
156	Spreadsheet Solution 8-16:		
157	Cost of Finished Goods Budget		
158		X	Y
159	Material A	+G80*G71	+G80*H71
160	Material B	+H80*G72	+H80*H72
161	Direct Labour	+G74*G75	+H74*H75
162	Machinery Overhead	+G68/60*$AF$155	+H68/60*$AF$155
163	Assembly Overhead	+G69/60*$AG$155	+H69/60*$AG$155
164		----------------------------------	----------------------------------
165	Factory Cost per unit	@SUM(AI159..AI163)	@SUM(AJ159..AJ163)

Spreadsheet solution 8.17 Raw materials purchasing budget

	AK	AL	AM
166	Spreadsheet Solution 8-17:		
167	Raw Materials Purchasing Budget		
168			
169		A	B
170	Closing Stock	800	1,200
171	Production Requirements	18,200	45,500
172	Less Opening Stock	(1,300)	(5,500)
173		---------------	---------------
174	Purchase Requirements	17,700	41,200
175			
176	Cost per unit (£)	2.50	1.50
177			
178	Purchase Costs	44,250	61,800

Spreadsheet solution 8.18 Raw materials purchasing budget

	AK	AL	AM
166	Spreadsheet Solution 8-18:		
167	Raw Materials Purchasing Budget		
168			
169		A	B
170	Closing Stock	+G78	+H78
171	Production Requirements	+W131	+X131
172	Less Opening Stock	-G79	-H79
173		----------------------------------	----------------------------------
174	Purchase Requirements	@SUM(AL170..AL172)	@SUM(AM170..AM172)
175			
176	Cost per unit (£)	+G80	+H80
177			
178	Purchase Costs	+AL174*AL176	+AM174*AM176

year. Existing stock levels and planned closing stock levels are also taken into account.

The relevant section of the spreadsheet model appears in Spreadsheet Solution 8.17 (with formulae given in Spreadsheet Solution 8.18).

Cost of goods sold budget

As the final pieces of the jigsaw begin to fit together, we are now able to produce a cost of goods sold budget which brings together some of the functional budget holders' targets. As there are considerations regarding opening and closing stocks of finished goods, certain assumptions about the method of stock accounting need to be made. For simplicity we have assumed that all the items in the opening stock have been sold by the year end; in other words, we have assumed that closing stock consists only of those items produced during the year but left unsold at the year end.

This budget within the spreadsheet model appears in Spreadsheet Solutions 8.19 and 8.20.

Spreadsheet solution 8.19   Cost of goods sold budget (using FIFO)

	AN	AO	AP	AQ	AR	AS	AT
179	Spreadsheet Solution 8-19: Cost of Goods Sold Budget (using FIFO)						
180							
181		X		Total	Y		Total
182		(units)	£	£	(units)	£	£
183	Opening Stocks	500	23.00	11,500	400	34.00	13,600
184	Cost of Production	5,600	34.10	190,960	7,000	48.35	338,450
185		----------------		----------------	-------		----------------
186		6,100		202,460	7,400		352,050
187	Less Closing Stocks	(600)	34.10	(20,460)	(1,400)	48.35	(67,690)
188		----------------		----------------	-------		----------------
189	Cost of Sales	5,500		182,000	6,000		284,360

Spreadsheet solution 8.20   Cost of goods sold budget (using FIFO)

	AN	AO	AP	AQ	AR	AS	AT
179	Spreadsheet Solution 8-20: Cost of Goods Sold Budget (using FIFO)						
180							
181		X		Total	Y		Total
182		(units)	£	£	(units)	£	£
183	Opening Stocks	+G65	+G66	+AP183*AO183	+H65	+H66	+AS183*AR183
184	Cost of Production	+N116	+$AI$165	+AP184*AO184	+O116	+$AJ$165	+AS184*AR184
185		-----------------------		------------------------	-----------------------		-------------------------
186		+AO183+AO184		+AQ183+AQ184	+AR183+AR184		+AT183+AT184
187	Less Closing Stocks	-G64	+$AI$165	+AO187*AP187	-H64	+$AJ$165	+AR187*AS187
188		-----------------------		------------------------	-----------------------		-------------------------
189	Cost of Sales	+AO186+AO187		+AQ186+AQ187	+AR186+AR187		+AT186+AT187

Budget profit and loss account

When all the other necessary budgets have been prepared, they can be summarized in the form of forecast final accounts for the coming year. This enables senior management to evaluate the planned performance for the coming year and the position the company expects to be in if the budgets are achieved.

Spreadsheet solution 8.21 Budgeted profit and loss account

	AU	AV	AW	AX
190	Spreadsheet Solution 8-21: Budgeted Profit & Loss Account			
191				
192		X	Y	Total
193		£	£	£
194	Sales	220,000	312,000	532,000
195	Less Cost of Sales	182,000	284,360	466,360
196		--------------	--------------	--------------
197	Gross Profit	38,000	27,640	65,640
198				
199	Less Selling & Administration			23,640
200				--------------
201	Net Profit			42,000
202				
203	Taxation			21,000
204				--------------
205	Net Profit after Taxation			21,000
206				=====

Spreadsheet solution 8.22 Budgeted profit and loss account

	AU	AV	AW	AX
190	Spreadsheet Solution 8-22: Budgeted Profit & Loss Account			
191				
192		X	Y	Total
193		£	£	£
194	Sales	+L105	+L106	+L108
195	Less Cost of Sales	+AQ189	+AT189	+AW195+AV195
196		-----------------------	-------------------------	-------------------------
197	Gross Profit	+AV194-AV195	+AW194-AW195	+AX194-AX195
198				
199	Less Selling & Administration			+H100
200				-------------------------
201	Net Profit			+AX197-AX199
202				
203	Taxation			+AX201*0.5
204				-------------------------
205	Net Profit after Taxation			+AX201-AX203
206				=========

See Spreadsheet Solutions 8.21 and 8.22 for the final accounts section of the model. We have assumed for the sake of simplicity that the marginal rate of taxation is 50%.

The cash budget

Although we could now proceed to the preparation of the budgeted balance sheet, leaving the closing cash balance as a balancing figure, it may be worthwhile preparing a separate cash budget.

Spreadsheet solution 8.23   Cash budget

	AY	AZ	BA	BB	BC	BD	BE
208	Spreadsheet Solution 8-23: Cash Budget						
209							
210		Quarter 1	Quarter 2	Quarter 3	Quarter 4	Total	Residuals
211							
212	Opening Balance	64,200	(22,558)	(18,021)	(13,483)	64,200	
213							
214	Receipts						
215	Debtors (19X7)	7,300				7,300	
216	Debtors (19X8)	88,667	133,000	133,000	133,000	487,667	44,333
217		----------------	----------------	----------------	----------------	----------------	
218		160,167	110,442	114,979	119,517	559,167	
219							
220	Payments						
221							
222	Creditors (19x7)	7,600				7,600	
223	Raw Materials	17,675	26,513	26,513	26,513	97,213	8,838
224	Direct Labour	76,475	76,475	76,475	76,475	305,900	
225	Factory Overhead	19,565	19,565	19,565	19,565	78,260	
226	Equipment	40,000				40,000	
227	Selling Etc	5,910	5,910	5,910	5,910	23,640	
228	Taxation (19X7)	15,500				15,500	
229		----------------	----------------	----------------	----------------	----------------	
230		182,725	128,463	128,463	128,463	568,113	
231							
232	Closing Balance	(22,558)	(18,021)	(13,483)	(8,946)	(8,946)	

Cash shortages are the main cause of failure of small firms in particular and can be irrecoverable, even if the firm is profitable. The cash budget contains information which should be very useful for management information. It may even prevent the firm from going into liquidation. Cash shortages can be planned for and any finance requirements agreed with the bank before a working capital crisis emerges.

The cash budget is given in Spreadsheet Solutions 8.23 and 8.24.

The reader will note that at this point we have broken our golden rule about keying in figures rather than cell references and formulae. We need to reflect the various periods of credit we give our customers and receive from our suppliers. We have assumed that sales accrue evenly over the period and all customers are allowed one month's credit.

We have incorporated the delay in receiving payment in the model in row 216: only two months of the current year's sales will be received in the first quarter so the formula in cell AZ 216 is ⟨+$AX$194/12*2⟩ and for the second quarter cell BA 216, ⟨+$AX$194/4⟩ to represent three months' sales.

Similarly, all raw materials are on credit with payment due one month after delivery. This, too, needs to be reflected in the model: for full details of the necessary formulae see row 223 in Spreadsheet Solution 8.24. Note also the fact that other categories of expense may need to be divided into the four quarters.

Spreadsheet solution 8.24   Cash budget

	AY	AZ	BA	BB	BC	BD	BE
208	Spreadsheet Solution 8-24: Cash Budget						
209							
210		Quarter 1	Quarter 2	Quarter 3	Quarter 4	Total	Residuals
211							
212	Opening Balance	+G40	+AZ232	+BA232	+BB232	+AZ212	
213							
214	Receipts						
215	Debtors (19X7)	+G39				@SUM(AZ215..BC215)	
216	Debtors (19X8)	+$AX$194/12*2	+$AX$194/4	+$AX$194/4	+$AX$194/4	@SUM(AZ216..BC216)	-BD216+AX194
217							
218		@SUM(AZ212..AZ216)	@SUM(BA212..BA216)	@SUM(BB212..BB216)	@SUM(BC212..BC216)	@SUM(BD212..BD216)	
219							
220	Payments						
221							
222	Creditors (19x7)	+F44				@SUM(AZ222..BC222)	
223	Raw Materials	(+$AL$178+$AM$178)/12*2	(+$AL$178+$AM$178)/12*3	(+$AL$178+$AM$178)/12*3	(+$AL$178+$AM$178)/12*3	@SUM(AZ223..BC223)	+AL178+AM178-BD223
224	Direct Labour	+$AD$141/4	+$AD$141/4	+$AD$141/4	+$AD$141/4	@SUM(AZ224..BC224)	
225	Factory Overhead	(+$AF$146+$AG$146)/4	(+$AF$146+$AG$146)/4	(+$AF$146+$AG$146)/4	(+$AF$146+$AG$146)/4	@SUM(AZ225..BC225)	
226	Equipment	+G92				@SUM(AZ226..BC226)	
227	Selling Etc	+$H$100/4	+$H$100/4	+$H$100/4	+$H$100/4	@SUM(AZ227..BC227)	
228	Taxation (19X7)	+F45				@SUM(AZ228..BC228)	
229							
230		@SUM(AZ222..AZ228)	@SUM(BA222..BA228)	@SUM(BB222..BB228)	@SUM(BC222..BC228)	@SUM(BD222..BD228)	
231							
232	Closing Balance	+AZ218-AZ230	+BA218-BA230	+BB218-BB230	+BC218-BC230	+BD218-BD230	

Spreadsheet solution 8.25   Balance sheet as at 31 March 19X8

	BF	BG	BH	BI	BJ
233	Spreadsheet Solution 8-25: Balance Sheet as at 31 March 19X8				
234		Cost	Depn	NBV	
235	Fixed Assets	£	£	£	
236	Land & Buidlings	65,000	0	65,000	
237	Plant & Equipment	335,000	126,500	208,500	
238		---------------	---------------	---------------	
239		400,000	126,500	273,500	
240	Current Assets				
241	Stock				
242	Raw Materials	3,800			
243	Finished Goods	88,150	91,950		
244	Debtors		44,333		
245	Cash		(8,946)		
246			---------------		
247			127,338		
248	Current Liabilities				
249	Creditors	8,838			
250	Taxation	21,000			
251		---------------	29,838		
252			---------------	97,500	
253				---------------	
254				371,000	
255				=====	
256	Financed by:				
257	Share Capital			250,000	
258	Retained Profit			121,000	
259				---------------	
260				371,000	
261				=====	

Budgeted balance sheet

Once all the other budgets have been prepared they can be brought together to produce
the final outcome of the process: the budgeted balance sheet. This is reproduced in
Spreadsheet Solutions 8.25 and 8.26.

'What if?' questions

Note: Return all variables to the original values before attempting each question.

1. The sales manager believes that if the selling price for product Y were to rise
    to £55, then 5500 units could be sold. Is this worthwhile? Examine the effect
    of the changes in price and output levels on the following:

    (a) materials usage budget;
    (b) direct labour budget;

Spreadsheet solution 8.26 Balance sheet as at 31 March 19X8

	BF	BG	BH	BI	BJ
		Cost	Depn	NBV	
234		£	£	£	
233	Spreadsheet Solution 8-26: Balance Sheet as at 31 March 19X8				
235	Fixed Assets				
236	Land & Buildings	+F31	+G31	+BG236-BH236	
237	Plant & Equipment	+F32+G92	+G32+AF148+AF149+AG148	+BG237-BH237	
238					
239		@SUM(BG236..BG237)	@SUM(BH236..BH237)	@SUM(BI236..BI237)	
240	Current Assets				
241	Stock				
242	Raw Materials	(+AL176*AL170)+(AM176*AM170)			
243	Finished Goods	-AQ187-AT187	+BG243+BG242		
244	Debtors		+BE216		
245	Cash		+BD232		
246					
247			@SUM(BH243..BH245)		
248	Current Liabilities				
249	Creditors	+BE223			
250	Taxation	+AX203			
251			@SUM(BH249..BH250)		
252				+BH247-BH251	
253				+BI252+BI239	
254				==============	
255					
256	Financed by:				
257	Share Capital			+H52	
258	Retained Profit			+H53+AX205	
259					
260				@SUM(BI257..BI258)	
261				==============	

(c) raw materials purchasing budget;
(d) budgeted profit and loss account.

2. Following a management consultant's report, stock levels for finished goods may be reduced by 50% from their budgeted position. Examine the effect on the following:

(a) factory overhead budget;
(b) cost of finished goods budget;
(c) cost of goods sold;
(d) budgeted profit and loss account;
(e) cash budget.

'What if?' solutions

1. (a) The quantity of material A used falls to 17,700 kg and material B to 43,250 kg. The cost of material A used now becomes £44,250 and for B £64,875.

   (b) The total direct labour hours expended on Y falls to 39,000 at a cost of £185,250.

   (c) The purchase requirement for A becomes 17,200 kg at a cost of £43,000 and for B 38,950 kg at a cost of £58,425.

   (d) Net profit after tax increases from £21,000 to £26,161.

2. (a) The absorption rate per hour for machining increases to £12.02 and for assembly to £10.92. This is due to the reduction in machine hours worked as fewer units of both X and Y need to be produced.

   (b) As a result of (a) the factory cost per unit rises to £34.69 for X and £49.33 for Y.

   (c) As a consequence of (b) the cost of goods sold rises to £289,872.

   (d) Net profit after tax falls to £16,770.

   (e) However, the cash budget's closing balance is £25,046. So the management consultant's advice has resolved a liquidity problem at the expense of lower profitability.

Conclusion

The concept of budgeting is vital to management control. The use of computers can aid the speed and accuracy of budget reporting. From simple contexts to relatively complex models, budgets can be produced using a spreadsheet package.

This chapter has illustrated, albeit with a fairly simplistic example, how the various relationships between output, income, costs, assets and liabilities can be modelled in the most adaptable manner. Our example used an annual budgeting cycle, but the same principles could equally well apply to models dealing with shorter time horizons, such as quarterly, monthly or weekly reports, as to long-term, strategic plans.

In practice, a spreadsheet model using numerous input values relating to all aspects of sales, production and other expense and capital items can provide the flexibility to update budget information for management information purposes.

As a planning tool, a properly constructed spreadsheet model can be used for budgeting purposes to explore many 'what if?' scenarios, the full implications of which are dealt with easily and automatically.

Exercises

Question 8.1

Company XYZ produces three products, X, Y and Z. For the coming accounting period budgets are to be prepared on the following information.

Budgeted sales
    Product X: 2000 at £100 each
    Product Y: 4000 at £130 each
    Product Z: 3000 at £150 each

Standard usage of raw material

	RM11	RM22	RM33
Product X	5	2	—
Product Y	3	2	2
Product Z	2	1	3
Standard cost per unit of material	£5	£3	£4

Finished stocks budget

	Product X	Product Y	Product Z
Beginning	500	800	700
End	600	1,000	800

Raw materials stock

	RM11	RM22	RM33
Beginning	21,000	10,000	16,000
End	18,000	9,000	12,000

	Product X	Product Y	Product Z
Standard hours per unit	4	6	8
Standard hourly rate labour	£3	£3	£3
Standard hourly rate variable overhead	£2	£2	£2

Fixed overhead budgeted at £292,000 absorbed on the basis of direct labour hours.

(a) You are required to prepare the following:
   (i) Sales budget — quantity and volume
   (ii) Production units budget
   (iii) Material usage budget
   (iv) Material purchases budget
   (v) Production cost budget, detailing standard product cost per unit.

(b) Explain how budgets may be used to enable cost control to be exercised in each department of a business, paying particular attention to the term 'control'.

Answer on page 268   *(AAT)*

Question 8.2

(a) Company Z is preparing budgets for the coming year. 120,000 direct labour hours will be 100% level of expected production time, but a flexible budget at 90%, 110% and 120% is required so that cost allowances can be set for these possible levels.

   Budgeted cost details

1. Fixed cost per annum

	£
Depreciation	22,000
Staff salaries	43,000
Insurances	9,000
Rent and rates	12,000

2. Variable costs

Power	30p per direct labour hour
Consumables	5p per direct labour hour
Direct labour	£3.50 per direct labour hour

3. Semi-variable costs
   Analysis of past records, adjusted to eliminate the effect on inflation shows the following:

		Direct labour hours	Total semi-variable costs £
Last year	19X8	110,000	330,000
	19X7	100,000	305,000
	19X6	90,000	280,000
	19X5	87,000	272,500
	19X4	105,000	317,500
	19X3	80,000	255,000

Prepare a cost budget at 100%, flexed to show cost allowances at 90%, 110% and 120% of expected level.

(b) The following budgeted profit and loss account has been prepared for company B for the first six months of the coming year.

	Jan £	Feb £	Mar £	Apr £	May £	June £
Sales	22,000	24,000	25,000	29,000	18,000	23,000
Less costs:						
Materials	8,000	9,000	9,500	10,000	6,000	8,500
Labour	3,900	4,000	4,200	4,700	3,700	4,100
Overhead	4,600	4,700	4,900	5,200	3,800	4,500
	16,500	17,700	18,600	19,900	13,500	17,100
Profit	5,500	6,300	6,400	9,100	4,500	5,900

The material cost above is arrived at as follows:

	Jan £	Feb £	Mar £	Apr £	May £	June £
Opening stock	3,000	5,000	3,000	2,500	3,500	1,500
Purchases	10,000	7,000	9,000	1,000	4,000	11,000
	13,000	12,000	12,000	13,500	7,500	12,500
Closing stock	5,000	3,000	2,500	3,500	1,500	4,000
	8,000	9,000	9,500	10,000	6,000	8,500

Notes
1. All materials are paid for one month after delivery. December purchases £9000.
2. Customers are expected to pay two months after sale. Sales for the previous November were £18,000 and for December £19,000.
3. Labour costs are paid in the month wages are earned.
4. Included in the overhead figures is £1000 per month for depreciation. All other overhead costs are paid for in the month the cost is incurred.
5. Capital expenditure is planned for March of £7500 and June £27,200.
6. A tax payment is due in January of £8000.
7. The expected cash balance at the beginning of January is £2000.

   (i) Produce a cash budget for the first six months of the coming year.
   (ii) Discuss the action the firm should take in view of the cash budget you have prepared.

No answer provided   *(AAT)*

Question 8.3

(a) Explain what you understand to be the objectives of budgetary control.

(b) Write brief notes on *two* of the following:
  (i)   budget manual
  (ii) budget committee
  (iii) master budget

(c) A company manufactures a single product and has produced the following flexed budget for the year.

| | Level of activity | | |
	70%	80%	90%
Direct materials	17,780	20,320	22,860
Direct labour	44,800	51,200	57,600
Production overhead	30,500	32,000	33,500
Administration overhead	17,000	17,000	17,000
Total cost	111,080	120,520	130,960

Prepare a budget flexed at the 45% level of activity.

(d) A company plans to produce and sell 4000 units of product YZ during the next period. The selling price of product YZ is £10 per unit. One unit of YZ requires four units of material A, three units of material B, and two units of material C. Opening stocks or raw material are as follows:

| | Total value | |
	Units	£
Material A	20,000	40,000
Material B	15,000	15,000
Material C	10,000	5,000

The closing stock for each raw material is to be a level which would meet the production requirements for 3000 units of product YZ. There are no opening or closing stocks of product YZ.

Purchase prices for all raw materials during the period are expected to be 20% higher than the prices reflected in the opening stock values.

Sales and purchases are on credit, the opening balance being as follows:

Debtors   £30,000
Creditors   £20,000

The company expects to receive £45,000 from debtors during the period, and plans to pay £23,000 to its creditors.

(i) Prepare the budget for raw material purchases.
(ii) Calculate the closing balance for debtors and creditors.

No answer provided *(AAT)*

Question 8.4

You have recently been appointed treasurer of a local authority and have been requested by the chairman of the finance committee to report briefly on techniques which have been proposed by various members of his committee with a view to improving the system of budgetary control.

You are required to write a brief report to the chairman in which you should explain and discuss the use of the following:

(a) Zero-base budgeting.
(b) Regression analysis.
(c) Participative budgeting.

No answer provided *(AAT)*

Question 8.5

'The feedback process is an essential part of a management accounting system'. Discuss the significance and implications of this statement.

No answer provided *(ICSA)*

Question 8.6

A company is preparing an outline budget for the year ahead based upon some broad assumptions about its business. These assumptions are as follows:

Opening stock of finished goods	40,000 units
Closing stock of finished goods	50% increase over opening stock
Stock turnover	6 times (based on average stock)
Gross profit to sales	40%
Product costs:	
Raw materials	£0.16 per unit
Direct labour	£0.20 per unit
Fixed production overhead	£0.18 per unit
(based on budgeted production volume)	
Variable selling and administration expenses	4% of sales
Fixed selling and administration expenses	£81,000
Opening stock of raw materials	£20,000

(these are expected to remain at the same monetary value throughout the budget year)

Both opening and closing stock of finished goods will be valued at the above total unit production cost.

Fixed production overhead includes depreciation of fixed assets of £20,000. All fixed assets will be 2 years old at the end of the budget year and are depreciated on a straight-line basis at 10% per annum.

Creditors total £16,000, and are expected to remain at the same level. The balance of debtors at the beginning of the year is expected to be £20,000. The debtors' collection period will be 30 days (assume that sales will be even, with 360 days in the year). A bank overdraft of £18,000 is anticipated at the beginning of the budget year.

(a) Prepare the budgeted profit and loss account for the year ahead.
(b) Prepare the balance sheet as at the end of the budget year.
(c) Explain how the budgeted production overhead cost per unit of output would be established by a company which uses predetermined overhead rates for each production department in its factory, based upon direct labour hours.

Answer on page 273   *(ACCA)*

Question 8.7

You have been approached by a principal of an accountancy college that is going to teach the AAT, to advise on the financial implications of plans for the first year of operation.

You ascertain that the college staff will consist of the principal, an administration department under the control of a deputy principal, and two departments, accounting and business studies, each of these under a head of department. The teaching will be provided by staff within the department.

The principal gives you the following projected information for the first year. He is rather proud of his estimates, having referred to nobody else in the college.

Level	Number of students	Fee per student £
Preliminary	400	2,000
Intermediate	300	3,000
Final	250	4,000

For the preliminary and intermediate stages you are told that there are to be 20 students in each class and for the final level there are to be ten students in each class. The college year will consist of 30 weeks' tuition and each class will have the following:

Level	Hours tuition per week	Tuition cost per class hour £
Preliminary	16	20
Intermediate	20	22
Final	22	24

(a) Prepare budgets showing the following information to the principal for the college's first year of operation:

   (i)   College revenue by level and in total.
   (ii) Number of classes required at each level.
   (iii) Tuition costs for each level and in total.
   (iv) Total student hours and the tuition cost per student hour at each level.

(b) You are also told that other costs include the following:

	£
Rental of college	500,000
Administration salaries	132,000
Administration costs	800,000
Welfare expenses	400,000
Examination fees	100,000

All the tuition fees are collectable, with the exception of 2% that are expected to turn out to be bad debts, and 5% of the administration costs are for depreciation. All the remaining expenses are budgeted to be paid.

Prepare a cash budget for the year advising the principal upon the outcome and possible course of action open to him.

(c) Acting upon the information given, evaluate the principal's method of budgeting and advise him of any alternative course of action for year 2 so that he maximizes the benefit that a system of budgeting and budgetary control can bring.

Answer on page 279

(AAT)

Question 8.8

Describe the main features of a spreadsheet package.

What are the primary benefits to be derived from developing a computer spreadsheet for use in a system of budgetary control?

No answer provided

(ICSA)

9 | Standard costing and variance analysis

AIMS OF CHAPTER

- to describe the role of a standard costing system;
- to calculate flexed budgets;
- to compare actual and standard costs in order to produce the main variances from standard;
- to demonstrate the construction of spreadsheet models to perform variance analysis;
- to explain and illustrate the uses of variance analysis.

SPREADSHEET SKILLS ACQUIRED

- constructing a solution to conform to spreadsheet logic.

Introduction

Chapter 8 describes the important role of budgetary control in the running of an organization. This chapter explains a related though independent aspect of control information, standard costing. The two are related because they are concerned with providing information for control purposes, they tend to be forward-looking and usually they are run in tandem. They are independent since it is possible for an organization to have a budgetary control system without having a standard costing system and, though less likely, vice versa.

Standard costing

Standard costing is the term given to the management accounting approach whereby the costs of products/services are predetermined. The purpose of the exercise is to

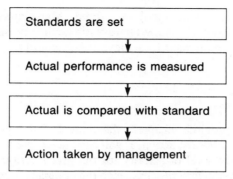

Figure 9.1 The standard cycle

calculate in advance what costs *should* be. This represents a *standard* against which actual costs can be measured. Any difference between actual and standard cost is called a *variance*. If the difference is to the company's advantage it is a *favourable* variance, if not it is an *adverse* or *unfavourable* variance.

The comparison of standard with actual provides management with vital information in that off-target performance can be identified. Those responsible can then be asked to explain why their performance has fallen below standard, and corrective action can be taken if necessary. Those who perform above the standard can be encouraged and rewarded.

Standard costing is therefore part of management's control cycle, as shown in Figure 9.1.

Setting the standards

The setting of the standards may be based on past experience of costs, but can you be sure that those costs were incurred under efficient operating conditions? Where operating procedures have changed, standards need to be revised and past costs are no longer relevant. Care therefore needs to be taken to ensure that standards reflect current operating conditions at a realistic level of efficiency.

Alternatively, the standards may be derived from detailed analysis of current operations, for example through an engineering study. This involves experts studying every aspect of a process, detailing the amount of material, labour and other services required to perform the process and costing out these items of input. Again care needs to be taken to ensure that the standards reflect realistic conditions rather than an idealistic environment. For example, allowance should be made for unavoidable machine breakdowns and maintenance.

A balance has to be drawn between setting standards that are too easily achieved and those which are unattainable. If the standards are too 'loose' then there will be no incentive for operatives to work at optimum efficiency. Favourable variances will be produced and management may be misled into thinking that all is well.

Impossibly 'tight' standards will always produce unfavourable variances which, after a while, will become accepted as normal. Management will disregard the information or at least not feel inclined to investigate the reasons for any occurrence. Operatives will not be motivated to achieve the standards.

Flexing the budget

As discussed in the previous chapter, the budget will have been set to reflect management's desired course of action. It will have been determined by management's assessment of the likely level of activity for the given period. The use of standard costing assists in the budgetary process since the company's cost structure will have been subjected to detailed examination. A company operating a standard costing system will invariably construct its budgeted profit and loss accounts using standard costs.

Actual sales and output will rarely match management's expectations or targets exactly. While comparison of actual performance versus budget can provide useful information, it is less relevant for controlling costs which vary with the level of activity.

For example, if the sales budget for the coming month is set at 50,000 units but subsequent sales amount to only 40,000 units it would be fairly meaningless to compare budgeted variable costs for 50,000 units with actual variable costs incurred in producing and selling 40,000 units. The favourable variances which are almost inevitable are not a measure of management's efficiency but have arisen simply because less has been produced and sold.

So the budget has to be *flexed* to reflect the level of actual sales, thus allowing like to be compared with like. Flexing was covered in detail in Chapter 8. The resulting income statement may be called a 'flexed budget profit and loss account' or a 'standard profit and loss account'.

Standard versus actual

Once the budget has been flexed, the comparison of standard and actual can begin. We shall consider the possible causes of the variances which arise from such a comparison and management's possible reactions to them later in this chapter. First let us review the calculation of these variances.

For a given cost item the variance between standard and actual may be expressed as follows:

$$SC - AC = V$$

where SC is standard costs, AC actual costs, and V the variance. Since costs are generally made up of two elements, quantity (of the input) and price (of the input), the total costs (both standard and actual) are calculated by multiplying the number of units of input (Q) by the price per unit of input (P). So the calculation of the variance for any one type of cost can be expanded as follows:

$$(SQ \times SP) - (AQ \times AP) = V$$

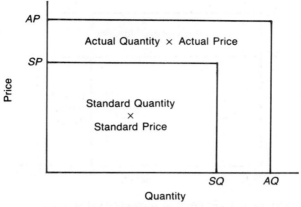

Figure 9.2 Standard versus actual

where again *S* is used to denote 'standard' and *A* 'actual'. The relationships between standard quantity and price and actual quantity and price are shown diagrammatically in Figure 9.2.

The smaller rectangle represents the standard cost of an expense item: the number of units of input that should be used multiplied by the cost per unit of input. The actual cost (the number of units actually used multiplied by the actual price) appears as the larger rectangle.

In the case illustrated both actual quantity and actual price exceed the standard amounts, but this need not always be the case. The point *AQ* on the horizontal axis may be to the left of *SQ*, representing a below-standard use of input. Similarly, the point *AP* on the vertical axis might occur below the point *SP*.

Principal variances for direct costs

In traditional manufacturing concerns the principal cost items relate to the major inputs into the manufacturing process, materials and labour.

Actual material and labour costs may vary from the standards set for two main reasons: either the actual quantity of input varied from standard, or the cost per unit of input varied from the standard cost per unit of input (for example, the actual wage rate paid per labour hour exceeded the standard rate).

The causes of the overall variance can be separated by expanding the term (V) for the variance itself:

$$V = ((SQ \times SP) - (AQ \times SP)) + ((SP \times AQ) - (AP \times AQ))$$

The first element of this equation,

$$(SQ \times SP) - (AQ \times SP)$$

measures the quantity-related part of the variance. How much should we have used compared with how much we actually used, measured in standard prices? Note that

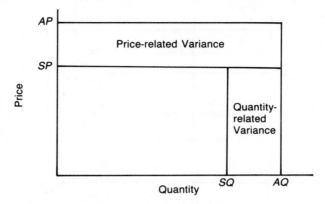

Figure 9.3 Price- and quantity-related variances

the common factor in the two expressions is the standard price per unit (*SP*). In the case of materials, this variance is called the *material usage variance*. In the case of labour, it is called the *labour efficiency variance*, since it tells us the cost (or saving), expressed at the standard rate of pay, of working more (or less) hours than should have been worked for a given quantity of output. It reflects the efficiency of the labour force in producing the output. Clearly if it took more hours than should have been taken, the labour force has not been as efficient as expected.

The second element of the total variance relates to the price per unit of input:

$$(SP \times AQ) - (AP \times AQ)$$

How much should the quantity used have cost compared with its actual cost? Note that the common factor in these expressions is the actual quantity (*AQ*). In the case of materials, this variance is known as the *materials price variance*. For labour, it is the *labour rate variance*. But what does it tell us? In the case of labour, the answer is: given the number of hours actually worked, the labour rate variance tells us how much of the overall variance for labour costs was due to a difference between the standard and actual rates of pay. Or, to put it another way, it tells us the difference between the anticipated cost and the actual cost of the number of hours actually worked.

The dissection of the total variance into its component parts is represented diagrammatically in Figure 9.3. The standard cost for the relevant output is represented by the rectangle bounded by the lines signifying a price of *SP* and quantity *SQ*. The actual cost is represented by the larger rectangle bounded by price *AP* and quantity *AQ*. The quantity-related variance is that rectangle bounded by price *SP* and quantities *SQ* and *AQ*. The price-related variance is the topmost rectangle, bounded by prices *SP* and *AP* and by quantity *AQ*.

The spreadsheet model

Conventional textbooks are written for solutions to be prepared manually, but to use the spreadsheet to good effect it is often necessary to adopt a different logic.

Many textbooks use the formula-based approach for the calculations of variances and it would seem natural to transform these into spreadsheet formulae. However, we prefer an alternative approach which aids presentation and, we hope, understanding. The preferred approach is based on a columnar form of presentation with standard costs ($SQ \times SP$) appearing alongside actual costs ($AQ \times AP$). A third column represents the standard cost of the actual quantity used ($AQ \times SP$). In this way the three expressions used in the original variance equation

$$((SQ \times SP) - (AQ \times SP)) + ((SP \times AQ) - (AP \times AQ))$$

are dealt with (note that the second and third expressions of this formula are identical). This results in the calculation of variances simply by subtracting one column from another.

Those preferring the formula-based approach, which uses embedded formulae in specific cells, should refer to the Appendix to this chapter (see page 154).

Example 9.1

Bennipool Ltd operates a standard costing system to control its main items of cost, raw materials and labour. It produces a product from two materials, A and B, in a given ratio which cannot be altered. Its overheads are insignificant. The budgeted level of activity is 12,000 units per period.

Each unit of the product should require 10 kg of material A and 5 kg of material B costing £6.00 and £7.85 per kilo, respectively. It should take 25 hours to produce one unit of the product. The standard rate of pay is £8.50 per hour.

For the period under review, the following data have been collected:

Units produced and sold:	10,000
Quantity of material A used:	103,000 kg costing £580,000
Quantity of material B used:	48,000 kg costing £380,000
Labour hours worked:	245,000, costing in total £2.1 million

Note that only the total costs are given for both materials and labour. This is often the approach used in examinations and may also reflect practice where aggregate figures are usually more readily available than individual unit costs.

The spreadsheet solution

Using the columnar approach outlined above, a spreadsheet model can be constructed to make the standard versus actual comparisons and to calculate the principal variances. A general description of the model is given in the control section (Spreadsheet Solution 9.1).

We now proceed to the input section (Spreadsheet Solution 9.2). Here we enter

Spreadsheet solution 9.1 Control section

	A	B
1	Spreadsheet Solution 9-1: Control Section	
2		
3	Example 9.1 - Bennipool Ltd.	
4		
5	Standard Costing and Variance Analysis	
6		
7	This model calculates standard costs of given levels of	
8	production and variances from actual costs.	
9		
10		
11		
12		
13	Location Table	Range Name
14	--	-------------------------
15	Input Section	INPUT
16	Output Section	OUTPUT
17		
18		
19	For Input Section Press F5 and type Input	

Spreadsheet solution 9.2 Input section

	D	E	F
21	Spreadsheet Solution 9-2: Input Section		
22			
23	STANDARD COSTS (per unit of output)		
24		Quantity	Price
25		(units)	£
26			
27	Material A (kg)	10	6.00
28			
29	Material B (kg)	5	7.85
30			
31	Labour (hours)	25	8.50
32			
33	ACTUAL COSTS		
34			
35	Quantities & Costs of Actual Production		
36			
37	Actual Production (units)	10,000	
38			
39		Quantity	Total Cost
40		(units)	£
41			
42	Material A	103,000	580,000
43			
44	Material B	48,000	380,000
45			
46	Labour	245,000	2,100,000
47			
48	Move to Output Section by Pressing F5 and typing Output		

the details of the standard costs, quantities and prices of inputs. Next we enter details of the actual activity level and costs.

Once this is done we can move to the output section (Spreadsheet Solution 9.3). We should arrange the rows representing the various cost items in the same order and with the same spacing as in the input section. This will allow the copy command to be used within the columns of the output section rather than having to enter separate formulae for each cell.

Column 1, Total Standard Cost, reflects the actual level of activity not the budgeted level. For variable costs the budgeted level of activity is not relevant. In this column we enter the formula to calculate the standard cost of materials and labour which should have been incurred for 10,000 units (that is, the number of actual units of output times the quantity of input per unit of output times the price per unit of input). If the cell reference to the actual production units is absolute and the spacing of the input rows and the output rows is identical then the formula for material A can simply be copied for material B and labour.

In column 2 we enter the actual costs using the relevant cell references of the input section. Again the copy command is used for the other cost items.

Column 3 represents the actual quantities used, valued at standard prices. The formula represents the multiplication of the relevant input cell references and is copied for material B and labour.

The total variance for each cost item will be displayed in the fourth column. This is calculated by deducting the second column (total actual cost or $AQ \times AP$) from the first column (total standard cost or $SQ \times SP$).

The remaining two columns break these total variances into the quantity-related and price-related variances, again simply by subtraction of columns. The former is found by deducting column 3 ($AQ \times SP$) from column 1 ($SQ \times SP$).

In Example 9.1 the material A usage variance appears as (18,000). The brackets indicate a negative number which means the variance is unfavourable or adverse; that is, more material has been used than should have been used. The standard quantity of material A for 10,000 units is 100,000 (10,000 units at 10 kg per unit). The actual quantity used was 103,000 kg. The excess 3000 kg being valued at standard price of £6.00 gives the £18,000 unfavourable variance.

The final column produces the price-related variances, calculated by deducting column 2 ($AQ \times AP$) from column 3 ($AQ \times SP$). For material A the £38,000 represents the 'saving' to the company (103,000 kg at £6.00 per kg should have cost a total of £618,000 but in fact cost only £580,000). This saving is referred to as a favourable variance.

All that remains is to produce column totals for the sake of completeness. The formula back-up is presented in Spreadsheet Solution 9.4.

'What if?' questions

Remember to change one variable at a time, note the effects of this change, then return the variable to its original value before moving to make the next change.

Spreadsheet solution 9.3   Output section

	G	H	I	J	K	L	M
							Variances
49	Spreadsheet Solution 9-3: Output Section						
50							
51							
52		Total	Total	Actual	Total	Usage/	Price/
53		Standard	Actual	Input at	Variance	Efficiency	Rate
54		Cost	Cost	Standard		Variance	Variance
55		SQ x SP	AQ x AP	AQ x SP		[SQxSP]-[AQxSP]	[AQxSP]-[AQxAP]
56		[1]	[2]	[3]	[1]-[2]	[1]-[3]	[3]-[2]
57							
58	Material A	600,000	580,000	618,000	20,000	(18,000)	38,000
59							
60	Material B	392,500	380,000	376,800	12,500	15,700	(3,200)
61							
62	Labour	2,125,000	2,100,000	2,082,500	25,000	42,500	(17,500)
63							
64	Total	3,117,500	3,060,000	3,077,300	57,500	40,200	17,300

Spreadsheet solution 9.4 Output section

	G	H	I	J	K	L	M
						Variances	
		Total Standard Cost SQ x SP [1]	Total Actual Cost AQ x AP [2]	Actual Input at Standard AQ x SP [3]	Total Variance [1]-[2]	Usage/ Efficiency Variance [SQxSP]-[AQxSP] [1]-[3]	Price/ Rate Variance [AQxSP]-[AQxAP] [3]-[2]
49	Spreadsheet Solution 9-4: Output Section						
50							
51							
52							
53							
54							
55							
56							
57							
58 Material A		+$E$37*(E27*F27)	+F42	+E42*F27	+H58-I58	+H58-J58	+J58-I58
59							
60 Material B		+$E$37*(E29*F29)	+F44	+E44*F29	+H60-I60	+H60-J60	+J60-I60
61							
62 Labour		+$E$37*(E31*F31)	+F46	+E46*F31	+H62-I62	+H62-J62	+J62-I62
63							
64 Total		@SUM(H58..H62)	@SUM(I58..I62)	@SUM(J58..J62)	+H64-I64	+H64-J64	+J64-I64

(a) What would happen to the material A variances if the actual quantity of material A used were 95,000 kg?

(b) What would happen to the material B variances if the standard quantity of material B were 4 kg per unit of output?

(c) What would happen to the material B variances if the standard price per kilo of material B were £6.75?

(d) What would happen to the total variances if the actual output were 10,500 units?

'What if?' solutions

Note: the effects of each change are examined in isolation and as if none of the other changes have been made.

(a) The total variance remains £20,000 because we have not changed either standard quantity or standard price, and actual total cost remains unchanged at £580,000. But now the usage variance is £30,000 and the price variance is (£10,000). The favourable materials usage variance arises because for 10,000 units of output we should have used 100,000 kg of material A; in fact we only used 95,000 kg. The difference (5000 kg) being valued at standard cost (£6.00 per kilo) gives us £30,000.

   The adverse price variance arises because the only variable we changed in the model was the quantity of material A used, not the total cost of that material. Now £580,000 bought us 95,000 kg of material A; we anticipated a cost of £6.00 per kilo so that such a quantity should have cost £570,000. We paid £10,000 more than we should have.

(b) This change affects the total standard cost ($SP \times SQ$). The total variance for material B is now (£144,500), comprising a usage variance of (£141,300) and a price variance of (£3200). The large adverse usage variance is caused by using 60% more material B than should have been used. The standard quantity for 10,000 units is 30,000 kg, while we actually used 48,000 kg. Valuing the difference at the standard price of £7.85 per kilo gives us (£141,300).

   The price variance remains as before since neither the standard price nor the actual price has changed.

(c) The total variance is now (£42,500), consisting of a usage variance of £13,500 and a price variance of (£56,000). Why has the usage variance changed? Because while the difference between standard and actual quantities remains the same the standard price per kilo has changed. Now the 2000 kg 'saved' are valued at £6.75 per kilo giving the usage variance £13,500.

   The 48,000 kg actually used cost £380,000, whereas under the revised standard this quantity should have cost £324,000.

(d) The total standard costs now reflect the new level of output but the actual costs have not changed. This results in changes to all the total variances. But notice that the price variances remain unchanged. This is not really surprising since none of the elements in the notation for the price-related variance $(AQ \times SP) - (AQ \times AP)$ has altered. This must mean that the changes in the total variances have been brought about by changes in the quantity-related variances.

These quantity-related variances compare what should have been used for a given output with what was actually used. Taking labour as an example, to produce 10,500 units should have taken 262,500 hours; in fact only 245,000 hours were taken. Valuing the difference of 17,500 hours at a standard rate per hour of £8.50 gives the efficiency variance, £148,750.

Other variances

Standards can be set for most types of cost, and variances calculated and analyzed. The following sections deal with the most common forms.

Variable overhead variances

In addition to materials and labour costs, which tend to vary directly with changes in the level of activity, there is a third type of variable cost: variable overheads.

Standards can be set and variances can be calculated for variable overheads in the same way as for materials and labour. There is one slight difference which arises due to the nature of overhead costs: such costs cannot be traced directly to units of production. Hence some form of allocation or overhead recovery is required, either a per-unit amount or an amount based on labour hours, material quantities or percentage of prime cost.

Where the basis of variable overhead allocation is simply a per-unit amount there is only one variance element which can arise. This is the *variable overhead expenditure variance*. This variance represents the difference between the overhead recovered on actual production and the actual overhead cost. An appropriate notation would be as follows:

$$(AQ \times SORR) - AC$$

where AQ is actual quantity, $SORR$ the standard overhead recovery rate, and AC the actual cost.

Where the basis for overhead recovery is materials or more usually direct labour, the overhead variance may also contain a quantity-related element. For example, if the basis of allocation is direct labour hours then above- or below-standard performance on labour hours will produce not only a labour efficiency variance but also a *variable overhead efficiency variance*.

If labour hours is the basis for overhead recovery, the two elements of the overhead variance can be expressed as follows. The expenditure variance is given by

$$(AH \times SORR) - AC$$

and the efficiency variance by

$$(SH \times SORR) - (AH \times SORR)$$

where H represents labour hours, A denoting actual and S standard, as usual.

Fixed overhead variances

Even though fixed overhead expenses do not vary directly with output there is still a need to control these expenses, and usually standards will be set and variances measured as with other expenses. The following gives an introduction to the nature of the problem and a simple solution. It should be noted that there are different views on how the fixed overhead variances may be analyzed; other texts may treat the variances in more depth or in a different way. With fixed overheads, the basic point to bear in mind is that variances may arise because either the original estimate of the basis for overhead recovery was wrong or the original estimate of the total expense was wrong.

Fixed overhead expenditure variance

If the estimate of the amount of fixed overheads is inaccurate then this will mean that the standard overhead recovery rate will either absorb too much or too little overhead, that is to say, application of the standard overhead recovery rate will charge too much or too little to the units actually produced.

The difference between the budgeted and actual fixed overhead is referred to as the *fixed overhead expenditure variance*. This can be expressed as:

$$BOE - AOE$$

where the first term represents the budgeted and the second term the actual overhead expenditure.

Fixed overhead volume variance

Any difference between the actual level of activity and the estimated or budgeted level will cause a variance in the actual overhead recovered. This variance is referred to as the *fixed overhead volume variance* and is calculated as the difference between the *original* budgeted output at the standard overhead recovery rate and actual output multiplied by the standard overhead recovery rate:

$$(BQ \times SORR) - (AQ \times SORR)$$

where BQ is the budgeted quantity and AQ the actual quantity.

An unfavourable variance represents the amount of overheads under recovered because the actual production level was below the original budgeted level, and a favourable variance would result from above-budgeted level of activity.

The calculations of this variance may become more complicated if the basis of overhead recovery is some measure of input activity such as labour hours. Variances in the basis of the input will cause variances in the overhead recovered.

Sales variances

Until now we have concentrated on differences between standard and actual costs, that is, input to the production process. But there are also likely to be differences in the output prices and quantities.

Sales price variance

It is possible that the selling price per unit will differ from the standard. Perhaps the company has had to reduce its prices to remain competitive. This variance is given by the following formula:

$$(AQ \times AP) - (AQ \times SP)$$

where P represents the price per unit. Note that we have reversed the order of the expressions so that standard is subtracted from actual. This is simply because we are dealing with revenue rather than expenditure, so that an above-standard variance is in the company's favour.

Sales volume variance

The divergence of budgeted and actual sales is a useful indicator for management action. However, of more concern to management is the divergence of budgeted and actual *profit* rather than sales. While a decline in sales volume may help to explain why actual profit is below budget, the absolute difference in budgeted and actual sales revenue has to be put in context: if sales volume is down then costs (to the extent that these are variable) should also be down. The *sales volume variance* is put in context with the other variables by the calculation of (for a company which operates absorption costing) the profit margin lost or gained on below- or above-budget performance:

$$(AQ \times \text{Standard Profit Margin}) - (BQ \times \text{Standard Profit Margin})$$

In the case of a company which bases its costing system on marginal costs, the sales volume variance is found by calculating the *contribution* which has been lost or gained through a change in volume:

$$(AQ \times \text{Standard Contribution per unit}) - (BQ \times \text{Standard Contribution per unit})$$

An overview of variances

Figure 9.4 displays how the calculation of individual variances combines to explain the total cost variance, that is, the difference between the total standard cost of actual

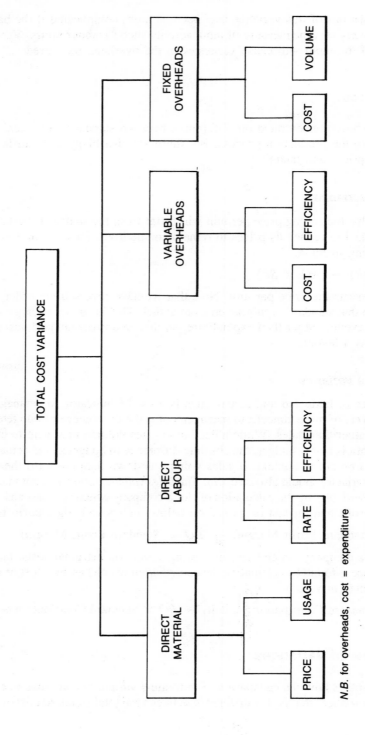

Figure 9.4   An overview of variances

N.B. for overheads, cost = expenditure

production and the total actual cost. We have treated variable and fixed overheads separately for ease of explanation. In practice, a single overhead recovery rate is used to absorb both variable and fixed overheads so that total overhead variance may be split into three components: expenditure, volume and efficiency.

Furthermore, in industries such as processed foods and chemicals, raw materials are introduced into the manufacturing process as a mix of ingredients. This permits the materials usage variance to be further analyzed, identifying differences arising from the mix of ingredients and the yield of that mix.

Presenting variance information to management

Once all the variances have been calculated they can be presented to management in a statement which explains why actual performance has varied from the preset budget. This will enable management to determine whether corrective action is required.

Example 9.2

Jodalease Ltd manufactures a single product with a standard selling price of £95 per unit. Twenty-five thousand were budgeted to be produced and sold. Direct standard costs per unit were:

Raw materials 10 kg @ £2
Labour 3 hours @ £5

Variable overheads had been estimated at £4 per labour hour. Fixed overheads were budgeted at £750,000 and were to be recovered at £30 per unit. Actual data relating to the period were as follows:

22,000 units were sold at £98 each.
250,000 kg of materials were used, costing £480,000.
70,000 labour hours were worked, at a total cost of £360,000.
Variable and fixed overheads amounted to £200,000 and £780,000, respectively.

There were no opening or closing stocks.

The management team requires explanations for the difference between budgeted and actual profit.

The spreadsheet solution

The control section is given as Spreadsheet Solution 9.5. The input section should contain the variables as shown in Spreadsheet Solution 9.6. Output section 1 is constructed as before, except that there is an additional column representing the budgeted income statement (see Spreadsheet Solution 9.7).

Spreadsheet solution 9.5   Control section

	A	B	C	D
1	Spreadsheet Solution 9-5: Control Section			
2				
3	Example 9.2 - Jodalease Ltd.			
4				
5	This model calculates standard costing variances			
6	including overhead variances.			
7				
8				
9				
10				
11				
12				
13				
14				
15				
16	Location Table	Range Name		
17	---	----------------		
18	Input	INPUT		
19	Output Section 1	OUTPUT1		
20	Output Section 2	OUTPUT2		

Variances for the variable costs, including variable overheads, are calculated as before by subtracting the relevant columns. The sales price variance is calculated by subtracting actual volume at standard price from the actual volume at actual price.

The sales volume variance and fixed overheads variances, however, cannot be calculated in this fashion since they require reference to the budgeted volume. The formula for the sales volume variance is $(G26 - F26) * (F28 - H47)$. This applies a simplified version of the formula given in the text: $(AQ - BQ) \times$ standard profit margin. The total sales variance is then the sum of the sales price variance and the sales volume variance. Note that the total variance is net budget actual.

The fixed overhead volume variance is the difference between the overhead recovered on actual output and the budgeted overhead. It represents the fixed overhead unrecovered on the 3000 unit fall in sales. The fixed overhead expenditure variance is the difference between the budgeted expenditure and the actual, $+K75 - L75$. The formula back-up for output section 1 is given as Spreadsheet Solution 9.8.

The net profit row is the sum of the columns. This shows the difference between the budgeted net profit of £450,000 and the actual net profit of £336,000, but the presentation of the variances which explain the difference may not be clear. We therefore need to arrange these variances into a statement for management.

Spreadsheet Solution 9.9 shows output section 2 in which the variances calculated in output section 1 are transferred and presented in a way which reconciles budgeted and actual net profit. Note that the variances caused by the actual output varying from the original budgeted output (the *volume* variances) are presented apart from the other

Spreadsheet solution 9.6   Input section

	E	F	G	H
21	Spreadsheet Solution 9-6: Input Section			
22				
23				
24		Budget	Actual	
25				
26	Production (units)	25,000	22,000	
27				
28	Selling Price per unit	95	98	
29				
30	Fixed Overheads	750,000		
31				
32	Standard Cost Per Unit			
33				
34		Quantity	Price	Total
35			£	£
36	Variable Costs:			
37				
38	Raw Materials	10	2.00	20.00
39				
40	Labour	3	5.00	15.00
41				
42	Variable Overheads - per		4.00	12.00
43	Labour hour			
44				
45	Fixed Overheads			30.00
46				---------------
47	Total per unit			77.00
48				
49	Actual Data:			
50		Quantity	Total Cost	
51		(units)	£	
52				
53	Material	250,000	480,000	
54				
55	Labour	70,000	360,000	
56				
57	Variable Overheads		200,000	
58				
59	Fixed Overheads		780,000	

variances. This isolates the variances which may be beyond management control: the unfavourable volume variances may have been caused by competitive pressures so that the company was not able to achieve budgeted sales. The remaining variances are more likely to be controllable. The formula back-up for this output section is presented in Spreadsheet Solution 9.10.

Spreadsheet solution 9.7   Output section 1

	I	J Budget	K Flexed Budget	L Actual	M Actual at Std	N Total Variance	O Quantity Variance	P Price Variance	Q Volume-Related
60	Spreadsheet Solution 9-7: Output Section 1								
61									
62		Budget	Flexed Budget	Actual	Actual at Std	Total Variance	Quantity Variance	Price Variance	Volume-Related
63									
64									
65	Sales	2,375,000	2,090,000	2,156,000	2,090,000	12,000		66,000	(54,000)
66	Less:								
67									
68									
69	Materials	500,000	440,000	480,000	500,000	(40,000)	(60,000)	20,000	
70									
71	Labour	375,000	330,000	360,000	350,000	(30,000)	(20,000)	(10,000)	
72									
73	Variable Overheads	300,000	264,000	200,000	280,000	64,000	(16,000)	80,000	
74									
75	Fixed Costs	750,000	660,000	780,000	660,000	(120,000)		(30,000)	(90,000)
76									
77	Under/over Recovery		90,000						
78									
79	Net Profit	450,000	306,000	336,000		(114,000)	(96,000)	126,000	(144,000)

Spreadsheet solution 9.8   Output section 1

	I	J Budget	K Flexed Budget	L Actual	M Actual at Std	N Total Variance	O Quantity Variance	P Price Variance	Q Volume-Related
60	Spreadsheet Solution 9-8: Output Section 1								
61									
62		Budget	Flexed Budget	Actual	Actual at Std	Total Variance	Quantity Variance	Price Variance	Volume-Related
63									
64									
65	Sales	+F26*F28	+G26*G28		+G26*F28	+Q65+P65		+L65-M65	(G26-F26)*(F28+H47)
66	Less:								
67									
68									
69	Materials	+F$26*F38*G38	+G$26*F38*G38	+G53	+F53*G38	+K69-L69	+K69-M69	+M69-L69	
70									
71	Labour	+F$26*F40*G40	+G$26*F40*G40	+G55	+F55*G40	+K71-L71	+K71-M71	+M71-L71	
72									
73	Variable Overheads	+F$26*F40*G42	+G$26*F40*G42	+G57	+F55*G42	+K73-L73	+K73-M73	+M73-L73	
74									
75	Fixed Costs	+F30	+G$26*H45	+G59	+G26*H45	+K75-L75		+J75-L75	+K75-J75
76									
77	Under/over Recovery		+J75-K75						
78									
79	Net Profit	+J65-@SUM(J69..J75)	+K65-@SUM(K69..K75)	+L65-@SUM(L69..L75)		+N65+@SUM(N69..N75)	+O65+@SUM(O69..O75)	+P65+@SUM(P69..P75)	+Q65+@SUM(Q69..Q75)

Spreadsheet solution 9.9   Output section 2

	R	S	T	U
80	Spreadsheet Solution 9-9: Output Section 2			
81				
82	Reconciliation of Budgeted and Actual Net Profit			
83			£	
84	Budgeted Profit		450,000	
85	Less Variances:			
86				
87				
88	Volume-related			
89				
90	Sales Volume	(54,000)		
91				
92	Volume	(90,000)		
93		------	(144,000)	
94	Other			
95				
96	Sales Price	66,000		
97				
98	Materials Use	(60,000)		
99				
100	Materials Price	20,000		
101				
102	Labour Efficiency	(20,000)		
103				
104	Labour Rate	(10,000)		
105				
106	Variable Overheads:			
107	Efficiency	(16,000)		
108	Expenditure	80,000		
109				
110	Fixed Overheads:			
111				
112	Expenditure Variance	(30,000)		
113		------	30,000	
114			------	
115	Actual Net Profit		336,000	
116			=====	

Spreadsheet solution 9.10   Output section 2

	R	S	T	U
80	Spreadsheet Solution 9-10: Output Section 2			
81				
82	Reconciliation of Budgeted and Actual Net Profit			
83			£	
84	Budgeted Profit		+J79	
85	Less Variances:			
86				
87				
88	Volume-related			
89				
90	Sales Volume	+Q65		
91				
92	Volume	+Q75		
93		------	@SUM(S90..S92)	
94	Other			
95				
96	Sales Price	+P65		
97				
98	Materials Use	+O69		
99				
100	Materials Price	+P69		
101				
102	Labour Efficiency	+O71		
103				
104	Labour Rate	+P71		
105				
106	Variable Overheads:			
107	Efficiency	+O73		
108	Expenditure	+P73		
109				
110	Fixed Overheads:			
111				
112	Expenditure Variance	+P75		
113		------	@SUM(S96..S112)	
114			------	
115	Actual Net Profit		@SUM(T84..T113)	
116			=========	

Investigation of variances

The purpose of standard costing is to direct management's attention to areas of activity where actual performance may be off target. Those managers responsible for particular areas of the business must be held accountable for the financial consequences of their actions. Corrective action may be required if the business is to be kept on track.

Management must assess the significance of any variances and decide if these warrant the time and cost of investigation and corrective action.

Investigation is required since although variance analysis can locate problem areas, it does not explain why problems have arisen. For example, an adverse material usage variance may have arisen for a number of reasons; if the use of poor-quality material results in more wastage, the purchasing manager may be at fault rather than the production manager. Whereas if the use of poorly trained operatives has caused excessive use of materials, then this suggests poor control by production management.

Favourable price variances arising because cheaper material was purchased, indicate that responsibility lies with the purchasing manager. Only investigation will determine whether savings in costs reflect astute purchasing or whether quality has been sacrificed for better prices.

Where unexpected price rises or on-costs, such as the supplier's handling and transportation charges, occur the appropriate corrective action required of management is the adjustment of the standards themselves. Standards must be kept up-to-date to reflect current operating conditions and costs, otherwise variances will inevitably occur. If standards are allowed to become out of date, confidence in the information provided by variance analysis will be lost, along with any motivation to achieve the standards set. Particular efforts are required during periods of rapid inflation.

Limitations of variance analysis

Although it has the advantage of being able to isolate and measure the effects of actual performance deviating from the expected targets, the technique of standard costing is not without its drawbacks.

Heterogeneous products/services

The application of standard costing is most suited to industries which produce a large number of identical or similar products/services. Industries or organizations producing customized or tailor-made products/services may find the process of predetermining their costs prohibitively expensive.

But just because the product or service produced is different for each customer it does not follow that standard costing techniques cannot be applied. For example, an office cleaning company with a number of clients, both large and small, may nevertheless be able to calculate some form of standard cost for labour and cleaning materials based on the square-footage of the client's office. In this way control can be exercised over the economy and efficiency of individual operatives or teams of operatives.

Joint variances

Where both a quantity- and a price-related variance arise for a given cost item a joint variance will occur. The approach we have adopted would treat the difference in price over the whole of the units used as a price-related variance for which the purchasing manager or personnel manager would be held responsible. But, taking the case of labour costs, is it the fault of the production manager for using too many labour hours or the personnel manager for exceeding the standard rate per hour? Since it may not be possible to assign responsibility to one individual it has been suggested that a 'pure' price variance be calculated:

$$(SQ \times SP) - (SQ \times AP)$$

This is represented diagrammatically in Figure 9.5.

The joint variance represents the additional cost of the additional units or hours used. It can be quantified by the calculation $(SQ - AQ) \times (SP - AP)$. There remains the difficulty of what to do about this joint variance. Should it be apportioned equally or ignored? Unfortunately there is no agreed answer to this.

Conclusion

In this chapter we have shown how management can control different areas of the business by setting standards of performance, measuring actual outcomes against these standards and analyzing the variances. Variance analysis identifies areas which may need management attention, in the form of either corrective action or praise and reward.

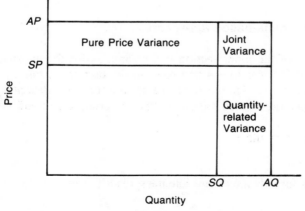

Figure 9.5 'Pure' price and joint variances

The precise causes of variances can only be determined by investigation of the circumstances, but without the information in the first place management would not know where to begin to look.

The study of standard costing can often be a tiresome experience for students who struggle to memorize set formulae without fully understanding what is being measured. The construction of spreadsheet models requires first an understanding of the relationships between quantity and price of inputs and the final outputs of a productive process. Once constructed, the model can perform many more calculations far more accurately and more quickly than could be achieved manually.

Appendix: An alternative spreadsheet approach

It should be noted that variance analysis formulae are commonly found in conventional texts. Such formulae can be used instead of the columnar approach preferred in the chapter.

The quantity-related part of this equation,

$$(SQ \times SP) - (AQ \times SP)$$

can be expressed more simply as

$$(SQ - AQ) \times SP$$

The second element of the total variance relating to the price per unit of input,

$$(SP \times AQ) - (AP \times AQ)$$

can be expressed more simply as

$$(SP - AP) \times AQ$$

These abbreviated formulae can be used in the output section of the spreadsheet, and in some circumstances this may be a more convenient approach.

Example 9.1 Formula-based approach

The construction of the input section is the same as for the approach described in the text. The labels for columns and rows in the output section are also the same. But within the output section we need to enter the formulae described above. Let us start with the quantity-related variances, the materials usage and labour efficiency variances.

The relevant formula is:

$$(SQ - AQ) \times SP$$

In our model this formula transforms into the spreadsheet formula for the usage variance for material A:

$$\langle ((E27 * E37) - E42) \times F27 \rangle$$

The standard quantity of material A which should have been used has to be found by multiplying the standard number of kilos of material A per unit of output by the number of units of actual output, $\langle (E27 * E37) \rangle$. The number of kilos actually used is given in the input section, cell reference E42. The difference between standard and actual quantities of material A must be valued at standard price per kilo, cell F27.

For the price/rate variances, the formula given above is:

$$(SP - AP) \times AQ$$

For material A, the formula to be entered in our model is:

$$\langle (F27 - (F42/E42)) * E42 \rangle$$

The only difficulty here is that no actual price per kilo of material is available, so this has to be calculated by dividing the actual total cost of material A used by the actual quantity of material A used, (F42/E42). This is deducted from the standard price per kilo (F27) and the result applied to the actual quantity used.

A word of warning

As with any formulae, the danger for students is the temptation to learn them by rote rather than by concentrating on gaining an understanding of their significance and what they are attempting to measure or represent. Of course, such temptation should be avoided at all costs. There is a very real risk that one's memory may not be infallible and in the heat of the examination room any combination of the formulae, save the correct one, may be recalled.

Exercises

Question 9.1

The standard cost of timber for a particular piece of furniture is £6.00, comprising 4 metres at £1.50 per metre. The standard time allowed an operator to construct the piece of furniture is 20 minutes. The standard rate of pay is £7.50 per hour. In the period under review, 1350 units of furniture were made. The actual costs for this period were:

Timber: £8480 for 5300 metres
Labour: £3503 for 452 hours worked.

(a) Calculate the following:

    (i)   material cost variance
   (ii)   material usage variance
  (iii)   material price variance
  (iv)   labour cost variance
   (v)   labour efficiency variance
  (vi)   labour rate variance.

(b) Suggest possible causes of these variances.

(c) Calculate the effect on the first three variances in (a) if 6625 metres were bought for £8480.

No answer provided

Question 9.2

(a) Chanamy Ltd manufacture a single product, Z. From the following data, calculate the material and labour variances:

Standard selling price of one unit of Z	£5.99
Standard cost of product Z	
Material cost	£0.60 per kg
Material required for one unit of Z	1.5 kg
Wage rate per hour	£8.75
Time required for one unit of Z	40 minutes

The following were recorded for last month:

No. of units produced and sold	7020
Sales income	£42,000
Materials used	10,500 kg @ £0.57 per kg
Wages paid	4500 hours @ £8.95

(b) Produce a statement showing the variances calculated in (a) above and a reconciliation of the budgeted and actual contribution from sales. Budgeted sales for last month were 7300 units.

No answer provided

Question 9.3

(a) Explain what is meant by the 'control cycle'.

(b) 'The setting of standard costs should be based on past experience of actual costs'. Discuss.

(c) Why is it useful to analyze total variances into their constituent parts?

(d) 'If a standard costing system is truly to aid management control then the standards should reflect ideal conditions'. Discuss.

No answer provided

Question 9.4

The following standard costs apply in a business that manufactures a single product.

Standard weight to produce one unit	12 kg
Standard cost per kilo	£9
Standard hours to produce one unit	10
Standard rate per hour	£4

Actual production and costs for one accounting period.

Material used	3770 kg
Materials cost	£35,815
Hours worked	2755
Wages paid	£11,571

The actual output was 290 units.

(a) Calculate relevant material and labour cost variances, and present these in a format suitable for presentation to the management of the company.

(b) Explain how standard costs for material and labour might be compiled.

Answer on page 280 *(AAT)*

Question 9.5

You have been asked to examine the performance of a subsidiary company for May 19X1. The subsidiary supplies kitchen units to the building industry. The standard cost of one unit for May was as follows:

	£
Direct materials: 5 kg £4.00	20
Direct labour: 4 hours @ £6.00	24
Overheads: recovered at £4.00 per labour hour	16
	60

The standard selling price of one unit was £100 and budgeted sales were 1200 units. All overheads are fixed in nature.

The actual results were as follows:

1300 units were made and sold for a total of £130,000.
Direct material used was 6600 kg at a total cost of £25,080.
Direct labour was 5330 hours at a cost of £32,513.
Actual fixed overheads were £22,000.

(a) Calculate the following:

   (i) material price variance
  (ii) material usage variance

    (iii)   labur rate variance
    (iv)   labour efficiency variance
    (v)   fixed overhead expenditure variance
    (vi)   fixed overhead capacity variance
    (vii)   fixed overhead efficiency variance.

(b) Prepare a variance report for management for May 19X1 reconciling the standard profit expected at actual production level with actual profit, clearly showing the total variance for each element of cost (though sub-variances are not required).

(c) Using your results from (a) and (b), comment upon the performance of the subsidiary company for May 1991.

Answer on page 282   *(AAT)*

Question 9.6

Stanco plc uses a standard costing system, and for the single product that the firm produces the following standard costs apply:

	£
Direct materials: 5 kilos at £2 per kilo	10
Direct wages: 4 hours at £3 per hour	12
Variable overhead: 4 hours at £1 per hour	4
Fixed overhead: 4 hours at £2 per hour	8
Total standard cost	34
Selling price	40

In October production and sales are budgeted at 5000 units and actual data for the month are as follows:

    Production and sales 5400 units
    Actual selling price per unit £42
    Actual materials consumed 30,000 kilos costing £57,000
    Actual labour hours 23,300, wages cost £72,500
    Actual variable overhead cost £24,800
    Actual fixed overhead cost £38,000

(a) Prepare a statement reconciling the budget profit with the actual profit, detailing all variances.

(b) Prepare a report on the statement you have prepared detailing the expected management action that might be necessary to attempt to deal with variances.

No answer provided   *(AAT)*

10 | *Profit reporting: the impact of stock valuation*

AIMS OF CHAPTER

- to show the different methods of identifying which items remain in stock;
- to calculate the cost of stocks using different methods;
- to show the impact on profit measurement of marginal and absorption costing;
- to demonstrate the construction of spreadsheet models to perform stock valuations.

SPREADSHEET SKILLS ACQUIRED

- simple and nested @IF statements.

Introduction

Stock valuation is a critical area in the preparation of financial reports both for external and management purposes. It is critical because the calculation of the amount assigned to the items which remain in stock has a direct impact on profit measurement. This is the result of the application of the accounting concept known as *matching* or *accruals*.

Under this concept the profit of an accounting period is measured by deducting from the sales revenue generated by the units sold, the costs which have been incurred in producing and selling those units. The costs relating to the units which remain unsold should not be treated as expenses for this period but should be carried forward to a future period to be recognized as expenses as and when the units are eventually sold. This procedure ensures that profit is a *fair* measure of performance.

Types of stock

Generally in a typical manufacturing company there are three main categories of stock. The *raw materials* stock consists of the basic inputs to the production process which have yet to reach the production line itself. For example, the raw materials stock of a pie manufacturer would include the flour, uncooked meat, vegetables and any other ingredients required for the making of the products.

Items which are partially complete are known as *work-in-progress*. In our example of the pie manufacturer this might include the pastry which has been made from the flour, meat which has been cooked but not put into the pies, and pies which have been filled but not yet cooked.

The items which have completed the production process are *finished goods*. These items are in a condition for sale. Our pie manufacturer's finished goods stock would include all the pies which have been baked and packaged and now simply await dispatch to a customer.

The reason for dividing stock items into these different categories is that in practice responsibility for the different areas of the production process belongs to different individuals. Thus the stock of raw materials may be under the supervision of the stores manager, the production manager would be responsible for controlling the amount of material passing through the production process, and responsibility for levels of finished goods stock rests with the warehouse or dispatch manager.

Of course, the whole process must be coordinated. Orders for raw materials must reflect planned production and sales levels after allowing for delivery time to the factory, the processing time and time taken for delivery to the customer. Without planning and coordination:

- raw materials stock may become excessive leading to spoilage in the case of perishable materials;

- the level of raw materials may fall below what is needed to sustain production causing temporary shut-downs of the production line;

- work-in-progress levels may lead to under- or overstocking of finished goods;

- high stocks of finished goods increase the risk of spoilage;

- low stocks of finished goods may lead to unsatisfied customer demand.

Management needs information to monitor and to control all these areas of responsibility. Poor planning and coordination will inevitably lead to unnecessary costs. It is important not to forget that money tied up in stocks is depriving the business of resources which may be urgently needed or more profitably used in other areas. Many companies have gone out of business simply because they ignored the dangers of poor stock control. This is summed up in the often-quoted saying that 'stocks are the graveyard of business'.

Different bases of stock identification

The need to value closing stock may cause a number of problems, the first of which is to identify which items remain in stock at the end of an accounting period. One solution is to conduct a physical inventory count, to identify each item in stock and then trace the particular items back to the original purchase documentation and value the stock on that basis. This method may not be feasible in many businesses where a large number of identical items are bought at various times during the year.

Example 10.1

A company specializes in buying and selling sets of Christmas tree lights. When possible, it tries to take advantage of lower prices earlier in the year and makes the following purchases:

1 June	200 units @ £10	= 2000
1 September	100 units @ £11	= 1100
1 December	150 units @ £12	= 1800
Total	450 units	4900

On 21 December it sells 350 units, leaving 100 units unsold at the close of business on 31 December. Since there may be no way of identifying exactly which items are left at the end of the year, to perform the valuation we need to make an assumption about how the stock has moved.

For example, if the company ensures that the stock on its shelves is rotated whenever a new batch of purchases is received, it would be safe to assume that the items on hand at the end of the year represent the latest purchases, the items in the earlier purchases having been moved to the front of the shelves and having been sold or issued to production first. This is known as the *first-in, first-out* (FIFO) method. Valuing the stock at the latest purchase price would give us a total value of £1200 (100 units @ £12) and a cost of sales of £3700 (total purchases of £4900 less closing stock of £1200).

A company which adopts a different stock rotation method may consider that FIFO is not appropriate for its circumstances. For example, a building materials supplier which buys and sells sand and gravel, materials which are not likely to deteriorate with age, may have a storage area where new deliveries of the sand and gravel are dumped on the top of the pile. Sales to customers are removed from the top of the pile. The stock of sand and gravel at the bottom of the pile effectively represents the very earliest purchases, unless at some point it was reduced to zero, that is, the storage bin emptied, and should be valued at those purchase prices. The sales to customers are taken from the top of the pile and should be valued at the latest purchase prices. This is the *last-in, first-out* (LIFO) method of stock valuation.

Applying the LIFO method to our example would have the effect of valuing the closing stock of 100 units at the earliest price of £10 per unit, £1000 in total. The cost of the units sold would be taken as the most recent purchases and, where (as in our case) prices are rising, would result in a higher charge against sales revenue and lower profits.

It has been argued that charging the cost of goods sold with the more recent purchase prices is one way of allowing for the effects of inflation since sales revenue at current prices is matched with cost of sales based (very nearly) on current prices. The drawback to this argument is that, under LIFO, the closing stock which appears in the balance sheet is stated at the earliest prices. Thus while LIFO may give a more realistic measure of a company's profitability, it provides a less realistic view of the company's net worth as shown by its balance sheet.

An alternative valuation basis may be appropriate where there is no clear pattern of stock movement, that is, the stock unsold at the end of the year may be a mixture of the different purchases made during the year. To enable the valuation basis to follow the physical movement of the stock some form of averaging is required. However, it would not be appropriate simply to take an average of the different purchase prices because the batches of purchases have varied in the quantity of units in each batch. We therefore take a *weighted average* to reflect the different sizes of the batches of purchases. This is fairly straightforward, being calculated by dividing total purchase costs, £4900, by 450 units giving a weighted average cost per unit of £10.89. This is the cost which will be applied to both the closing stock to give a valuation of £1089 and the cost of units sold, 350 units @ £10.89 = £3811.

The spreadsheet solution

The spreadsheet model we construct will value stock on each of the three bases described above, FIFO, LIFO and weighted average. This will be done in separate output sections. The format of each will be the same.

With the control section set up (Spreadsheet Solution 10.1), we can move to the input section (Spreadsheet Solution 10.2), where we key in the details of the purchases

Spreadsheet solution 10.1   Control section

	A	B
1	Spreadsheet Solution 10-1: Control Section	
2		
3	Example 10.1	
4		
5	This model calculates stock values using different	
6	bases for identifying which items remain in stock;	
7	FIFO, LIFO and weighted average.	
8		
9		
10		
11		
12		
13	Location Table	Range Name
14	---	----------------------
15	Input Section	Input
16	Output Section 1 - FIFO	FIFO
17	Output Section 2 - LIFO	LIFO
18	Output Section 3 - Wtd. Average	WTDAV

Spreadsheet solution 10.2 Input section

	C	D	E	F
	C	D	E	F
20	Spreadsheet Solution 10-2: Input Section			
21				
22	Stock Receipts	Units	Value	Total Cost
23	------------------------			
24	June 1	200	10	2000
25	September 1	100	11	1100
26	December 1	150	12	1800
27			---------------	-------------------
28		450		4900
29	Stock Issues			
30	------------------------			
31	December 21	350		

and issues of the stock. The quantities, unit prices and total cost for each batch of purchases are included.

Output section 1 (Spreadsheet Solution 10.3), starts at cell G33. Labels for the number of 'Units in Closing Stock', the 'Valuation of the Closing Stock' and the 'Cost of Sales' are entered in column G. The units in closing stock are calculated by the formula, $\langle +\$D\$28 - \$D\$31 \rangle$. Note that if we use absolute cell references, we can copy this formula to the other output sections which we will construct later.

Under the FIFO method the items in stock are assumed to belong to the latest batches of purchases. If the number of units in stock exceeds the number of units in the latest batch of purchases, we assume that all of this batch remains in stock, with the remaining items of stock coming from previous batches.

To perform this valuation we can make use of the **@IF** function. The formula to be entered in cell H37 is:

$$\langle @IF(H35\langle D26, H35 * E26, @IF(H35 < (D26 + D25), F26 + ((H35 - D26) * E25), F26 + F25 + (H35 - (D26 + D25)) * E24)) \rangle$$

What this apparently complicated formula means is that if the closing stock is less in number than the latest purchase then all units in stock are valued at the latest price; if not then it depends on whether the remaining stock relates to the previous batch or batches of purchases and this is dealt with in the second **@IF** statement.

Spreadsheet solution 10.3 Output section 1

	G	H	I
	G	H	I
33	Spreadsheet Solution 10-3: Output Section 1		
34			
35	Units in Closing Stock	100	
36			
37	Valuation of Closing Stock	1200	
38			
39	Cost of Sales	3700	

Spreadsheet solution 10.4   Output section 2

	I	J	K
41	Spreadsheet Solution 10-4: Output Section 2		
42			
43	Units in Closing Stock	100	
44			
45	Valuation of Closing Stock	1000	
46			
47	Cost of Sales	3900	

Spreadsheet solution 10.5   Output section 3

	K	L	M
49	Spreadsheet Solution 10-5: Output Section 3		
50			
51	Units in Closing Stock	100	
52			
53	Valuation of Closing Stock	1,089	
54			
55	Cost of Sales	3,811	

The cost of sales is simply the total cost of purchases minus the valuation of the closing stock; the formula in cell H39 is $+F28-H37$.

Output section 2 (Spreadsheet Solution 10.4), deals with the LIFO valuation basis and may be set up by copying the range for output 1. The LIFO valuation involves a similar formation of @IF statements except that the direction of valuation starts with the earliest batches of purchases. The formula in cell J45 needs to be edited using the F2 key and should read:

⟨@IF(J43 < D24,J43 ∗ E24,@IF(J43 < (D24+D25),F24+((J43−D24) ∗ E25),
F24+F25+((J43−(D24+D25)) ∗ E26)))⟩

The output section 3 (Spreadsheet Solution 10.5), deals with the weighted average cost of stock. The formula for this is much simpler than with FIFO and LIFO. The weighted average cost per unit is found by dividing the total cost of purchases by the total number of units purchased; this is then used to value the number of units in stock. Cell L53 contains the formula:

⟨(F28/D28) ∗ L51⟩

The spreadsheet model we have constructed can be run to calculate stock valuations for any scenario involving up to three stock purchases and one stock issue. This is fairly typical of a number of textbook exercises but is, of course, quite unrealistic. To deal with situations with a large number of purchases and issues the spreadsheet formulae would quickly become unwieldy. In practice, therefore, it is unlikely that spreadsheets would be used to perform this aspect of stock valuation. Instead specific computer programs tend to be written to control and value stock items.

'What if?' questions

1. If 200 units are issued on 21 December, what are the closing stock valuation and cost of sales figures under the three methods?

2. If 150 units are issued on 21 December, what are the closing stock valuation and cost of sales figures under the three methods?

'What if?' solutions

1.

	Closing Stock	Cost of Sales
FIFO	£2,900	£2,000
LIFO	£2,550	£2,350
Weighted Av.	£2,722	£2,178

2.

	Closing Stock	Cost of Sales
FIFO	£3,400	£1,500
LIFO	£3,100	£1,800
Weighted Av.	£3,267	£1,633

The valuation process

An important point to note is that although we have referred throughout this chapter to stock *valuation*, the calculation is based on *costs* not *value*. In the case of profitable products, the eventual sales value of the items of stock will exceed cost. To value stock at selling price before the sale has been made would be to anticipate future profits before they have been earned. While this may hold some attraction for management, it offends the fundamental accounting concept of prudence which dictates that a cautious approach is required in valuing assets and measuring profit. So the basic principle is that stock should be valued at cost.

However, there is a slight twist to this valuation principle where the net realizable value of the stock is less than its cost — net realizable value means the eventual selling price less any additional costs required to bring the stock to the point of sale. In such cases a loss is likely to be made on the sale of the item. In these situations, the basis of stock valuation is net realizable value not cost. Applying this rule has the effect of recognizing the likely eventual loss before it is actually incurred. This, too, is cautious and is consistent with the prudence concept. So the basic stock valuation principle can be revised to *cost or net realizable value, whichever is the lower.*

This principle is applicable to all items of stock and work-in-progress on an individual basis, that is, line by line.

Example 10.2

A company has a number of lines of product in stock. Having counted these items, the management accountant has calculated the costs and estimated the net realizable values (NRVs) of each line of stock item as follows:

Item	Cost £	NRV £
A	1,500	2,900
B	2,500	4,500
C	3,000	2,000
D	4,500	8,500
E	500	1,500
F	8,000	6,000
G	7,500	15,000
H	4,200	7,500
Total	31,700	47,900

It would not be appropriate to value the stock on the basis of the comparison of the total cost with the total NRV because 'profits' on some lines would mask 'losses' on others. Instead, we must take each line of stock and compare cost with NRV. Thus for items A, B, D, E, G and H cost is the basis for valuation and for items C and F NRV will be used since this is lower than cost. In total this will give us a stock valuation of £28,700. The difference between this figure and the total cost of £31,700 is made up of the losses or write-downs on the items C (£1000) and F (£2000).

If the total cost of £31,700 had been used to value stock for income measurement, this would have resulted in profit being overstated by £3000 since it fails to recognize the need to provide for the eventual losses on lines C and F.

The spreadsheet solution

It is an easy exercise to construct a spreadsheet model to perform the comparison of cost and NRV. The control section is shown as Spreadsheet Solution 10.6.

The input section of the model should contain all the details of the lines of stock, their cost and NRV, as shown in Spreadsheet Solution 10.7.

The output section of the model will give us the stock valuation having applied the lower of cost and NRV on a line-by-line basis. To do this, enter a formula in the cell alongside the label for each item, which will take the lower of the two figures relating to each item. This uses a simple @IF statement. For example, for item A the formula in cell G38 is:

@IF(D25<E25,D25,E25)

Spreadsheet solution 10.6 Control section

	A	B
1	Spreadsheet Solution 10-6: Control Section	
2		
3	Example 10.2	
4		
5	This model calculates stock values for a range	
6	of stock items based on the principle of the lower	
7	cost and net realizable value.	
8		
9		
10		
11		
12		
13	Location Table	Range Name
14	--	--------------------
15	Input	INPUT
16	Output - Stock Valuation	OUTPUT

Spreadsheet solution 10.7 Input section

	C	D	E	F	G
21	Spreadsheet Solution 10-7: Input Section				
22					
23	Item	Cost	NRV		
24	---------------	---------------	---------------		
25	A	1,500	2,900		
26	B	2,500	4,500		
27	C	3,000	2,000		
28	D	4,500	8,500		
29	E	500	1,500		
30	F	8,000	6,000		
31	G	7,500	15,000		
32	H	4,200	7,500		

Spreadsheet solution 10.8 Output section

	F	G	H	I	J
34	Spreadsheet Solution 10-8: Output Section				
35					
36	Item	Value			
37	---------------	---------------			
38	A	1,500			
39	B	2,500			
40	C	2,000			
41	D	4,500			
42	E	500			
43	F	6,000			
44	G	7,500			
45	H	4,200			
46		---------------			
47	Total	28,700			
48		=====			

This formula is then copied to the other cells in column G. The output section is presented in Spreadsheet Solution 10.8.

Absorption versus marginal costing methods

Issues surrounding absorption and marginal costing have already been introduced. In this section we examine the impact of these alternative methods of costing on stock valuation.

For internal reporting purposes companies may choose whichever basis of stock valuation they wish. Their choice will be determined after consideration of the company's circumstances, the nature of the stock and the production process and management's need for and use of information. An additional consideration is the cost of obtaining the data on which to base the valuation. For example, many retail companies find it easier to start by valuing their stocks at selling prices and then adjust for the profit margin.

For external reporting purposes companies are required by accounting standards to value their stocks according to the absorption method. This, it is argued, gives a more accurate estimate of the actual cost of the stock. So those companies which have used marginal costing for management reports are required to adjust their stock valuations to a full-cost basis for their published annual accounts.

The choice of methods for internal reporting can have a significant impact on the profits reported in a given period. This is because, by using absorption costing, part of the overheads incurred in a period will be absorbed into the valuation of closing stock. This portion of the overheads is effectively excluded from the calculation of the period's income; it will be carried forward (in the stock valuation) to be charged against income in a future period when the stock is sold. Marginal costing does not involve allocation of overheads, so under this method the stock is valued only at marginal (or variable) cost. Thus absorption costing will produce higher stock valuations.

This will obviously impact on the profit and loss account. When stock levels are rising (closing stock exceeds opening stock), the cost of sales will be lower under absorption costing than under marginal costing. When stock levels fall, marginal costing will produce a lower cost of sales and therefore higher profits.

Example 10.3

Abmar Ltd uses marginal costing for internal reports but period-end adjustments are required to value the closing stock in accordance with accepted external reporting practice. During each of the last three periods, 12,000 units were produced. Sales, at £75.00 per unit, for the three periods were 10,000, 13,500 and 12,500 units, respectively. There were no opening stocks at the start of the first period. Direct costs per unit were:

Table 10.1 *Abmar Ltd: calculation of gross profit*

	Period 1	Period 2	Period 3
Sales	750,000	1,012,500	937,500
Less:			
Materials	180,000	180,000	180,000
Labour	96,000	96,000	96,000
Variable Overheads	72,000	72,000	72,000
Cost of Production	396,000	396,000	396,000
Less Closing Stock	(58,000)	(14,500)	—
Add Opening Stock	—	58,000	14,500
Cost of Sales	338,000	439,500	410,500
Gross Profit	412,000	573,000	527,000

	£
Materials	15.00
Labour	8.00
Variable overheads	6.00

Fixed production costs for each period amounted to £48,000.

Under the marginal costing policy of Abmar Ltd the calculations of the periods' gross profit would be as shown in Table 10.1. The closing stock valuations have been calculated using marginal cost per unit of £29.00. For external reporting purposes this needs to be adjusted to include an element of production overheads, in line with the absorption cost method.

Under the marginal cost method the entire fixed overhead is treated as a cost of the period: none of it is carried forward in the closing stock valuation. The closing stock represents one-sixth (2000/12,000) of the total production and so, under the absorption costing method, should bear the same proportion of the total production costs. The adjustment required for the first period is £8000 to be added to the closing stock valuation (and consequently added to the gross profit). This amount is one-sixth of the total fixed costs of £48,000.

Now if we consider the next period, when again production is 12,000 but sales are 13,500, we can see the impact of a fall in stock levels on the profit measurement under the two methods. The difference between sales and production is made good by the reduction in stock levels — 2000 units in stock at the beginning of the second period compared with 500 units at the end.

The adjustment required for period 2 is £6000. This is caused by the inclusion of overheads in both opening and closing stocks under the absorption costing method. In period 1 £8000 of overheads were excluded from cost of sales but are now brought into account as the opening stock valuation becomes part of the cost of sales in period 2. The closing stock of period 2 carries £2000 of overheads into the next period. The net effect is an additional £6000 expense recognized in period 2 under the absorption costing method.

In effect, the adjustment is an additional £4.00 per unit in opening and closing stocks thus:

	£	£	£
Gross profit	412,000	573,000	527,000
Adjustments:			
to closing stock	8,000	2,000	—
to opening stock	—	(8,000)	(2,000)
Adjusted gross profit	420,000	567,000	525,000

The spreadsheet solution

The spreadsheet solution for Example 10.3 produces gross profit calculations on both absorption cost and marginal cost bases. The control section is given in Spreadsheet Solution 10.9.

Set up the input section as shown in Spreadsheet Solution 10.10, listing stock movements across the three periods and the per-unit data. The closing stock (in units) is calculated for each period by deducting the units sold from the units of opening stock and the units produced.

Spreadsheet solution 10.9   Control section

	A	B	C	D
1	Spreadsheet Solution 10-9: Control Section			
2				
3	Example 10-3			
4				
5	This model calculates cost of sales and stock valuations			
6	based on both marginal and absorption costing methods.			
7				
8	Abmar Ltd sells a product for £75.00 per unit. Variable			
9	costs are:			
10	Materials £15.00			
11	Labour £8.00			
12	Variable Overheads £6.00			
13				
14	Fixed overheads are £48,000 and 12,000 is the normal			
15	level of production.			
16				
17	Location Table		Range Name	
18	--		----------------	
19	Input Section		INPUT	
20	Output Section 1 - Absorption		ABSORB	
21	Output Section 2 - Margin		MARGIN	

Spreadsheet solution 10.10 Input section

	E	F	G	H
21	Spreadsheet Solution 10-10: Input Section			
22				
23		Period 1	Period 2	Period 3
24				
25	Sales (units)	10,000	13,500	12,500
26				
27	Opening Stock (units)	0	2,000	500
28				
29	Production (units)	12,000	12,000	12,000
30				
31	Closing Stock (units)	2,000	500	0
32				
33	Total fixed costs	48,000	48,000	48,000
34				
35	Selling Price per unit .	75.00		
36				
37	Cost per unit:			
38				
39	Materials	15.00		
40				
41	Labour	8.00		
42				
43	Variable Overheads	6.00		
44		----------------		
45	Total variable cost per unit	29.00		
46				
47	Fixed Overheads	4.00		
48		----------------		
49	Total cost per unit	33.00		

Next construct two simple income statements, output sections 1 and 2, showing sales and costs of production by creating formulae referenced to the input section. For details see the output sections and the formulae back-up shown in Spreadsheet Solutions 10.11 to 10.14.

Under the absorption costing method the cost of the closing stock is the full (total) cost per unit multiplied by the number of units in stock. The closing stock valuation under the marginal costing method can be calculated by multiplying the units of the closing stock by the variable cost per unit.

Note that if we add a column for each method to calculate the aggregate figures for the three periods there is no difference in total gross profit between the two methods. This because from the start to the end of the three periods there is no change in stocks (zero opening stock in period 1 and zero closing stock in period 3). The same overall effect would be observed if stock levels remained relatively stable.

Spreadsheet solution 10.11   Output section 1

	I	J	K	L	M
51	Spreadsheet Solution 10-11: Output Section 1				
52					
53	ABSORPTION COSTING	PERIOD 1	PERIOD 2	PERIOD 3	TOTAL
54					
55	Sales	750,000	1,012,500	937,500	2,700,000
56		---------------	-----------------	------------------	------------------
57	Less Cost of Production:				
58					
59	Materials	180,000	180,000	180,000	540,000
60					
61	Labour	96,000	96,000	96,000	288,000
62					
63	Variable Overheads	72,000	72,000	72,000	216,000
64					
65	Fixed Costs	48,000	48,000	48,000	144,000
66		---------------	-----------------	------------------	------------------
67	Cost of Production	396,000	396,000	396,000	1,188,000
68					
69	Closing Stock	(66,000)	(16,500)	0	(82,500)
70					
71	Opening Stock	0	66,000	16,500	82,500
72		---------------	-----------------	------------------	------------------
73	Cost of Sales	330,000	445,500	412,500	1,188,000
74		---------------	-----------------	------------------	------------------
75	Gross Profit	420,000	567,000	525,000	1,512,000
76		---------------	-----------------	------------------	------------------

Spreadsheet solution 10.12   Output section 1

	I	J	K	L	M
51	Spreadsheet Solution 10-12: Output Section 1				
52					
53	ABSORPTION COSTING	PERIOD 1	PERIOD 2	PERIOD 3	TOTAL
54					
55	Sales	+F25*$F35	+G25*$F35	+H25*$F35	@SUM(J55..L55)
56		-------------------------	-------------------------	-------------------------	-------------------------
57	Less Cost of Production:				
58					
59	Materials	+F29*$F39	+G29*$F39	+H29*$F39	@SUM(J59..L59)
60					
61	Labour	+F29*$F41	+G29*$F41	+H29*$F41	@SUM(J61..L61)
62					
63	Variable Overheads	+F29*$F43	+G29*$F43	+H29*$F43	@SUM(J63..L63)
64					
65	Fixed Costs	+F33	+G33	+H33	@SUM(J65..L65)
66		-------------------------	-------------------------	-------------------------	-------------------------
67	Cost of Production	@SUM(J59..J65)	@SUM(K59..K65)	@SUM(L59..L65)	@SUM(J67..L67)
68					
69	Closing Stock	-F31*$F49	-G31*$F49	-H31*$F49	@SUM(J69..L69)
70					
71	Opening Stock	+F27*$F49	-J69	-K69	@SUM(J71..L71)
72		-------------------------	-------------------------	-------------------------	-------------------------
73	Cost of Sales	@SUM(J67..J71)	@SUM(K67..K71)	@SUM(L67..L71)	@SUM(J73..L73)
74		-------------------------	-------------------------	-------------------------	-------------------------
75	Gross Profit	+J55-J73	+K55-K73	+L55-L73	@SUM(J75..L75)
76		-------------------------	-------------------------	-------------------------	-------------------------

Spreadsheet solution 10.13   Output section 2

	N	O	P	Q	R
77	Spreadsheet Solution 10-13: Output Section 2				
78					
79	MARGINAL COSTING	PERIOD 1	PERIOD 2	PERIOD 3	TOTAL
80					
81	Sales	750,000	1,012,500	937,500	2,700,000
82		--------------	--------------	--------------	--------------
83	Less Cost of Production:				
84					
85	Materials	180,000	180,000	180,000	540,000
86					
87	Labour	96,000	96,000	96,000	288,000
88					
89	Variable Overheads	72,000	72,000	72,000	216,000
90					
91	Fixed Costs	48,000	48,000	48,000	144,000
92		--------------	--------------	--------------	--------------
93	Cost of Production	396,000	396,000	396,000	1,188,000
94					
95	Closing Stock	(58,000)	(14,500)	0	(72,500)
96					
97	Opening Stock	0	58,000	14,500	72,500
98		--------------	--------------	--------------	--------------
99	Cost of Sales	338,000	439,500	410,500	1,188,000
100		--------------	--------------	--------------	--------------
101	Gross Profit	412,000	573,000	527,000	1,512,000
102					

Spreadsheet solution 10.14   Output section 2

	N	O	P	Q	R
77	Spreadsheet Solution 10-14: Output Section 2				
78					
79	MARGINAL COSTING	PERIOD 1	PERIOD 2	PERIOD 3	TOTAL
80					
81	Sales	+F25*$F35	+G25*$F35	+H25*$F35	@SUM(O81..Q81)
82		--------------	--------------	--------------	--------------
83	Less Cost of Production:				
84					
85	Materials	+F29*$F39	+G29*$F39	+H29*$F39	@SUM(O85..Q85)
86					
87	Labour	+F29*$F41	+G29*$F41	+H29*$F41	@SUM(O87..Q87)
88					
89	Variable Overheads	+F29*$F43	+G29*$F43	+H29*$F43	@SUM(O89..Q89)
90					
91	Fixed Costs	+F33	+G33	+H33	@SUM(O91..Q91)
92		--------------	--------------	--------------	--------------
93	Cost of Production	@SUM(O85..O91)	@SUM(P85..P91)	@SUM(Q85..Q91)	@SUM(O93..Q93)
94					
95	Closing Stock	-F31*F45	-G31*F45	-H31*G45	@SUM(O95..Q95)
96					
97	Opening Stock	+F27	-O95	-P95	@SUM(O97..Q97)
98		--------------	--------------	--------------	--------------
99	Cost of Sales	@SUM(O93..O97)	@SUM(P93..P97)	@SUM(Q93..Q97)	@SUM(O99..Q99)
100		--------------	--------------	--------------	--------------
101	Gross Profit	+O81-O99	+P81-P99	+Q81-Q99	@SUM(O101..Q101)
102		--------------	--------------	--------------	--------------

'What if?' questions

1. Under the two methods what is the effect on the gross profit of each period if production remains at 12,000 units per period and sales for each period are 11,000 units? Explain the results.

2. Under the two methods what is the effect on the gross profit of each period if there are 3000 units in opening stock in period 1 (the value per unit is the same as for other periods), production remains at 12,000 units per period and sales for period 1 are 12,000 units, period 2 13,000 units and period 3 14,000 units? Explain the results.

'What if?' solutions

1. Under the absorption costing method the gross profit for each period is £462,000 per period and under the marginal costing method it is £458,000 per period. The difference in gross profit of £4000 per period is caused by the gradual increase in stocks over the three periods of 1000 units per period. For this reason, the total gross profits are not the same; the absorption costing method producing the higher total gross profit.

2. The gross profits are as follows:

	Period 1	Period 2	Period 3
Absorption	£504,000	£546,000	£588,000
Marginal	£504,000	£550,000	£596,000

Since there is no change in stocks in period 1 there is no difference between gross profit under the two methods. In period 2 stock levels fall by 1000 units causing an additional £4000 (1000 @ £4) to be charged to cost of sales under the absorption method. In period 3, stocks fall by 2000 units and £8000 more is charged to cost of sales under the absorption method than under the marginal method. For the three periods in total, therefore, gross profit under the absorption method is £12,000 less than under the marginal method. This is the amount of overheads carried in the opening stock of period 1 (3000 @ £4), there being no closing stock at the end of period 3.

Conclusion

Stock valuation is probably one of the most critical issues in management accounting practice since changes in stock values have a direct impact on income measurement.

In this chapter, we have reviewed various aspects of stock valuation. Spreadsheet models can be used to perform valuations provided the set of data is not unduly complex. In practice, however, specialist computer programs may be required to handle the large number of stock movements.

Nevertheless, the models we have constructed should be capable of dealing with many of the exercises typically set at an introductory level and in any event should allow the reader quickly to see the changes to certain variables and thereby to gain a greater understanding of the significance of stock valuation problems.

Part V

Information for decision-making purposes

11 | *Pricing decisions*

AIMS OF CHAPTER _____

- to identify the factors involved in reaching a decision on price;
- to contrast the accountant's and economist's pricing models;
- to determine the optimum selling price;
- to examine cost-based pricing decisions including cost-plus;
- to consider the limitations of cost-plus pricing;
- to introduce the importance of a pricing policy.

SPREADSHEET SKILLS ACQUIRED _____

- data tables with two variables.

Introduction

This chapter concentrates on the total revenue function which, using linearity assumptions, is determined by quantity sold multiplied by price per unit. The problem facing the firm is what price to charge for its product or service. The management accountant, along with other professionals in the organization, has a key role to play in providing information relevant to the company's pricing policy.

The selling price is one component of what is termed the *marketing mix*. Customers will not buy the product if it does not meet their needs, or if they are not aware of its existence or if they cannot obtain it conveniently. So price is one of the four *P*s of the marketing mix: price, product, promotion and place. Neglecting any one of these areas will impact upon the total revenue earned by the firm.

Factors that influence the pricing decision

Some firms, especially smaller businesses, have little choice other than to accept the

PERFECT------IMPERFECT------OLIGOPOLY------MONOPOLY
Market trader   Printing   Pharmaceuticals   Water
Food retail   Cars   Petrol   Electricity

Figure 11.1 The competition continuum

price dictated by similar products in the marketplace. Economists state that these firms are *price takers* and are operating in a state of *perfect competition*. In contrast, the *monopoly* supplier has total control over price and hence profit. In practice these states represent the ends of a continuum, as shown in Figure 11.1.

In between these extremes are firms which operate in a state of *imperfect competition*. A company operating in an industry where barriers to entry are high and only a few large firms exist, is known as an *oligopoly*.

Cost information is important to the pricing decisions of the management of any company, regardless of the state of the particular industry. Even if the firm is a price taker an analysis of costs is still necessary if the firm is to operate profitably. In imperfect and oligopolistic markets, non-price competition may have a significant impact on costs. For example, the goods 'given away' with petrol vouchers are variable costs and the advertising campaign that accompanies the offer will be a fixed cost. Monopolistic companies are always aware of allegations of overpricing; these are best refuted by reference to the costs of manufacturing the product or providing the service.

The economist's pricing model

The accountant's assumption of linearity for the total revenue function is strongly contested by economists who argue that demand is *elastic*. The theory of elasticity of demand hypothesizes that the quantity demanded by the market is dependent upon the price charged. Specifically, it states that the lower the price charged, the higher the quantity demanded. This results in a downward sloping demand curve as shown in Figure 11.2. Demand elasticity, or sensitivity to price changes, is given by the slope of the demand curve. A perfectly inelastic demand curve would be vertical

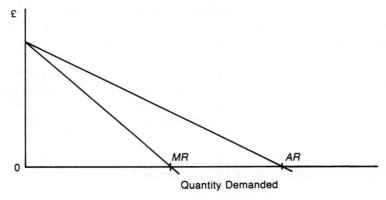

Figure 11.2 The economist's demand curve

(a slope of 0) while a perfectly elastic demand curve would be horizontal ($b = \infty$).

Unlike the total cost function, the demand curve has a negative b-coefficient. Note that the demand curve is *not* the total revenue curve, but the *average revenue (AR)* curve. *AR* is defined as the total revenue divided by quantity. With a downward sloping demand curve, the price charged must fall in order to increase the number of units demanded and hence the *marginal revenue (MR)* (the revenue gained from selling one extra unit) will fall. The relationship is such that *MR* falls twice as fast as *AR*.

Optimal selling price determination

We can use our spreadsheet to model the total revenue (*TR*) and total cost (*TC*) functions and graphically to present the point at which profit is maximized. The profit maximization assumption is often made in economics, but there are many other objectives that the firm can achieve through the pricing decision (see section on pricing policy below).

Economists have refined their analysis and have stated what is sometimes referred to as the *marginalist principle*. This states that profit is maximized at the point where marginal revenue equals marginal cost.

Example 11.1

This is a hypothetical example using the following variables:

$TC = 2500 + 12.5x$

$AR = 40 - 0.05x$

Having described the model in the control section, (Spreadsheet Solution 11.1), these variables are entered into our input range (see Spreadsheet Solution 11.2). Note that to produce a range of quantities in the output section, we have keyed into the input section the start value and incremental size of output levels. This approach allows these figures to be varied as necessary.

We need to construct an output section which shows *TR*, *TC*, Profit, *MR* and *MC* for various combinations of quantity and price (see Spreadsheet Solutions 11.3 and 11.4).

The levels of quantity demanded are calculated by reference to the start value and the incremental size given in the input section. Note the use of the absolute cell reference, $D$18, for the incremental size.

The price column is prepared by incorporating the formula for *AR* for different quantity levels.

We determine profit by deducting *TC* from *TR* for the first quantity level. Note that sales of 250 and 300 units both produce the maximum profit of £1250. To display the result in a more visually appealing way, graph the *TC* and *TR* functions (as in Figure 11.3). Note that the *TC* function is linear whereas the *TR* function is curvilinear.

Spreadsheet solution 11.1 Control section

	A	B
1	Spreadsheet Solution 11-1: Control Section	
2		
3	Example 11.1	
4		
5	This spreadsheet is used to determine the optimal price	
6	for a product using the marginalist principle.	
7		
8		
9		
10	Location Table	Range Name
11	--	----------------------------------
12	Input Section	INPUT
13	Output Section 1	OUTPUT1

Spreadsheet solution 11.2 Input section

	C	D
15	Spreadsheet Solution 11-2: Input Section	
16		
17	Quantity Start Value	100
18	Incremental Size	50
19		
20	Total Cost Intercept	2500
21	Total Cost Slope	12.5
22		
23	Average Revenue Intercept	40
24	Average Revenue Slope	-0.05
25		

Spreadsheet solution 11.3 Output section 1

	E	F	G	H	I	J	K
26	Spreadsheet Solution 11-3: Output Section 1						
27							
28	Quantity	Price	TR	TC	Profit	MR	MC
29							
30	100	35.00	3,500.00	3,750.00	(250.00)	-	-
31	150	32.50	4,875.00	4,375.00	500.00	1,375.00	625.00
32	200	30.00	6,000.00	5,000.00	1,000.00	1,125.00	625.00
33	250	27.50	6,875.00	5,625.00	1,250.00	875.00	625.00
34	300	25.00	7,500.00	6,250.00	1,250.00	625.00	625.00
35	350	22.50	7,875.00	6,875.00	1,000.00	375.00	625.00
36	400	20.00	8,000.00	7,500.00	500.00	125.00	625.00
37	450	17.50	7,875.00	8,125.00	(250.00)	(125.00)	625.00
38	500	15.00	7,500.00	8,750.00	(1,250.00)	(375.00)	625.00

Spreadsheet solution 11.4 Output section 1

26 Spreadsheet Solution 11-4: Output Section 1

	E	F	G	H	I	J	K
28	Quantity	Price	TR	TC	Profit	MR	MC
30	+D17	+$D$23+($D$24*E30)	+F30*E30	+$D$20+($D$21*E30)	+G30-H30	-	-
31	+E30+$D$18	+$D$23+($D$24*E31)	+F31*E31	+$D$20+($D$21*E31)	+G31-H31	+G31-G30	+H31-H30
32	+E31+$D$18	+$D$23+($D$24*E32)	+F32*E32	+$D$20+($D$21*E32)	+G32-H32	+G32-G31	+H32-H31
33	+E32+$D$18	+$D$23+($D$24*E33)	+F33*E33	+$D$20+($D$21*E33)	+G33-H33	+G33-G32	+H33-H32
34	+E33+$D$18	+$D$23+($D$24*E34)	+F34*E34	+$D$20+($D$21*E34)	+G34-H34	+G34-G33	+H34-H33
35	+E34+$D$18	+$D$23+($D$24*E35)	+F35*E35	+$D$20+($D$21*E35)	+G35-H35	+G35-G34	+H35-H34
36	+E35+$D$18	+$D$23+($D$24*E36)	+F36*E36	+$D$20+($D$21*E36)	+G36-H36	+G36-G35	+H36-H35
37	+E36+$D$18	+$D$23+($D$24*E37)	+F37*E37	+$D$20+($D$21*E37)	+G37-H37	+G37-G36	+H37-H36
38	+E37+$D$18	+$D$23+($D$24*E38)	+F38*E38	+$D$20+($D$21*E38)	+G38-H38	+G38-G37	+H38-H37

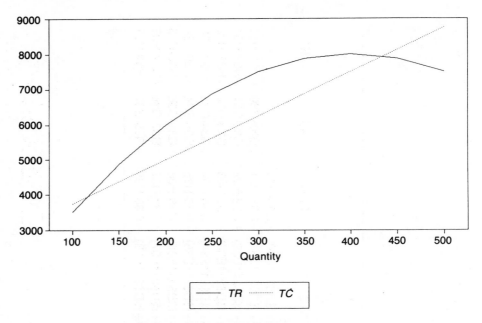

Figure 11.3 Profit maximization

Perhaps we can distinguish between the two points of maximum profit using the marginalist principle. The last two columns of the output section use formulae to calculate *MC* and *MR*. The first quantity level for which we can calculate marginal revenue or marginal cost is 150.

Note that the quantity of 300 (price £25) produces *MR* and *MC* of equal amounts (£625) which is where one of the maximum profit levels occurs. However, the result is not that accurate since the increments of quantity are quite large. We will refine this approach later (see the next 'What if?' section).

Graphing *MR*, *MC* and profit gives a visual display of the marginalist principle. To avoid 'kinks' in your graph insert *MR* and *MC* values for the first quantity level. This can be done manually. An alternative is to start your graph on the second quantity level. See Figure 11.4.

'What if?' question

The management of the company may need a more precise estimate of the point of maximum profit. Calculate the exact output level at which profit is maximized by fine-tuning the increments in the input section of the spreadsheet.

'What if?' solution

We know from Spreadsheet Solution 11.3 that profit is maximized somewhere

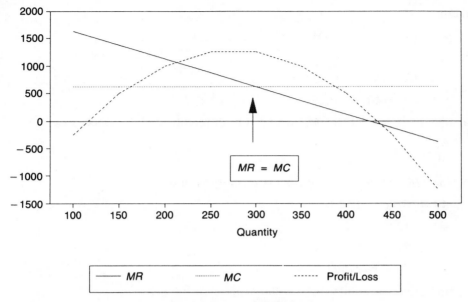

Figure 11.4   The marginalist principle

between 250 and 300 units. So the first change to the input section is to make the quantity start value 250 and the incremental size 10. Now view the output section. You should see that again two levels appear to give the highest profit, 270 and 280. This tells us that the highest profit is produced somewhere between these two points. Run the model again after changing the input section by making 270 the quantity start value and the incremental size, 1. Now we can see that 275 is the single point at which profit is maximized, at £1,281.25 and a price of £26.25.

Using simple calculus for optimal price determination

We need not use the spreadsheet at all to determine the optimal selling price. We now know that this is where $MR = MC$. If we can derive expressions for these functions involving x (quantity) as the unknown variable then we can solve for x.

In our example TC is given by the following expression:

$$TC = 2500 + 12.5x$$

Differentiating with respect to x will give an expression for MC:

$$\frac{\mathrm{d}TC}{\mathrm{d}x} = 12.5$$

TR is a different problem as we only have an expression for AR, that is, price. We can substitute for price in the normal expression for TR:

$$TR = px$$

where:

$$p = AR = 40 - 0.05x$$

Hence:

$$TR = (40 - 0.05x)x$$
$$TR = 40x - 0.05x^2$$

To find an expression for *MR* we need to differentiate with respect to *x*:

$$\frac{\mathrm{d}TR}{\mathrm{d}x} = 40 - 0.1x$$

Placing *MR* and *MC* equal gives the quantity required:

$$40 - 0.1x = 12.5$$
$$40 - 12.5 = 0.1x$$
$$27.5 = 0.1x$$
$$x = 275$$

To find price, substitute for *x* in the expression for *AR*:

$$p = AR = 40 - 0.05x$$
$$p = AR = 40 - 0.05(275)$$
$$p = 40 - 13.75$$
$$p = 26.25$$

The demand curve can only be a crude estimate of likely demand and our original solution produced a figure for the price of between £25 and £27.50. This would be adequate for management's needs and, depending upon the product, the eventual decision may be to select a price 'point' of, say, £25.99.

Cost-plus pricing

The management accountant's role is one of information provider. In using the economist's model to calculate the optimal price level a number of estimates have been made which may not be very robust. In estimating the total cost function we have already discovered that there is a margin of error in the coefficients. The estimate of total revenue or the demand function is even more susceptible to error as it relies on so many explanatory variables. In addition to customers' circumstances, for instance disposable income and taste, there is also competitor reaction to worry about. Any carefully researched demand curve is likely to be just a snapshot of estimated demand at any point in time, and the demand curve can move or change shape very rapidly and without warning.

In some cases, such as the launch of a new product, estimates of demand will vary widely as the market is totally untested. Some products do not have a market as such, but just one customer; for example, the government is the main if not sole customer for many civil engineering and military hardware projects.

For these reasons the management accountant will often use a cost-based pricing model to provide more information to management. This is often a first stage in determining the final price and is not relied upon totally. For example, if a new product is going to cost the firm more to produce than the market will bear, then managers have to rethink the product specification, the production process and the marketing initiative; it may even be necessary to consider scrapping the idea.

The logic of cost-plus pricing is very straightforward. The full cost of the product or service is measured, to which is added a percentage representing the desired profit margin. This has given rise to the term *target pricing*. An example of a cost-plus price calculation is given in Example 11.2 below.

Example 11.2

A company wishes to set its selling price to give it a 15% mark-up on the cost of its product. Its per-unit variable costs are as follows:

	£
Direct Materials	3.50
Direct Labour	4.50
Variable Production Overheads	3.00
Variable Non-production Overheads	2.75

Fixed overheads are recovered as follows:

Production	100% of direct labour costs
Non-production	50% of the full cost of production

The selling price of the product is calculated as shown below:

Production costs per unit:

	£	
Direct Materials	3.50	
Direct Labour	4.50	
Variable Production Overheads	3.00	
Fixed Production Overheads	4.50	
Total Production cost		15.50
Non-production costs:		
Variable Non-production Overheads	2.75	
Fixed Non-production Overheads	7.75	
Total Non-production Overheads		10.50
Total cost		26.00
Profit Mark-up 15%		3.90
Selling price		29.90

The spreadsheet solution

Set up the control and input sections as shown in Spreadsheet Solutions 11.5 and 11.6. The construction of the output section involves no advanced spreadsheet skills which need to be described, but remember that it should only include cell references (see Spreadsheets 11.7 and 11.8).

Variations

A variation on the above method is to add a mark-up to the full cost of production to cover non-manufacturing overheads and still produce a profit. In this instance the

Spreadsheet solution 11.5   Control section

	A	B
1	Spreadsheet Solution 11-5: Control Section	
2		
3	Example 11.2	
4		
5	This spreadsheet illustrates the cost-plus method of pricing.	
6		
7		
8	Location Table	Range Name
9	--------------	----------
10	Input Section	INPUT
11	Output Section 1	COSTPLUS
12	Output Section 2 - 'What If?' Table	WHATIF

Spreadsheet solution 11.6   Input section

	C	D	E
15	Spreadsheet Solution 11-6: Input Section		
16			
17		£	
18	Direct Materials	3.50	
19			
20	Direct Labour	4.50	
21			
22	Variable Production Overheads	3.00	
23			
24	.Variable Non-Production Overheads	2.75	
25			
26	Fixed Production Overheads	100.00%	of Direct Labour Costs
27			
28	Fixed Non-Production Overheads	50.00%	of Full Cost of Production
29			
30	Profit Mark-Up %	15.00%	of Total Cost

Spreadsheet solution 11.7 Output section 1

	F	G
31	Spreadsheet Solution 11-7: Output Section 1	
32		
33		£
34	Direct Materials	3.50
35		
36	Direct Labour	4.50
37		
38	Prime Cost	8.00
39		
40	Variable Production Overheads	3.00
41		
42	Fixed Production Overheads	4.50
43		
44	Full Cost of Production	15.50
45		
46	Variable Non-Production Overheads	2.75
47		
48	Fixed Non-Production Overheads	7.75
49		
50	Total Cost	26.00
51		
52	Profit Mark-Up	3.90
53		
54	Selling Price	29.90
55		=====

Spreadsheet solution 11.8 Output section 1

	F	G
31	Spreadsheet Solution 11-8: Output Section 1	
32		
33		£
34	Direct Materials	+D18
35		
36	Direct Labour	+D20
37		
38	Prime Cost	+G34+G36
39		
40	Variable Production Overheads	+D22
41		
42	Fixed Production Overheads	+D20*D26
43		
44	Full Cost of Production	@SUM(G38..G42)
45		
46	Variable Non-Production Overheads	+D24
47		
48	Fixed Non-Production Overheads	+D28*G44
49		
50	Total Cost	@SUM(G44..G48)
51		
52	Profit Mark-Up	+D30*G50
53		
54	Selling Price	+G52+G50
55		=========

production unit cost is £15.50 and the mark-up necessary to produce the same selling price is:

$$\frac{14.40}{15.50} \times 100 = 93\% \text{ (approx.)}$$

Often this method is preferred as production costs are easier to estimate than the other overheads.

Disadvantages of cost-plus pricing

On the face of it, the simplicity and apparent accuracy of cost-based pricing methods is attractive, but the main disadvantage is the absence of any market considerations. However, it can produce a price level which market researchers can test for consumer response and the mark-up can be varied as a result.

Another disadvantage is the need to allocate fixed overheads based on some estimate of production levels. When fixed overheads represent a high proportion of total costs, errors or inaccuracies in estimating the basis of allocation may have serious implications for costing and pricing. In Example 11.2, fixed overheads account for 47% of total cost on which the selling price is based; the eventual profit level is very sensitive to production and sales estimates.

Fixed overheads are incurred regardless of production or sales levels, and it is dangerous to treat them on a unit basis. If the volume of production and sales exceeds the initial estimate then the eventual profit margin will be more than 15%.

A vicious circle can result if too high a price is charged initially: sales volume may be lower than anticipated, forcing fixed costs per unit to rise, which in turn raises the selling price per unit, which reduces sales volume still further, and so on.

Firms producing more than one product have an additional problem of apportioning common overheads among different product lines. An unfair apportionment can result in sub-optimal pricing decisions (see Chapter 13).

'What if?' question

In our example there are two types of fixed overhead, production and non-production, that need to be recovered. What would be the impact on price if the two overhead absorption rates both varied between 50% and 150%?

'What if?' solution

This question requires two variables to be altered simultaneously. This can be performed using a data table containing 2 variables. This is prepared in the same way as the one-variable data table (see Chapter 7). However, as we have two variables we require two ranges of substitute values and two input cells (cells D26 and D28). The result is presented in Spreadsheet Solution 11.9.

Spreadsheet solution 11.9

	H	I	J	K	L	M
56	Spreadsheet Solution 11-9: Output Section 2 - 'What If?' Table					
57						
58			Fixed Non-Production Overhead Absorption Rate			
59						
60		+G54	50.00%	75.00%	100.00%	125.00%	150.00%
61	Fixed	50.00%	26.02	29.83	33.64	37.45	41.26
62	Production	60.00%	26.80	30.73	34.67	38.61	42.55
63	Overhead	70.00%	27.57	31.64	35.71	39.78	43.84
64	Absorption	80.00%	28.35	32.55	36.74	40.94	45.14
65	Rate	90.00%	29.12	33.45	37.78	42.10	46.43
66		100.00%	29.90	34.36	38.81	43.27	47.73
67		110.00%	30.68	35.26	39.85	44.43	49.02
68		120.00%	31.45	36.17	40.88	45.60	50.31
69		130.00%	32.23	37.07	41.92	46.76	51.61
70		140.00%	33.01	37.98	42.95	47.93	52.90
71		150.00%	33.78	38.88	43.99	49.09	54.19

Marginal cost-plus pricing

To avoid the problems of overhead allocation, some firms use a cost-based price model that ignores fixed costs and adds a mark-up to marginal costs. This is sometimes referred to as *relevant cost-plus pricing*. This is very common in the retail trade where the marginal costs are easily determined. The amount of the mark-up depends on the nature of the goods. High-turnover products tend to have lower mark-ups than low-turnover goods. So a grocer may apply a mark-up of 33% to the fruit and vegetables he buys, while a jeweller may apply over 100% to his stock purchases.

This method is also used in cases of short-term decision-making where full-cost pricing may have been used, but now the firm needs to reduce stock levels to generate cash flow.

The method ties in very well with cost−volume−profit analysis as the firm knows what sales it requires to meet its fixed costs and hence break even.

A contingency approach to cost-based pricing methods

As is often the case in practice, there is no single correct solution to the problem as to what is the best price. The role of the management accountant is to provide as much information as possible to enable managers to reach the 'best' pricing decision. This may be the price that maximizes profit, or maximizes sales. However, managers need to be aware of the marginal cost in the short and long term as well as the target profit margin.

In the short term, managers can 'afford' to reduce prices to a level just above marginal cost, as shown in the example below.

Example 11.3

A company calculates the minimum short-term selling price for its product as follows:

	£	£
Direct Materials	3.50	
Direct Labour	4.50	
		8.00
Variable Production Overheads		3.00
Variable Non-production Overheads		2.75
Minimum Short-term Selling Price		13.75

Any price above £13.75 will produce a contribution to overheads and is hence desirable. However, this strategy is not enough for the long term, when fixed costs need to be covered. So the minimum price for the long term is given below:

	£	£
Direct Materials	3.50	
Direct Labour	4.50	
		8.00
Variable Production Overheads		3.00
Variable Non-production Overheads		2.75
Marginal Cost		13.75
Fixed Production Overheads	4.50	
Fixed Non-production Overheads	7.75	
		12.25
Minimum Long-term Selling Price		26.00

This price will only guarantee that the company will break even, but if the company requires a set rate of return then a profit margin must be added, as in Example 11.2 where a 15% mark-up was applied.

Pricing policy

The eventual price chosen will be management's prerogative based on its perception of, and reaction to, market conditions.

Products follow a 'product life cycle' of five stages: introduction, growth, maturity, saturation and decline. The optimal price may be different for each stage. During the launch or introduction of a new product the firm may chose to sell the product cheaply to ensure a wider market base for the later stages of the product life cycle. This is known as *penetration* pricing.

The opposite strategy may be chosen whereby the new product is priced at a premium. This may exploit the novelty of the product when it is perceived as being in vogue. This is known as price *skimming*. In later stages of the product life cycle the price is lowered to reach a wider market base. This is the sort of strategy followed by 'high tech' products such as CD players or the latest advance in computers. This strategy has the advantage of recovering the overheads incurred in developing the new product and bringing it to market. It also allows cash to be generated which can be invested in production methods which may reduce manufacturing costs and allow adequate returns to be made on the product when it is in the maturity and saturation phases.

Conclusion

In this chapter we have considered a number of factors which will affect management's pricing strategy, both in theory and in practice. Spreadsheet models can readily adapt to changes in variables which would be either very difficult or tedious to perform manually.

Exercises

Question 11.1

In the last quarter of 19X5/19X6 it is estimated that YNQ will have produced and sold 20,000 units of its main product by the end of the year. At this level of activity it is estimated that the average unit cost will be as follows:

	£
Direct material	30
Direct labour	10
Overhead: fixed	10
variable	10
	60

This is in line with the standards set at the start of the year.

The management accountant of YNQ is now preparing the budget for 19X6/19X7. He has incorporated into his preliminary calculations the following expected cost increases:

Raw material: price increase of	20%
Direct labour: wage rate increase of	5%
Variable overhead: increase of	5%
Fixed overhead: increase of	25%

The production manager believes that if a cheaper grade of raw material were to be used, this would enable the direct material cost per unit to be kept to £31.25 for 19X6/X7. The cheaper material would, however, lead to a reject rate of 5% of the completed output, and it would be necessary to introduce an inspection stage at the end of the manufacturing process to identify the faulty items. The cost of this inspection process would be £40,000 per year (including £10,000 allocation of existing factory overhead).

Established practice has been to reconsider the product's selling price at the time the budget is being prepared. The selling price is normally determined by adding a mark-up of 50% to unit cost. On this basis the product's selling price for 19X5/X6 has been £90, but the sales manager is worried about the implications of continuing the cost plus 50% policy for 19X6/19X7. He estimates that demand for the product varies with price as follows:

Price	£80	£84	£88	£90	£92	£96	£100
Demand	25	23	21	20	19	17	15

(a) You are required to decide whether YNQ should use the regular or the cheaper grade of material and to calculate the best price for the product, the optimal level of production and the profit that this should yield. Comment briefly on the sensitivity of the solution to possible errors in the estimates.

(b) Indicate how one might obtain the answer to part (a) from an appropriately designed cost—volume—profit graph. You should design such a graph as part of your answer but the graph need not be drawn to scale providing that it demonstrates the main features of the approach that you would use.

Answer on page 285   *(ACCA)*

Question 11.2

Sniwe plc intend to launch a commemorative product for the 19X2 Olympic games onto the UK market commencing 1 August 19X0. The product will have variable costs of £16 per unit.

Production capacity available for the product is sufficient for 2000 units per annum. Sniwe plc has made a policy decision to produce to the maximum available capacity during the year to 31 July 19X1.

Demand for the product during the year to 31 July 19X1 is expected to be price-dependent, as follows:

Selling Price per Unit	Annual Sales
£	units
20	2000
30	1600
40	1200
50	1100
60	1000
70	700
80	400

It is anticipated that in the year 31 July 19X2 the availability of similar competitor products will lead to a market price of £40 per unit for the product during that year.

During the year to 31 July 19X2, Sniwe plc intends to produce only at the activity level required to enable it to satisfy demand, with stocks being run down to zero if possible. This policy is intended as a precaution against a sudden collapse of the market for the product by 31 July 19X2.

In answering the following questions, ignore tax and the time value of money.

(a) Determine the launch price at 1 August 19X0 which will maximize the net benefit to Sniwe plc during the two-year period to 31 July 19X2 where the demand potential for the year to 31 July 19X2 is estimated as (i) 3600 units and (ii) 1000 units.

(b) Identify which of the launch strategies detailed in (a) will result in unsold stock remaining at 31 July 19X2.

Advise management of the minimum price at which unsold stock should be in order to alter the initial launch price strategy which will maximize the net benefit to Sniwe plc over the life of the product.

(c) Comment on any other factors which might influence the initial launch price strategy where the demand in the year to 31 July 19X2 is estimated at 1000 units.

Answer on page 290   *(ACCA)*

12 | *Short-term decisions: cost−volume−profit and break-even analysis*

- to introduce the concepts of cost−volume−profit and break-even analysis;
- to explain the meaning of the terms *contribution ratio* and *margin of safety* and to describe how they are calculated;
- to explain and illustrate the uses of break-even analysis;
- to explain the limitations of the approach and the assumptions on which it is based;
- to demonstrate the graphical presentation of break-even information.

SPREADSHEET SKILLS ACQUIRED _____

- development of algebraic notations and their conversion into spreadsheet formulae.

Introduction

Chapter 5 describes how different types of cost behave over a range of levels of activity. For example, you will remember that certain costs remain constant regardless of the level of the company's activity (fixed costs) while others change in direct proportion to the changes in activity level (variable costs). Chapter 6 explains how the behaviour of these various costs can be estimated. In this chapter we will see how knowledge of cost behaviour is useful to management in making short-term decisions. We will also present an algebraic approach to problem-solving which has a direct bearing on the construction of spreadsheet models.

The algebraic approach has been developed in response to the suggestion from some academics that the style of presenting accounting knowledge should change from the illustrative methods traditionally used to one which requires accounting students to deduce the solution for themselves. It is claimed that the illustrative method merely teaches the student to repeat an exercise which has been demonstrated. The alternative 'deductive' approach requires an understanding of financial concepts and relationships which are then applied to solve any particular problem. Typically these concepts and relationships are expressed in algebraic form. The advantage of this approach is that it requires the student to think logically and in a manner similar to that used in computer programs. Such skills can then be readily applied to obtain the best use of computer programs.

Revenues, costs and profits

Managers who are responsible for running a business with a view to making a profit are going to be interested in the level of costs associated with a given level of sales. Profit (P) is, of course, the difference between total revenue (TR) and total costs (TC), expressed notationally as follows:

$$P = TR - TC$$

Total revenue is determined by multiplying the quantity sold (Q) by the selling price per unit (sp):

$$TR = spQ$$

The total cost function is a little more complex. There are few businesses where costs are either all fixed or all variable, so in most cases there will be a mixture of these two types of cost. Therefore we can express the components of total cost, fixed cost (FC) and variable cost (VC), as follows:

$$TC = FC + VC$$

Note that the element of total cost that varies with output can also be written as:

$$VC = vcQ$$

where vc is variable costs per unit. We can now expand our original profit formula to reflect the impact of the level of activity on the level of profit:

$$P = spQ - (FC + vcQ)$$

The relationship between volume of activity and levels of costs and profits is known as the cost—volume—profit (CVP) relationship. Use of CVP will provide management with much-needed information for both planning and control purposes. Examples of questions for which management require answers include the following. How much of its product will the company need to sell in order to cover its costs? What will be the effect on profit of an increase in variable costs of, say, 10%? At a given level of activity, what price will the company need to charge for its product to make a specified amount of profit?

Break-even analysis

In particular, CVP will enable management to determine how much of a product needs to be sold to cover its costs. It is only once this point is passed that the business starts to show a profit. Algebraically, the break-even is the point where:

$$TR = TC$$

or, expressed another way:

$$spQ - (FC + vcQ) = 0$$

Contribution

Another way of viewing the break-even point is by concentrating on the *contribution*, that is, the amount by which the selling price per unit exceeds variable cost per unit (or, at the aggregate level, the excess of total revenue over total variable costs). The term 'contribution' refers to the fact that if selling price exceeds variable cost then each unit sold is contributing something towards meeting fixed costs. The break-even point occurs when total contribution is exactly equal to fixed costs.

If we let C denote the total contribution, the break-even point may also be expressed as follows:

$$C = FC$$
$$= (sp - vc)Q$$
$$= TR - VC$$

We will make use of these formulae in a spreadsheet application later on, but let us begin by constructing a model which will allow us to calculate total revenue, total costs and net profit/loss at different levels of output.

Example 12.1

A company has only one product line which sells at £100 per unit. Variable costs per unit are estimated at £50, while fixed costs are an estimated £750,000. The maximum possible output given the current production capacity is 25,000 units.

We can calculate the revenue, cost and profit for any level of sales by using the algebraic expressions described above. For example, for 15,000 units:

Total revenue	1,500,000
Less: Variable costs	750,000
Fixed costs	750,000
	1,500,000
Net profit	0

This just happens to be the exact level at which the company breaks even, but the use of a spreadsheet model makes life much easier by allowing the CVP relationship to be calculated for a number of output levels.

The spreadsheet solution

To construct our model we need to place in the input section the relevant variables and parameters: the selling price, variable and fixed costs and range of output levels. We can now begin to build the model itself. After designing the control section (Spreadsheet Solution 12.1), the input section should appear similar to the one shown in Spreadsheet Solution 12.2.

The output section can be constructed to map the costs and revenues for a number of output levels (see Spreadsheet Solutions 12.3 and 12.4).

The level of total costs and revenues will be determined by the level of units sold, so we begin by specifying a number of possible levels of sales within the range allowed by the present capacity. For ease of presentation this has been restricted to six levels, increments of 5000 from 0 to 25,000 (cell references G43–L43). In practice such a restriction would not apply and it would be quite simple to cover the whole range from 0 to 25,000 units in steps of 1000 units, which would perhaps present a more helpful picture to management.

The various items which are required to be inserted in the model are now dealt with by reference to the original elements of the break-even formula described above.

Total revenue from sales is given, as already stated, by

$$TR = spQ$$

Spreadsheet solution 12.1   Control section

	A	B	C
1	Spreadsheet Solution 12-1: Control Section		
2			
3	Example 12.1		
4			
5	This model calculates the break-even position		
6	and plots costs and revenues across a range of		
7	output levels.		
8			
9			
10			
11			
12			
13	Location Table	Range Name	
14	--	--------------------------------	
15	Input Section	INPUT	
16	Output Section	OUTPUT	
17			
18			
19	For Input Section Press F5 and type Input		

Spreadsheet solution 12.2　Input section

	C	D	E
21	Spreadsheet Solution 12-2: Input Section		
22			
23	Variables	Value	
24			
25			
26	Selling Price per unit	100.00	
27			
28	Variable Cost per unit	50.00	
29			
30			
31	Parameters		
32			
33	Minimum No. of units	0	
34	Incremental Increase	5,000	
35			
36	Fixed Costs	750,000	
37			
38	Move to Output Section by pressing F5		
39	and typing the range name OUTPUT1		

Since we are looking at a range of sales levels, beginning with a minimum as given in cell D33 in the input section and repeated in cell G43 in the output section, and since *sp* is given in cell D26, the formula we enter in cell G45, for example, is

$\langle +G43 * \$D\$26 \rangle$

Similar formulae appear across row 45.

We proceed in a like manner to deal with total variable costs, given by the formula

$$VC = vcQ$$

Thus our formulae in row 47 will be like those in row 45, with \$D\$28 substituted for \$D\$26.

The contribution for a given level of sales is then found by simply subtracting row 47 from row 45.

(Alternatively we could go straight to the calculation of total contribution (selling price per unit less the variable cost per unit × the number of units sold). Using the terms above:

$$C = (sp - vc)Q$$

This would dispense with rows 45 and 47 (sales and variable costs) and require the formula for the first cell in the 'Contribution' row to be:

$\langle (\$D\$26 - \$D\$28) * G43 \rangle$

However, for this example, let us assume that we need figures for sales and variable costs.)

Finally, by deducting fixed costs from contribution (whichever way this is

Spreadsheet solution 12.3 Output section

	F	G	H	I	J	K	L
41	Spreadsheet Solution 12-3: Output Section						
42					No. of Units		
43		0	5,000	10,000	15,000	20,000	25,000
44		----------	----------	----------	----------	----------	----------
45	Sales	0	500,000	1,000,000	1,500,000	2,000,000	2,500,000
46							
47	Variable costs	0	250,000	500,000	750,000	1,000,000	1,250,000
48							
49	Contribution	0	250,000	500,000	750,000	1,000,000	1,250,000
50							
51	Fixed Costs	750,000	750,000	750,000	750,000	750,000	750,000
52		----------	----------	----------	----------	----------	----------
53	Net Profit\Loss	(750,000)	(500,000)	(250,000)	0	250,000	500,000
54							
55	Total Costs	750,000	1,000,000	1,250,000	1,500,000	1,750,000	2,000,000

Spreadsheet solution 12.4 Output section

	F	G	H	I	J	K	L
41	Spreadsheet Solution 12-4: Output Section						
42					No. of Units		
43		+D33	+G43+$D$34	+H43+$D$34	+I43+$D$34	+J43+$D$34	+K43+$D$34
44		----------	----------	----------	----------	----------	----------
45	Sales	+G43*$D$26	+H43*$D$26	+I43*$D$26	+J43*$D$26	+K43*$D$26	+L43*$D$26
46							
47	Variable costs	+G43*$D$28	+H43*$D$28	+I43*$D$28	+J43*$D$28	+K43*$D$28	+L43*$D$28
48							
49	Contribution	+G45-G47	+H45-H47	+I45-I47	+J45-J47	+K45-K47	+L45-L47
50							
51	Fixed Costs	+$D$36	+$D$36	+$D$36	+$D$36	+$D$36	+$D$36
52		----------	----------	----------	----------	----------	----------
53	Net Profit\Loss	+G49-G51	+H49-H51	+I49-I51	+J49-J51	+K49-K51	+L49-L51
54							
55	Total Costs	+G47+G51	+H47+H51	+I47+I51	+J47+J51	+K47+K51	+L47+L51

calculated) we are left with the net profit/loss for each level of sales. It is clear that the level which produces neither profit nor loss, the break-even point, is 15,000 units or sales revenue of £1.5 million.

Note also that for zero sales the net loss is equivalent to fixed costs but the losses decline as output moves towards the 15,000 level. If fixed costs are unavoidable, this would mean that in the short term the company would be better off producing at levels below the break-even point than ceasing production and sales altogether, since every unit sold is making a contribution towards fixed costs.

Another point to note is the proportional effect on the 'bottom line' of changes in output. Thus at levels of activity above the break-even point the net profit rises at a greater rate than the increase in units sold. For example, increasing sales from 20,000 units to 25,000 units (a 25% rise) *doubles* the net profit. Conversely, below the break-even point a fall in sales will lead to a greater than proportional increase in net loss.

This is the result of fixed costs being held constant over a range of output levels, producing a *gearing* effect which becomes accentuated the greater the ratio of fixed to variable costs. A company which has a high level of fixed costs (as a proportion of its total costs) will experience more volatility in its net profits following changes in the level of activity than a company which has a relatively low ratio of fixed to variable costs.

Graphical presentation

In management accounting, a mass of financial and other data, such as production figures, has to be condensed by the management accountant for use by others, who often lack financial and accounting expertise. It may be far easier for managers to understand the information if it is presented in graphical form.

Let us take another look at the data presented in Example 12.1 above. We can graph any of the figures in the model by assigning the rows as values for the *range* under the graph menu.

If we are only interested in the break-even point, we need only graph the values for fixed costs and contribution since (taking the second break-even formula discussed above) the break-even point occurs where $C = FC$. In Figure 12.1, the break-even point is where the two lines cross. Such a presentation clearly demonstrates the fact that fixed costs remain constant over the range of sales levels and that contribution rises in a strictly linear and directly proportional fashion with increases in sales.

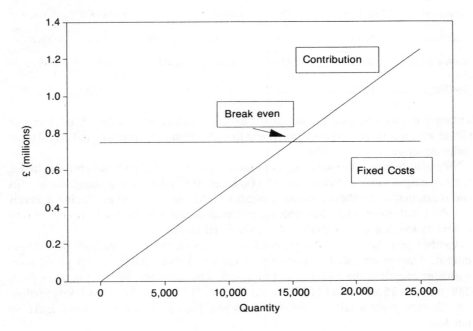

Figure 12.1 Contribution chart

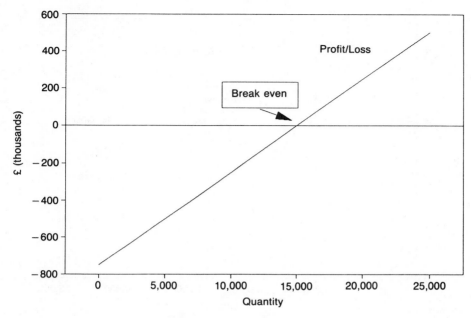

Figure 12.2 Profit chart

An even simpler presentation of the CVP relationship would graph the net profit/loss against sales, as shown in Figure 12.2. Notice that the slope of the line is the same as the slope of the contribution line in Figure 12.1 (this is because net profit is simply contribution less the constant, fixed costs). Notice also that the line below $Y = 0$ measures the extent of the loss, while the line above $Y = 0$ measures the net profit. Again the break-even point can clearly be seen: the point where the net profit/loss line intersects the $Y = 0$ line.

This presentation does not give us all the information which management may need; it omits, for example, sales revenue and total costs. Remember that the break-even point could also be described as occurring when

$$TR = TC$$

and that

$$TC = FC + VC$$

In our model the easiest way for us to calculate total costs is to add another row (row 55) which represents the sum of fixed and variable costs. We can then use this row and the row for sales revenue as series values to produce a graph (Figure 12.3) which will be familiar to readers of more conventional management accounting texts.

Note that if we were only interested in total costs, rather than the split between fixed and variable costs, we could have calculated this by expanding the term used in the original break-even formula:

$$TC = FC + (vcQ)$$

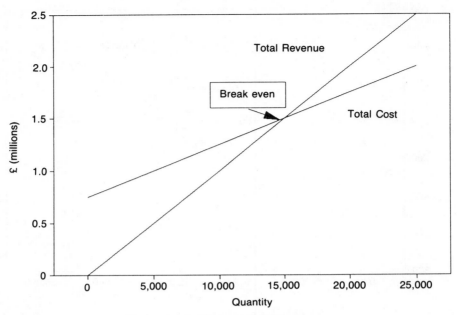

Figure 12.3 Conventional break even

We could then use this to construct a formula to calculate the total cost under each level of activity. This formula would be (for the first, that is, minimum level):

⟨ +$D36+($D28∗G43)⟩

The exact relationship between sales, costs and profit may not be particularly difficult to appreciate given the simplicity of the numbers used in this example, but of course in practice the figures and relationships would rarely be so straightforward.

'What if?' questions

1. Changing only the input section of the model, answer the following:

    (a) Suppose that the company is in a fiercely competitive market and may not be able to maintain its market share if its product retails at £100. What is the net profit if 20,000 units are sold at the reduced price of £95?

    (b) The managing director wishes to know how a proposed advertising campaign will affect the company's break-even point. The sales director proposes a TV promotion campaign which will enhance the image of the product so much that the selling price could be raised by £7.50 per unit. The cost of the campaign, including the rights to a 1960s rock song, will add £100,000 to the company's fixed costs. View the break-even graph with the changed variables and determine what will happen to the break-even point.

(c) The production director is considering contracting out the plant maintenance, currently performed by workers taken off the production line. To contract out would cost the company a fixed price per year of £150,000 but would result in a saving in variable costs of £5.00 per unit. What is the effect on the break-even point?

2. Make a small refinement to the model in Example 12.1 so that the sales revenue, costs and profit at any specified level of sales (in units) can be produced.

'What if?' solutions

1. (a) With 20,000 units being sold at £95, the net profit would be £150,000.

   (b) The break-even point has fallen slightly below 15,000 units.

   (c) Under this scenario the break-even point is above the 15,000 level.

2. All that is required is the insertion of a new row in the input section of the model to cope with an additional variable, 'Specified sales (units)'. This is then referenced in the output section in a new column M, alongside the existing range of activity levels (row 43). The cell formulae for the values of revenue, costs and profit are copied (from column L to column M, rows 45—53) to provide the necessary data for the specified volume of sales.

Further development of the spreadsheet model

In Example 12.1 there was no problem identifying the break-even point since one of the levels chosen (15,000 units) happened to be the break-even level; but this will not always be the case. What we need is a formula (see above) which we can insert in the model (in a second output section) in order to calculate the precise point at which the company will break even. There are other aspects of CVP which we can introduce by adapting the existing model to calculate: margin of safety; level of sales to produce a given profit; and the price to be charged to produce a given profit at a given level of sales. For this we should revise our control section as shown in Spreadsheet Solution 12.5 and expand our input section as shown in Spreadsheet Solution 12.6 by inserting rows for the additional items (the relevance of which is discussed below).

In output section 2 (Spreadsheet Solutions 12.7 and 12.8) we start by calculating the break-even point. The simplest way stems from the formula for describing the break-even point:

$$C = FC$$

Spreadsheet solution 12.5   New control section

	A	B	C
1	Spreadsheet Solution 12-5: New Control Section		
2			
3			
4	The Break-even Model		
5			
6	This model calculates the breakeven position of a company.		
7	It also allows the calculation of margin of safety and		
8	profit per specified level of sales. It enables "What if?"		
9	questions to be answered.		
10			
11			
12			
13	Location Table	Range Name	
14	--	---------------	
15	Input Section	INPUT	
16	Output Section 1	OUTPUT1	
17	Output Section 2	OUTPUT2	
18			
19	For Input Section Press F5 and type Input		

Spreadsheet solution 12.6   New input section

	C	D	E
21	Spreadsheet Solution 12-6: New Input Section		
22			
23	Variables	Value	
24			
25			
26	Selling Price per unit	100.00	
27			
28	Variable Cost per unit	50.00	
29			
30	Desired Profit	15,000	
31			
32	Current Sales (£)	2,000,000	
33			
34	Specified Sales (units)	20,000	
35			
36	Parameters		
37			
38	Minimum No. of units	0	
39	Incremental Increase	5,000	
40			
41	Fixed Costs	750,000	
42			
43	Move to Output Section by pressing F5		
44	and typing the range name OUTPUT1		

Spreadsheet solution 12.7 Output section 2

	M	N
61	Spreadsheet Solution 12-7: Output Section 2	
62		
63	Break-even Point Calculations	
64		
65	Contribution Per Unit	50
66		
67	Fixed Costs	750,000
68		
69	Break-even (Units)	15,000
70		
71	Break-even (£)	1,500,000
72		
73	Sales for Desired Profit (Units)	15,300
74		
75	Sales for Desired Profit (£)	1,530,000
76		
77	Margin of Safety %	25.00%
78		
79	Price for Specified P & V	88.25

Spreadsheet solution 12.8 Output section 2

	M	N
61	Spreadsheet Solution 12-8: Output Section 2	
62		
63	Break-even Point Calculations	
64		
65	Contribution Per Unit	+D26-D28
66		
67	Fixed Costs	+D41
68		
69	Break-even (Units)	+N67/N65
70		
71	Break-even (£)	+N69*D26
72		
73	Sales for Desired Profit (Units)	(D30+N67)/N65
74		
75	Sales for Desired Profit (£)	+N73*D26
76		
77	Margin of Safety %	(D32-N71)/D32
78		
79	Price for Specified P & V	(D30+D41+(D34*D28))/D34

and if

$$C = (sp - vc)Q$$

then break-even occurs where

$$(sp - vc)Q = FC$$

Then, dividing both sides of the equation by $(sp - vc)$, break-even in terms of units (Q_{bu}) is given by:

$$Q_{bu} = \frac{FC}{sp - vc}$$

Break-even point in terms of sales value $(Q_{bs} = spQ_{bu})$ is obtained by multiplying both sides of the equation by the selling price per unit:

$$Q_{bs} = \frac{FC}{sp - vc} \times sp$$

In our model we begin by calculating the contribution made by each unit sold, $(sp - vc)$. Insert the formula to calculate contribution per unit, $\langle +D26 - D28 \rangle$, in cell N65 alongside the appropriate label (cell M65). For the sake of clarity we have repeated 'fixed costs' to show the level of fixed costs by reference back to the appropriate cell in the input section. Since the break-even point is that at which total contribution is exactly equal to fixed costs, it follows that the break-even point in terms of number of units sold is fixed costs divided by contribution per unit.

So the formula we enter in cell N69 is $\langle +N67/N65 \rangle$. The result is the number of units which need to be sold in order to break even. We can convert this to the sales value by multiplying the result in cell N69 by the selling price per unit given in cell D26 (see cell N71).

The second method of arriving at the same answer is based on reordering the equation derived above:

$$Q_{bs} = \frac{FC}{sp - vc} \times sp$$

by dividing by sp, to read

$$Q_{bs} = \frac{FC}{sp - vc/sp}$$

The denominator represents contribution as a proportion of selling price. It shows (provided selling price exceeds variable cost per unit) the amount of every £1 of sales which will contribute to fixed costs. This is called the *contribution ratio*, although perhaps a better term would be contribution *margin* because it is usually expressed as a percentage.

Thus by dividing fixed costs by the contribution ratio we arrive at the level of sales required to break even (that is, to provide a contribution at a given proportion per £1 of sales, sufficient to cover exactly fixed costs).

If we were to use this in output section 2 of our model, in place of contribution per unit, the formula we would need to insert in cell N65 (against a label 'Contribution ratio') would be ⟨(+D26−D28)/D26⟩ (the cell needs to be formatted to show a percentage).

If in cell N69 we now divide the fixed costs by the contribution ratio we will end up with the level of sales (in money terms) required to produce sufficient contribution to cover fixed costs. To convert this to the number of units required to break even we need (in cell N71) to divide the break-even sales by the selling price per unit.

Calculation of sales to achieve desired profit

The break-even approach has other useful applications. For instance, it can indicate to management the level of sales required to reach a specified or target level of net profit.

We can enter the desired profit as a variable in the input section of the model by inserting a row. In cell C32 enter the appropriate label and in cell D30 the value of the desired profit, ⟨15000⟩.

At this stage we can also insert another item of data which we will use later: the current level of sales. Let us assume that the company is currently operating at 80% of its maximum capacity, that is, sales are £2 million.

The formula to calculate the number of units to be sold in order to produce sufficient contribution to cover fixed costs *and* to yield a required net profit, can be expressed thus:

$$Q_P = \frac{FC + P}{sp - vc}$$

where P is the required level of profit and Q_P the level of sales (in units) which will produce P.

To use this in our spreadsheet, the formula to be inserted in cell N73 would be ⟨(D30+N67)/N65⟩. Note that for clarity fixed costs are represented in cell N67 by reference to the input section.

Again this can be expressed in sales in terms of value simply by multiplying the result by the selling price per unit (cell D26).

Margin of safety

The break-even approach allows another important indicator to be produced which is of benefit to the more cautious of managers. This is the *margin of safety*, which can be defined as the percentage by which current sales will have to fall before the break-even point is reached (assuming, of course, that the company is currently making a net profit). If sales fall by a percentage higher than the margin of safety then the company will make a loss.

To calculate the margin of safety in our model we enter the relevant formula in cell N77, ⟨(D32 − N71)/D32⟩. Cell N77 is formatted to express the solution as a percentage. The solution according to our model is 25%, that is, sales will have to fall by 25% from the current level of £2 million for the company to reach the break-even point.

A quick visual check of the data in output section 1 shows the margin of safety calculated in cell N77 is correct: a 25% fall in current sales will take us to the £1.5 million level which is the break-even point. If you are still not convinced, then change the value of current sales in cell D32 to 1,500,000 and look at the margin of safety now: it should be 0%.

Calculation of selling price

The management accountant may be asked to calculate the selling price of a product to produce a specified profit at a given level of sales. This may occur where management is concerned about profitability and there is some scope for adjustment of the selling price without adversely affecting the company's competitive position.

Remember the original CVP equation:

$$P = spQ - (FC + vcQ)$$

If management is prepared to specify both the level of sales (Q) they expect to achieve and the profit desired (P), all the management accountant needs to do is substitute the known variables in the CVP equation:

$$sp = \frac{P + FC + vcQ}{Q}$$

To incorporate this into our model we have inserted an additional row in the input section for 'Specified Sales', now cell D34. In output section 2, make cell N79 the location for our solution, 'Price for Specified Profit and Volume'. The formula would then be ⟨(D30+D41+(D34∗D28))/D34⟩.

'What if?' questions

1. Devise a formula to calculate the net profit at a given level of sales (in units). The formula should fit in a single cell in output section 2 and contain references only to cells in the input section.

2. What is the net profit if sales of 17,500 units are made at the regular price?

3. What is the margin of safety if the current level of sales is £2.25 million?

4. At what price will 20,000 units need to be sold to generate a net profit of £200,000?

'What if?' solutions

1. The spreadsheet formula we need to devise is based on the profit formula

   $$P = spQ - (FC + vcQ)$$

   This is reordered to give us:

   $$= ((sp - vc)Q) - FC$$

   where Q is the specified quantity of sales. We need to extend output section 2 by adding the label in cell M81 'Profit for Specified Sales', and in cell N81 entering the formula $\langle((D26-D28)*D34)-D41\rangle$.

2. The net profit at 17,500 units is £125,000.

3. The margin of safety is 33%.

4. 20,000 units sold at £97.50 will produce a net profit of £200,000.

Limitations of the break-even approach

The limitations of the break-even approach stem from its underlying assumptions, which would appear to be a little unrealistic.

Assumption of linearity

Another look at Figure 12.2 will show you that costs, revenues and profits are dealt with as strictly linear relationships across the entire range of possible sales levels. From your reading of Chapters 5 and 11 you will remember that in practice costs and revenues are likely to behave other than in a linear manner.

For example, suppliers are likely to offer discounts to their best customers, these discounts often being dependent on the level of purchases made in a particular period (month/quarter/year). If the discount takes the form of, say, a 2.5% reduction in purchase price per unit for purchases in excess of 50,000 units per year, the effect of this discount is to reduce the slope of the variable cost line for this cost item.

The same will apply to sales to a company's customers. If the company operates in a competitive market, it may only be able to increase total sales by offering discounts or lowering prices. Graphically this will be represented by a decreasing slope at higher levels of sales. So both costs and revenues are likely to be curvilinear over the entire range.

So does this mean that the whole of the preceding section has no relevance to the real world? Accountants justify maintaining the linearity of their graphs by stating that in practice the range of focus will not be the entire range of sales but will be a relatively small band within the entire range, called the *relevant range*.

Assumption of single product/product mix

The break-even approach assumes that the company has only one product. It *can* be applied to a multi-product company, but only if there is a given mix of products which remains constant across the entire range of sales levels. For example, a company has two products, A and B, which sell in a ratio of 2:1. If at higher levels of total sales it is found that proportionally more of product B is sold than product A, then the break-even analysis approach will be invalid.

No change in stocks

In building the model earlier in this chapter you may have been surprised that no allowance was made for opening or closing stocks. This is because the break-even approach assumes that the costs being calculated are the costs of sales, that is, either there is no opening/closing stock or there is no change in the stock levels. This is unrealistic since many businesses relate their stock-holding levels to their sales so that, for example, they always have sufficient stocks of finished goods to meet, say, two weeks' sales; if total sales increase so will stocks.

Conclusion

In practice management requires information about the financial effect of proposed plans. Use of a spreadsheet model immediately produces the required information, such as the effect on net profit of a reduction in selling price or the change in break-even point following an increase in fixed costs.

However, we must not overlook the fact that there are limitations to the break-even approach. These do not totally invalidate the approach but restrict its application to certain situations and to a narrow or relevant range of sales levels. Notwithstanding these limitations, CVP analysis can provide much useful information relevant to short-term planning and control.

Having worked through this chapter you should now appreciate the relationships between costs, profits and volume. There has been a heavy emphasis on the expression of relationships using algebraic notation. While this may at first appear unnecessarily confusing, it is essential for you to view relationships in this way since this facilitates construction of spreadsheet models.

Exercises

Question 12.1

The directors of Barque Ltd, a manufacturing company, are considering the introduction of a new product to their range. This product can be made by either of two methods, and the production director has supplied the following information about these alternatives:

	Method 1	Method 2
Investment in place (£ thousand)	3,000	1,000
Annual fixed costs, excluding depreciation (£ thousand)	420	370
Variable cost per unit (£)	0.50	1.00

In both cases the plant has a maximum output of 250,000 units per annum, an expected life of 10 years and a zero residual value. The selling price per unit is £5.

The sales director says that the market for the new product is very unpredictable, but he expects sales to be between 100,000 and 250,000 units a year. However, he is sure that if, in addition to the fixed costs identified by the production director, an advertising campaign costing £135,000 each year is undertaken, then annual sales would be at least 200,000 units while the maximum sales would remain at 250,000.

(a) For each production method, assuming that the advertising campaign is undertaken, calculate:
  (i) the break-even point in units;
  (ii) the maximum possible profit.

(b) For each production method, assuming that the advertising campaign is *not* undertaken, calculate:
  (i) the break-even point in units;
  (ii) the maximum possible profit.

(c) Explain to the management the course of action which you would recommend, on the assumption that the directors wish to take the minimum possible risk.

Answer on page 294   (CIB)

Question 12.2

A cinema chain, based in Oxford, owns three cinemas in the towns of Newbury, Reading and Basingstoke. It has prepared budgets for the coming year based upon a ticket price of £4.00 (all figures in thousands of pounds):

	Reading	Newbury	Basingstoke	Total
Budgeted receipts	1,600	1,200	800	3,600
Costs				
Film hire	500	400	390	1,290
Wages and salaries	300	250	160	710
Overheads	500	400	350	1,250
	1,300	1,050	900	3,250

Included in the overhead figures are the Oxford head office fixed costs that amount to £720,000. These have been allocated to each cinema on the basis of budgeted ticket receipts. All other costs are variable.

The mangement is concerned about the Basingstoke cinema and the fact that it is showing a budgeted loss, and is considering closing the cinema and selling the site to a property developer.

(a) Prepare marginal costing statements to show contributions for each cinema and contribution and profit for the overall chain on the following bases:
 (i) the original budget;
 (ii) if the Basingstoke cinema is closed.

(b) On the grounds of profitability do you think that the Basingstoke cinema should be closed? Give a reasoned explanation of your decision.

(c) What is the contribution per ticket sale at each cinema?

(d) What is the margin of safety in revenue for the chain at the budgeted level of activity if the Basingstoke cinema is:
 (i) kept open?
 (ii) closed down?

(e) If the Basingstoke cinema is kept open management wants an increase in profitability. One suggestion is that receipts at the cinema can be increased by 50% by an advertising campaign directed at Basingstoke that will add £40,000 to the chain's fixed costs. Do you think the advertising should be undertaken to improve the cinema's profitability? Give reasons for your decisions.

Answer on page 296   *(AAT)*

AIMS OF CHAPTER

- to identify the characteristics of short- and medium-term decision-making situations;
- to examine relevant or opportunity costs and contrast them with sunk or past costs;
- to consider situations where there are no scarce resources;
- to consider situations where there is one scarce resource, requiring the use of limiting factor analysis;
- to consider situations where there are many scarce resources, requiring the use of linear programming.

SPREADSHEET SKILLS ACQUIRED

- more nested @IF statements;
- optimization functions;
- introduction to simple macros.

Introduction

A decision implies that a choice has to be made between two or more options. In making that choice managers need quantitative and qualitative information. The production of quantitative information is the subject of this chapter, but where appropriate we will also consider intangible consequences of decisions which may be difficult to quantify but may nevertheless be important.

In the long term, management has to make *strategic* decisions. Such decisions are important for the survival of the business, for example the decision as to which new products to develop or which new markets to exploit. Long-term decisions are also characterized by large amounts of irreversible capital investment. Management accountants use numerous specialized techniques to assist management to determine the optimal decision. These are discussed in detail in Chapter 14.

In the short term, the number of options facing management is often more limited. These decisions can be *operational* or *tactical*. Examples of operational decisions are whether to accept a bulk discount from suppliers and whether to run an extra shift to meet an unexpected order. They are very short-term decisions taken almost daily. A tactical decision is more medium-term, and examples include whether or not to stop producing a product, whether or not it is worth processing a joint product further, and how to make the most of one or more scarce resources.

The main characteristic of both operational and tactical decisions is the presence of fixed costs that will not be affected by the choices available to management. This means that in preparing information for managers, the management accountant needs to decide which costs are relevant.

Relevant costs

Decisions can only affect the future, they cannot influence the past. Therefore in making all decisions the only appropriate costs and revenues to consider are those that may change as a consequence of the decision. Relevant costs are those which have an impact on the firm's future cash flows.

Many costs are not relevant because they have been incurred as the result of a previous managerial decision, for example the depreciation of plant and machinery. These are described as *sunk* costs.

Other costs may not be relevant because the company is committed to incurring them in the short term; for example, lease payments on rented property will be incurred whether or not the premises continue to be occupied. These are referred to as *unavoidable* costs.

Differences between the relevant costs of various options are called *differential costs*. Another term used extensively in short-term decision-making is *opportunity cost*. This is an economic term that represents the benefit forgone in choosing one option in preference to the next best option. It can be described as a *differential profit*.

To see how relevant costs are used, we will examine a number of short-term decisions common to many businesses, starting with the assessment of whether to drop a product.

Example 13.1: the shut-down decision

Flapjack Ltd makes three products with costs and revenues as shown in Table 13.1. Fixed costs are absorbed on the basis of units produced.

The managers are considering shutting down the production of product Z which is making a loss, and they are also considering whether product Y is worth producing as it is only breaking even. In effect the managers are facing three choices: drop product Z; drop product Z and product Y; do nothing. It is important to realize that

Table 13.1 *Flapjack Ltd: costs of and revenues from product range*

	X	Y	Z	Total
Sales (units)	5,000	2,000	3,000	10,000
	£	£	£	£
Sales Revenue	55,000	18,000	21,000	94,000
Variable Costs	(20,000)	(6,000)	(6,000)	(32,000)
Fixed Costs	(30,000)	(12,000)	(18,000)	(60,000)
Net Profit/(Loss)	5,000	0	(3,000)	2,000

Table 13.2 *Options before Flapjack management*

	Do Nothing	Drop Z	Drop Z and Y
Sales (units)	10,000	7,000	5,000
	£	£	£
Sales Revenue	94,000	73,000	55,000
Variable Costs	(32,000)	(26,000)	(20,000)
Fixed Costs	(60,000)	(60,000)	(60,000)
Net Profit/(Loss)	2,000	(13,000)	(25,000)

in all decisions, doing nothing is always an option, and by comparing the other choices against this option we can produce a series of differential cash flows (see Table 13.2).

The 'do nothing' option is the total column from Table 13.1. However, the 'drop Z' option adds the cash flows from the sales revenue and variable costs of X and Y and the fixed costs of £60,000. Under this option there are fewer units to bear the fixed costs and this results in a net loss to the company of £13,000. The difference between doing nothing and dropping product Z is £15,000. This is made up as follows:

	£
Cash inflows forgone (revenue from Z)	21,000
Less:	
Cash outflows avoided (variable costs of Z)	6,000
Differential revenue loss	15,000

The final option, to drop both Z and Y, compounds the problem and the differential revenue loss becomes £27,000 comprising:

	£
Cash inflows forgone (revenue from Y and Z)	39,000
Less:	
Cash outflows avoided (variable costs of Y and Z)	12,000
Differential revenue loss	27,000

Table 13.3 *Contributions of Flapjack products*

	X	Y	Z	Total
Sales (units)	5,000	2,000	3,000	10,000
	£	£	£	£
Sales Revenue	55,000	18,000	21,000	94,000
Variable Costs	(20,000)	(6,000)	(6,000)	(32,000)
Contribution	35,000	12,000	15,000	62,000
Fixed Costs				(60,000)
Net Profit				2,000

The feature of this analysis is that since the fixed costs are incurred anyway, they are not relevant to this short-term decision. It is better, therefore, to ignore fixed costs altogether and concentrate on the contribution of each product (see Table 13.3).

From this contribution statement we can see that it is worth £15,000 to the firm to keep producing Z. In other words, the opportunity cost of producing Z is £15,000. The opportunity cost of producing Y is £12,000 which is lower than the opportunity cost of Z. So if the managers were to find an alternative use for the factory space occupied by Y, that alternative use would have to contribute more than £12,000 for it to be feasible.

The spreadsheet solution

Set up your control and input sections as shown in Spreadsheet Solutions 13.1 and 13.2. We can now construct the output section to measure the costs and revenues of X, Y and Z. We can also measure the total differential costs and revenues under the three options (see Spreadsheet Solutions 13.3 and 13.4).

The 'Do Nothing' column (K) represents the current state, with the other options simply calculated by inserting references to the relevant columns under products X, Y or Z. Note that fixed costs under each option are given by the cell reference for fixed costs in the input section.

Spreadsheet Solutions 13.5 and 13.6 give the alternative approach discussed above which concentrates on contribution. It is clear from the information in this output section that in the short term provided a product is covering its variable costs it should be produced.

Joint product decisions

The costing of joint products has been dealt with in Chapter 7. Our concern now is with a typical situation involving a manufacturing process: there may be a number of stages of the process at which the product can be sold. Generally the greater the amount of subsequent refinement, the higher the eventual sales value but of course

Spreadsheet solution 13.1 Control section

	A	B
1	Spreadsheet Solution 13-1: Control Section	
2		
3	Example 13.1	
4		
5	This spreadsheet models the alteratives for dropping a segment.	
6		
7		
8		
9		
10	Location Table	Range
11	--------------	-----
12		
13	Input Section	INPUT
14	Output Section	OUTPUT

Spreadsheet solution 13.2 Input section

	C	D	E	F
20	Spreadsheet Solution 13-2: Input Section			
21				
22		X	Y	Z
23	Sales (Units)	5,000	2,000	3,000
24				
25	Selling Price	11	9	7
26	Variable Costs	4	3	2
27				
28	Total Fixed Costs	60,000		

Spreadsheet solution 13.3 Output section

	G	H	I	J	K	L	M
29	Spreadsheet Solution 13-3: Output Section						
30							
31		X	Y	Z	Do Nothing	Drop Z	Drop Z & Y
32	Sales (Units)	5,000	2,000	3,000	10,000	7,000	5,000
33							
34	Sales Revenue	55,000	18,000	21,000	94,000	73,000	55,000
35							
36	Variable Costs	(20,000)	(6,000)	(6,000)	(32,000)	(26,000)	(20,000)
37	Fixed Costs	(30,000)	(12,000)	(18,000)	(60,000)	(60,000)	(60,000)
38		----------------	----------------	----------------	----------------	----------------	----------------
39	Net Profit	5,000	0	(3,000)	2,000	(13,000)	(25,000)

Spreadsheet solution 13.4   Output section

	G	H	I	J	K	L	M
29	Spreadsheet Solution 13-4: Output Section						
30							
31		X	Y	Z	Do Nothing	Drop Z	Drop Z & Y
32	Sales (Units)	+D23	+E23	+F23	@SUM(H32..J32)	+H32+I32	+H32
33							
34	Sales Revenue	+D23*D25	+E23*E25	+F23*F25	@SUM(H34..J34)	+H34+I34	+H34
35							
36	Variable Costs	-D23*D26	-E23*E26	-F23*F26	@SUM(H36..J36)	+H36+I36	+H36
37	Fixed Costs	(+H32/$K$32)*$K$37	(+I32/$K$32)*$K$37	(+J32/$K$32)*$K$37	-D28	-D28	-D28
38							
39	Net Profit	@SUM(H34..H37)	@SUM(I34..I37)	@SUM(J34..J37)	@SUM(K34..K37)	@SUM(L34..L37)	@SUM(M34..M37)

Spreadsheet solution 13.5   New output section

	G	H	I	J	K
29	Spreadsheet Solution 13-5: New Output Section				
30					
31		X	Y	Z	Total
32	Sales (Units)	5,000	2,000	3,000	10,000
33					
34	Sales Revenue	55,000	18,000	21,000	94,000
35					
36	Variable Costs	(20,000)	(6,000)	(6,000)	(32,000)
37		------------------	------------------	------------------	------------------
38	Contribution	35,000	12,000	15,000	62,000
39					
40	Fixed Costs				(60,000)
41					------------------
42	Net Profit				2,000

Spreadsheet solution 13.6   New output section

	G	H	I	J	K
29	Spreadsheet Solution 13-6: New Output Section				
30					
31		X	Y	Z	Total
32	Sales (Units)	+D23	+E23	+F23	@SUM(H32..J32)
33					
34	Sales Revenue	+D23*D25	+E23*E25	+F23*F25	@SUM(H34..J34)
35					
36	Variable Costs	-D23*D26	-E23*E26	-F23*F26	@SUM(H36..J36)
37		------------------	------------------	------------------	------------------------------
38	Contribution	+H34+H36	+I34+I36	+J34+J36	+K34+K36
39					
40	Fixed Costs				-D28
41					------------------------------
42	Net Profit				+K38+K40

the more additional costs are incurred. The decision which managers must make is whether to process the product further or whether to sell it at an intermediate stage.

Example 13.2

A firm produces two products A and B from a single process. To produce a whole batch costs £4000 which results in 300 units of A and 400 units of B. In their current form A and B sell for £10 and £7, respectively, but they could be processed further to sell for £22 and £14. However, this would result in additional processing costs of £6 and £8. What should the managers do?

To solve the problem we will use the same methodology as deployed in Example

Table 13.4   *Additional processing decision*

	Product A	Product B
Production (units)	300	400
Intermediate Sales Value*	£3,000	£2,800
Potential Sales Value	£6,600	£5,600
Costs of Further Processing	1,800	3,200
	4,800	2,400
Differential Cash Flow	1,800	(400)

*Before additional costs are incurred.

11.1 above, namely the preparation of a statement that produces differential cash flows. The calculation is shown in Table 13.4. The joint costs of production (up to the intermediate stage) are not relevant. Calculation shows that it is better further to process product A, whereas product B should be sold at its intermediate stage.

A single scarce resource: limiting factor analysis

The above short-term decisions are made under the assumption that the firm can obtain additional factors of production as required. A feature of the short term is making do with what is available. Firms often face a temporary market shortage of supplies of certain raw materials or components; sometimes it is skilled labour which is in short supply. In the medium term, extra machinery or a new production process may take time to acquire and to bring on-line.

A resource is only scarce if it has a positive opportunity cost: in other words, extra availability would generate cash flows over and above the acquisition costs. A limited amount of manpower does not necessarily imply that labour is scarce. Restructuring of working practices could reduce the amount of idle time or the workforce could be better utilized producing more profitable goods.

Example 13.3

A company produces four products with cost and other details, shown in Table 13.5, which ignore any fixed or non-relevant costs. It would appear from the evidence that the company should first produce product F, which has the highest contribution. This should be produced until demand is satisfied, at which point the company should produce G, then H, then E.

Let us assume that in the short term materials are readily obtainable, but labour is limited to 120,000 hours. Applying the above rationale of concentrating on the product with the highest contribution per unit would produce the product mix shown in Table 13.6. The labour runs out before the demand on product G is satisfied. No units of

Table 13.5 *Calculation of contribution per product*

Product	E £	F £	G £	H £
Selling Price	470	350	540	400
Less:				
Labour	300	150	240	180
Materials	120	90	200	125
Contribution per Unit	50	110	100	95
Labour Hours Used	100	50	80	60
Maximum Demand	1,000	800	600	1,100

Table 13.6 *Total contribution based on contribution per unit*

Product	Cont/Unit	Units	Labour Hours	Total Contrib. £
F	110	800	40,000	88,000
G	100	600	48,000	60,000
H	95	533	3,200	50,667
E	50	—	—	—
Total			120,000	£198,667

Table 13.7 *Total contribution based on contribution per labour hour*

Product	Contribution per Labour Hour	Labour Used (Hours)	Units	Contribution (Total)
F	2.20	40,000	800	88,000
H	1.58	66,000	1,100	104,000
G	1.25	14,000	175	17,500
E	0.50	—	—	—
Totals		120,000		£210,000

E are produced. The total contribution is £198,667. However, is this making the best use of the scarce resource of labour?

Instead of concentrating on contribution per unit, we calculate the contribution per labour hour in order to produce a production plan that uses labour most efficiently (Table 13.7). So with the same amount of labour and the same demand constraints we are able to increase the contribution by £11,333. This approach is known as *limiting factor analysis*.

The spreadsheet solution

Whereas limiting factor analysis is theoretically straightforward, to use the spreadsheet to perform the algorithms involved requires the use of nested @IF statements combined with a fairly complex model structure.

The control and input sections for Example 13.3 appear in Spreadsheet Solutions 13.7 and 13.8. The input section records details of the labour and materials costs per unit, the maximum labour hours and, for each product, the selling prices, amounts of labour and materials usage and maximum demand.

The output section, the solution to the problem, is shown in Spreadsheet Solutions 13.9 and 13.10. Columns K—Q replicate the data in the input section using absolute cell references. This results in the calculation of the contribution per labour hour given in the range R38..R41, which has been given a range name 'cont'. Column T calculates the labour hours which would be used if the maximum demand for each product were to be met.

Column U produces the cumulative total of hours required to produce the maximum number of units demanded for each product, that is, without regard for the limited amount of labour hours available. This cumulative figure is used in Column V which

Spreadsheet solution 13.7   Control section

	A	B	C	D	E
1	Spreadsheet Solution 13-7: Control Section				
2					
3	Example 13.3				
4					
5	This spreadsheet models a situation of a single limiting factor.				
6					
7	The aim is to maximize the contribution made given just one				
8	constraint.				
9					
10	Location Table		Range		
11	--------------		-----		
12	Input Section		INPUT		
13	Output Section		OUTPUT		
14	Macro Section		MACRO		

Spreadsheet solution 13.8   Input section

	F		G	H	I	J
18	Spreadsheet Solution 13-8: Input Section					
19						
20	Labour Cost Per Hour		3			
21	Material Cost Per Unit		1			
22	Maximum Labour Hours		120,000			
23						
24			Selling	Materials	Labour	Maximum
25	Product		Price	Usage	Hours	Demand
26		E	470	120	100	1,000
27		F	350	90	50	800
28		G	540	200	80	600
29		H	400	125	60	1,100

Spreadsheet solution 13.9 Output section

Spreadsheet Solution 13-9: Output Section

	Selling Price	Labour Cost	Materials Cost	Contribution per unit	Labour Hours	Maximum Demand	Contribution/Labour Hour	Rank	Hours Used	Cumulative Hours Used	Optimal Usage	Production Plan	Contribution
F	350	150	90	110	50	800	2.20	1	40,000	40,000	40,000	800	88,000
H	400	180	125	95	60	1,100	1.58	2	66,000	106,000	66,000	1,100	104,500
G	540	240	200	100	80	600	1.25	3	48,000	154,000	14,000	175	17,500
E	470	300	120	50	100	1,000	0.50	4	100,000	254,000	0	0	0
											120,000		210,000

Spreadsheet solution 13.10 Output section

Spreadsheet Solution 13-10: Output Section

	Selling Price	Labour Cost	Materials Cost	Contribution per unit	Labour Hours	Maximum Demand	Contribution/Labour Hour	Rank	Hours Used	Cumulative Hours Used
F	+$G$27	+$G$20*P38	+$G$21*$H$27	+L38-M38-N38	+$I$27	+$J$27	+O38/P38		+P38*Q38	+T38
H	+$G$29	+$G$20*P39	+$G$21*$H$29	+L39-M39-N39	+$I$29	+$J$29	+O39/P39		+P39*Q39	+T39+U38
G	+$G$28	+$G$20*P40	+$G$21*$H$28	+L40-M40-N40	+$I$28	+$J$28	+O40/P40		+P40*Q40	+T40+U39
E	+$G$26	+$G$20*P41	+$G$21*$H$26	+L41-M41-N41	+$I$26	+$J$26	+O41/P41		+P41*Q41	+T41+U40

	Optimal Usage	Production Plan	Contribution
F	@IF((+$G$22-U37)>0,@IF((+U38<$G$22,+$G$22,+T38,(+$G$22-U37)),0)	+V38/P38	+W38*O38
H	@IF((+$G$22-U38)>0,@IF((+U39<$G$22,+$G$22,+T39,(+$G$22-U38)),0)	+V39/P39	+W39*O39
G	@IF((+$G$22-U39)>0,@IF((+U40<$G$22,+$G$22,+T40,(+$G$22-U39)),0)	+V40/P40	+W40*O40
E	@IF((+$G$22-U40)>0,@IF((+U41<$G$22,+$G$22,+T41,(+$G$22-U40)),0)	+V41/P41	+W41*O41
	@SUM(V38..V41)		@SUM(X38..X41)

determines the optimal usage for the limited hours available. Note that at this stage we have not sorted the data into descending order of contribution per limiting factor; this will be done once we have completed the structure of the output section.

Next in column V we need to construct a nested @**IF** statement for each product, which compares the cumulative labour hours used with the maximum available. For the first product in the range, the @**IF** statement in cell V38 is:

$$\langle @IF((+\$G\$22-U37)>0,@IF(+U38<\$G\$22,+T38,(+\$G\$22-U37)),0)\rangle$$

Note that the condition $(\$G\$22-U37)>0$ is a little artificial since there is no value in cell U37, but we have constructed the formula like this to allow it to be copied for the other three rows in column V.

Let us try to explain this complicated formula. The first condition simply tests whether the total number of hours available less the cumulative hours brought forward from the row above is greater than zero (remember that, in the first row, the cell reference U37 is a contrivance). If the condition is true, the result depends on the outcome of the inner @**IF** statement; if it is not true, the answer is zero. The inner @**IF** statement tests whether the cumulative hours required for this and the product(s) above are less than the total available hours. If this condition holds, the answer is the total number of hours required to produce the maximum number of units of that product; if it is not true, the answer is the total available hours less the cumulative hours from the row above.

Now, this explanation is very long-winded and at this stage may appear more confusing than enlightening, but let us progress to the next stage when the picture will become clearer.

To determine the optimal production plan we need to sort the data into a ranking based on contribution per labour hour and calculate the total contribution. This is done by first naming that part of the output range containing all the formulae, that is, K38..R41. This is given the range name 'block'. To sort the 'block' into descending 'cont' order we need to type:

$$\langle /\text{Data, Sort, } \textbf{D}\text{ata Range, } \textbf{block}, [\text{Enter}], \text{Primary Key, } \textbf{cont}, \textbf{D}, [\text{Enter}], \text{Go}\rangle$$

Column W calculates the number of units of each product to be produced under the optimal plan by dividing the total number of hours allocated to that product by the number of hours required for each unit.

Column X calculates the resulting contribution per product under this plan, by multiplying the contribution per unit by the number of units in the relevant row in column W.

In order to answer the 'What if?' questions below, the data sort must be performed each time.

'What if?' questions

1. Product F currently requires 50 labour hours, but a new production process increases this to 70 labour hours. What is the new production plan and the total contribution?

2. After recent pay negotiations, the rate per labour hour increases to £3.50. What is the new production plan and the total contribution?

'What if?' solutions

1. The new production plan is: H, 1100 units; G, 600 units; F, 86 units; and no units of E. This gives a total contribution of £168,786.

2. The new production plan is: F, 800 units; H, 1100 units; and G, 175 units. None of E is produced. This gives a total contribution of £150,000.

To avoid unnecessary keystrokes, you may wish to create a macro such as that shown in Spreadsheet Solution 13.11. You can see that the macro (cell AA47) only contains the keystrokes required for the Data Sort with the tilde '~' used for the [Enter] key. Notice the use of the range names 'block' and 'cont' for the sort range and primary key, respectively. The Appendix to this chapter (see page 234) gives more information about creating and using macros.

Spreadsheet solution 13.11 Macro section

	Y	Z	AA	AB	AC
45	Spreadsheet Solution 13-11: Macro Section				
46					
47	SORT MACRO /M		/dsdblock ~ pcont ~ d ~ g		

Many scarce resources: linear programming

Given more than one scarce resource, limiting factor analysis is not appropriate except in the rare cases where the coefficient ranking is the same for both resources. To obtain the optimal solution we therefore must turn to a technique called *linear programming*.

The mathematics of linear programming is similar to matrix manipulation and students of management accounting were often taught a manual method of solution called the *simplex method*. This was a long-winded algorithm that was prone to computational error. Its complexity meant that the topic was only covered at more advanced stages of study.

Now, however, the most up-to-date spreadsheet packages contain the functions necessary for matrix manipulation and optimization. Some use familiar linear programming terminology in the appropriate sub-menu. One such package is Quattro-Pro. Other popular spreadsheets, such as Lotus 1−2−3, have add-ins which perform linear programming routines, for example, What's Best.

This makes the handling of linear programming much more accessible to the majority of students who may not feel comfortable with the apparent complexity of the simplex approach. It now seems likely that in the near future the topic of linear programming will move into earlier parts of the accounting syllabus. For this reason we give some coverage of the topic below.

If your spreadsheet package cannot perform optimization then the solution can be produced graphically or using simultaneous equations. These are illustrated first. The example is then extended to cover optimization using the spreadsheet.

Two products with scarce resources

We can use a similar approach to solve problems involving two products in situations where more than one resource is scarce.

Example 13.4

A company has two products, X and Y, that contribute £40 and £44, respectively, per unit to profit after deduction of the variable costs. Each product requires three resources (materials, labour and machine time), all of which are limited. Product X requires 16 units of material, 12 hours of labour and 15 hours of machine time. Product Y requires 8 units of material, 16 hours of labour and 20 hours of machine time. In the short term 3000 units of material, 5000 labour hours and 6000 hours of machine time are available.

Formulating the problem

The first stage is to formulate the problem as a linear programme, commencing with stating the *objective function*. Linear programming assumes that you wish to maximize or to minimize an expression. This expression must be linear since the technique does not work for curvilinear expressions.

We wish to maximize the total contribution of the combined sales of products X and Y:

Maximize $40X + 44Y$

where X is the number of units of product X made and sold, and Y is the number of units of product Y made and sold.

The second step is to state the constraints. We know that it takes 16 units of material to produce one unit of X and 8 units of material for one unit of Y. There are 3000 units of material available. So we can express this algebraically as:

Material $\quad 16X + 8Y \leq 3000$

We produce the same expressions for all the constraints, and the entire linear programme is produced below:

Maximize $40X + 44Y$

subject to:

Material	$16X + 8Y \leq 3000$
Labour	$12X + 16Y \leq 5000$
Machine	$15X + 20Y \leq 6000$

We can now begin to solve the problem either graphically or by the use of simultaneous equations.

Graphical solution

This method of solution requires the constraints to be graphed. This produces a number of intersecting lines. This may be done using the spreadsheet or by drawing the graph manually. The result is given in Figure 13.1.

Once the constraints are graphed we now need to find the combination of X and Y that will maximize the contribution. This involves drawing an *isoprofit* line. This is a line which produces the same profit (or contribution) at any combination of X and Y along its length.

For example, at the extremes a profit of £10,560 would result from either 240 units of Y (10,560/44) or 264 units of X (10,560/40). This gives us one point on each axis:

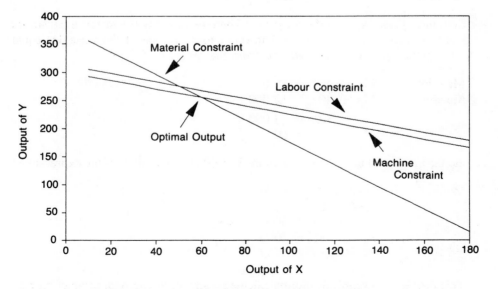

Figure 13.1   Graphical solution to Example 13.4

$X = 0, Y = 240$
$Y = 0, X = 264$

By joining these points we produce the isoprofit line for £10,560 and we can use a ruler to find a line parallel with the isoprofit line which takes us to the furthest extent of the feasible region (moving away from the origin until we exceed one or more of our constraints).

We find that we touch the corner of the intersection of the constraint for material and machine time. The coordinates of this point on the X and Y axes are $X = 60$ and $Y = 255$. Substituting these values into the objective function gives the profit at this point as:

$$40(60) + 44(255) = £13,620$$

Simultaneous equation solution

Another method is to use simultaneous equations to produce the values at the point of intersection of the constraints. This involves a process of trial and error, unless the relevant constraints are known. Often this method is used in conjunction with the graphical method, which can quickly identify the relevant constraints but which can be imprecise as to the exact position of optimization.

We know the constraints involved are:

Material	$16X + 8Y \leq 3000$
Machine	$15X + 20Y \leq 6000$

We first make these expressions equalities. Then we multiply the material constraint by 5 and the machine constraint by 2 in order to make one of the variables equal in both expressions. Now subtract one from the other:

Material	$80X + 40Y = 15,000$
Machine	$30X + 40Y = 12,000$
	$50X = 3,000$
	$X = 60$

To find the number of units of Y, substitute $X = 60$ in one or other of the expressions:

Material	$16(60) + 8Y = 3000$
	$960 + 8Y = 3000$
	$8Y = 3000 - 960$
	$8Y = 2040$
	$Y = 255$

This proves the graphical solution calculated above; the optimal production plan produces 60 units of X and 255 units of Y.

Dual prices

One attribute of linear programming is that it can produce other information that is useful to managers in the short term. For example, linear programming can produce a *dual price* for each of the constraints which is a measure of the maximum price to be paid for an additional extra unit of the scarce resource. This is calculated using *marginal rates of substitution*.

For example, it may be possible to run the machine for an extra hour at an additional cost, but what is the maximum that we should pay for the extra hour? Holding the material constraint constant and increasing the machine constraint by one to 6001 hours would shift the machine constraint very slightly and produce an output plan of 59.96X and 255.08Y. You can show this by reworking the simultaneous equations above. This produces a new objective function value of £13,621.92, an increase of £1.92. In other words, one extra hour of machine time would produce £1.92 more profit, therefore it is worth paying up to £1.91 for one more hour of machine time.

Put another way, we have reduced the output of X by 0.04 and increased the output of Y by 0.08. The effect on contribution is therefore:

Number less X × contribution per unit 0.04 × 40 = (1.60)
Number more Y × contribution per unit 0.08 × 44 = 3.52
                                                    1.92

We can repeat the exercise for the material constraint. The new output plan is for 60.1X and 254.925Y:

Number more X × contribution per unit 0.10 × 40 = 4.00
Number less Y × contribution per unit 0.075 × 44 = (3.30)
                                                     0.70

An extra unit of material is worth £0.70.

Of course, in practice these units would be ordered in larger quantities and the number of X and Y produced would be in whole numbers at least, but it is still useful to know the dual price. The dual price is sometimes called the *shadow price* or *opportunity cost*.

Linear programming using spreadsheets

This section presents a general guide to using your spreadsheet to perform linear programming. For exact instructions, consult your spreadsheet 'User's Guide' or its equivalent or the 'Help Menus' which are often very comprehensive. In the latter case the [Print Screen] key is useful for producing hard copy of the information on screen.

Use a similar presentation for the formulated linear program on the screen as on paper. However, head the appropriate number of columns with labels to indicate the variables used. Note that it is not possible to put in 44X + 40Y, but only the coefficients 44 and 40.

Use the extreme left-hand column for narrative explanations such as objective function, materials constraint, and so on. Normally the constraint coefficients must appear in one block, with the rows representing each constraint and a separate column for each variable.

The inequality relations ($< =$, $> =$) should be placed in the column adjacent to the block containing the constraint coefficients in separate cells. Place the right-hand values in the cells in the column to the right.

The linear program is therefore input by dividing it into its constituent elements using separate cells and a matrix layout.

Turning to the 'optimization' routine, you will need to specify the ranges containing these elements, as well as output ranges which will give the value of the objective function, the solution variables and the dual prices. You will also have to specify whether the problem requires a maximization or minimization solution.

It may be possible to specify additional dual values which enable the sensitivity of the solution to be tested, that is, how far the variables are allowed to vary before the optimal solution is no longer feasible. Prompt messages on the input lines often present brief explanations of the menu choices.

The beauty of using the spreadsheet model is that the output values can be used in further manipulations, for example to present a profit and loss account.

More than two products with scarce resources

The situation can be further complicated where scarce resources affect the production of more than two products.

Example 13.5

The information shown in Table 13.8 has been obtained for the four products of a firm. In addition, the following prices are known:

Price of Limited Material:	£0.50 per unit
Labour (Skilled):	£6.50 per hour
Labour (Unskilled):	£2.50 per hour

Fixed costs are expected to total £10,000. There are 50,000 units of the limited material in stock and no supplies are arriving in the foreseeable future. In the short term, skilled labour is limited to 4650 hours and unskilled labour to 4930 hours.

Given the current situation, how many units of each product should the firm produce? There is a feeling among the managers that the company should concentrate on production of the most profitable products. Produce a profit and loss account to reflect this product mix using the absorption costing method of dealing with fixed costs.

Additional labour hours may be obtained providing the firm is willing to pay a

Table 13.8 *Per-unit costs of and revenues from four products*

	A	B	C	D
		Product Name		
Variable Costs				
Limited Material	5.50	4.50	7.50	3.50
Unlimited Material	3.40	5.60	3.60	2.50
Labour (Skilled)	6.50	9.75	6.50	13.00
Labour (Unskilled)	5.00	3.75	2.50	5.00
Variable Overheads	4.60	6.40	4.90	6.00
Total Variable Cost	25.00	30.00	25.00	30.00
Selling Price	32.00	34.00	31.00	37.00
Contribution per Unit	7.00	4.00	6.00	7.00
Fixed Costs (15% VC)	3.75	4.50	3.75	4.50
Profit/Loss per Unit	3.25	(0.50)	2.25	2.50

rate of 'time and a half'. More material may be acquired from a 'black market' supply at 25p a unit. The managers are not sure whether the firm should take advantage of either of these opportunities.

The spreadsheet solution

First formulate the linear program using separate cells as stated. Use narratives and formulae to produce constraint coefficients. Your input will look something like this:

	A	B	C	D		
Objective Function	7	4	6	7		
Constraints						
Material	11	9	15	7	< =	50000
Labour (Skilled)	1	1.5	1	2	< =	4650
Labour (Unskilled)	2	1.5	1	2	< =	4930

Specify the appropriate ranges for your optimization routine and type in labels near to the ranges that will accommodate the output. Try to be as logical with the layout as possible; for example, use the column headings already available. Your output solution should be as follows:

	A	B	C	D
Variable Solution	280	0	2750	810

Objective Function Value   24130

Dual Prices	
Material	0.22
Labour (Skilled)	0.87
Labour (Unskilled)	1.87

From the dual prices it is clear that neither of the opportunities to increase capacity is worthwhile in the short term.

Using cell references you can produce a profit and loss account in another output range to the variable solution row, this time using the preferred marginal costing method to deal with fixed costs:

Profit and Loss Account

	A	B	C	D	Total
Turnover	8,960	0	85,250	29,970	124,180
Limited Material	1,540	0	20,625	2,835	25,000
Unlimited Material	952	0	9,900	2,025	12,877
Labour (Skilled)	1,820	0	17,875	10,530	30,225
Labour (Unskilled)	1,400	0	6,875	4,050	12,325
Variable Overhead	1,288	0	13,475	4,860	19,623
	1,960	0	16,500	5,670	24,130
Less Fixed Costs					10,000
Net Profit					14,130

It would appear that the managers' intuitive solution is not optimal since the best use of the limited resources is to produce 2750 of C, 810 of D and 280 of A. This adequately covers fixed costs, producing a net profit of £14,130.

Conclusion

From time to time management will face shortages of some vital component in the production process, be it labour or raw materials or production facilities. In these situations it is important that the correct decisions are taken to make the most of limited resources. This is best done by focusing on relevant costs and in particular on the contribution to fixed costs provided by different products.

In more complex situations, with many products and more than one scarce resource, problem-solving naturally becomes more difficult. However, the use of spreadsheet technology can reduce that difficulty, allowing the problem to be modelled and the best solution to be found very quickly.

Appendix: Creating spreadsheet macros

Spreadsheets are mainly used in the work environment where users are often asked to execute repetitive tasks which are 'interactive'. This means that the user has to sit at the PC and repeat a number of keystrokes. A common example is the printing out of a large number of ranges one after the other. This is time-consuming and boring.

Consequently, software developers have included a facility that enables users to batch together commonly used sequences of keystrokes that can be activated using a single key.

This facility has been extended to include a programming mode with special programming commands. Our requirements are not so complex but we have introduced simple macros to give you a flavour of what can be achieved.

To write a macro is as simple as operating the spreadsheet. Some packages ask you to specify a *learn range* which will store the keystrokes as a label as you perform the functions. If you do not have this learn capability then you must type in the macro label from memory. The best course of action is to keep a written record of the keystrokes.

As the macro executes keystrokes, certain keys need to be indicated by special characters. The function keys are referred to by the function they perform and the cursor movement keys are written out longhand and enclosed in braces. Some examples are given below:

[Enter]

[F2]	{EDIT}
[F3]	{NAME}
[F4]	{ABS}
[F5]	{GOTO}
To move up	{UP}
To move down	{DOWN}
To move right	{RIGHT}
To move left	{LEFT}
To move up four cells	{UP 4}
To move screen left	{BIGLEFT}

The stored macro is usually in a named range which commences with '\' and is followed by a single letter, for instance '\S'. When you want to perform the macro you simply hold down the [Alt] key and press [S].

A macro stops when it comes to a blank cell or if an error has occurred. You can manually stop a macro by pressing [Ctrl] and [Break] while the macro is running.

Exercises

Question 13.1

(a) The managing director of your organization, a manufacturer of garden furniture, disagrees with you over the need for a costing system within your organization. He says that the only requirement for the classification of costs is by the financial accountant into cost of sales, distribution cost and administration expense for the published accounts, and that anything beyond that is unnecessary.

Write a report to the managing director stating why you believe he is wrong and specifying the following:
(i)   The manner in which he has classified cost in his statement.
(ii) Four alternative classifications of cost and the ways in which they can assist management decision-making, planning and control.

(b) A one-off order for 3000 garden chairs has been received from an overseas customer for the coming period. Your budgeted production for the period is for 16,000 chairs, which represents 80% of your capacity to manufacture garden chairs. Budgeted data for the period are as follows.

	£	£
Sales		672,000
Materials	192,000	
Labour	196,000	
Overheads	200,000	
		588,000
Net profit		84,000

You ascertain that £20,000 of labour and 20% of overheads are fixed in nature and all the other costs are variable.

Prepare a cost statement to show whether the order should be accepted if the customer is prepared to pay:
(i)   £30 per chair;
(ii) £36 per chair.
Give reasons for your decisions.

(c) What other factors need to be taken into consideration before the order is accepted or rejected?

No answer provided   *(AAT)*

Question 13.2

A firm produces three products, and for the coming year its budget shows the following:

	Total	Product A	Product B	Product C
Sales	100,000	60,000	25,000	15,000
Direct material	42,000	23,000	10,000	9,000
Direct labour	20,000	10,000	8,000	2,000
Variable overhead	10,500	4,000	5,000	1,500
Fixed overhead	15,000	7,500	6,000	1,500
Total costs	87,500	44,500	29,000	14,000
Profit (loss)	12,500	15,500	(4,000)	(1,000)

Fixed overheads are absorbed on the basis of a percentage on direct labour.

It is suggested that product B should be eliminated and you are required to do the following.

(a) Re-present the above statement if product B is eliminated.

(b) Produce a break-even chart for the company for the coming year, showing the break-even point based upon:
  (i) the original budget;
  (ii) if product B were eliminated.

(c) Show by calculation the break-even point at the original budget level and the break-even point if product B is eliminated.

(d) Discuss the limitations that management should be aware of when using break-even charts.

(e) Explain the term 'margin of safety'.

No answer provided

Question 13.3

The management of Springer plc is considering next year's production and purchase budgets.

One of the components produced by the company, which is incorporated into another product before being sold, has a budgeted manufacturing cost as follows.

	£
Direct material	14
Direct labour (4 hours at £3 per hour)	12
Variable overhead (4 hours at £2 per hour)	8
Fixed overhead (4 hours at £5 per hour)	20
Total cost	54 per unit

Trigger plc has offered to supply the above component at a guaranteed price of £50 per unit.

(a) Considering cost criteria only, advise management whether the above component should be purchased from Trigger plc. Any calculations should be shown and assumptions made, or aspects which may require further investigation should be clearly stated.

(b) Explain how your advice would be affected by each of the two *separate* situations shown below.
  (i) As a result of recent government legislation, if Springer plc continues to manufacture this component the company will incur additional inspection and testing expenses of £56,000 per annum, which are not included in the above budgeted manufacturing costs.

(ii) Additional labour cannot be recruited and if the above component is not manufactured by Springer plc, the direct labour released will be employed in increasing the production of an existing product which is sold for £90 and which has a budgeted manufacturing cost as follows.

	£
Direct material	10
Direct labour (8 hours at £3 per hour)	24
Variable overhead (8 hours at £2 per hour)	16
Fixed overhead (8 hours at £5 per hour)	40
Total cost per unit	90

All calculations should be shown.

(c) The production director of Springer plc recently stated the following.

We must continue to manufacture the component as only one year ago we purchased some special grinding equipment to be used exclusively by this component. The equipment cost £100,000, it cannot be resold or used elsewhere and if we cease production of this component we will have to write off the written-down book value which is £80,000.

Draft a brief reply to the production director, commenting on his statement.

No answer provided *(AAT)*

Question 13.4

(a) George manufactures commemorative medals. The following data relates to 19X0.

	£
Selling price	50
Variable production cost	30
Variable selling cost	5
Contribution per medal	15
Fixed production cost	5
(based on annual sales of 20,000 medals)	
Fixed selling cost	1
(based on annual sales of 20,000 medals)	
Profit per medal	9

  (i) Calculate the level of production needed for George to break even.
 (ii) George is thinking of doubling his production. To do so, he will have to occupy additional premises at an annual rent of £120,000. What will be the new break-even point and the margin of safety?

(b) The following standard data are available regarding products Able and Baker.

		Product	
		Able	Baker
Direct materials per unit		£10	£30
Direct labour	Rate per hour		
Grinding	£5.0	7 hours	5 hours
Finishing	£7.5	15 hours	9 hours
Selling price per unit		£206.5	£168
Budgeted production		1200 units	600 units
Maximum sales for the period		1500 units	800 units

Notes:
1. No closing stocks are anticipated.
2. The skilled labour used for the grinding processes is highly specialized and in short supply, although there is sufficient to meet the budgeted production. However, it will not be possible to increase the supply for the budgeted period.

(i) Prepare a statement showing the contribution from each product based on the budgeted production.
(ii) Prepare a statement showing the total contribution that could be obtained if the best use was made of the skilled grinding labour.

Answer on page 301   *(ICSA)*

Question 13.5

Reynald Ltd is currently preparing its budget for the year ending 30 September 19X2. The company manufactures and sells three products, Beta, Delta and Gamma.
The unit selling price and cost structure of each product is budgeted as follows:

	Beta £	Delta £	Gamma £
Selling price	100	124	32
Variable costs:			
Labour	24	48	6
Materials	26	7	8
Overhead	10	5	6
	60	60	20
Contribution per unit	40	64	12

Direct labour rate is budgeted at £6 per hour, and fixed costs at £1,300,000 per annum. The company has a maximum production capacity of 228,000 direct labour hours.

A meeting of the board of directors has been convened to discuss the budget and to resolve the problem as to the quantity of each product which should be made and sold. The sales director presented the results of a recent market survey which reveals that market demand for the company's products will be as follows:

Product	Units
Beta	24,000
Delta	12,000
Gamma	60,000

The production director proposes that since Gamma only contributes £12 per unit, the product should no longer be produced, and the surplus capacity transferred to produce additional quantities of Beta and Delta. The sales director does not agree with the proposal. Gamma is considered necessary to complement the product range and to maintain customer goodwill. If Gamma is not offered, the sales director believes that sales of Beta and Delta will be seriously affected. After further discussion the board decided that a minimum of 10,000 units of each product should be produced. The remaining production capacity would then be allocated so as to achieve the maximum profit possible.

(a) Prepare a budget statement which clearly shows the maximum profit which could be achieved in the year ending 30 September 19X2.

(b) Alpha, a component used by Reynald Ltd, is incorporated into a number of its completed products. Currently, Alpha is purchased from a supplier at £2.50 per component and some 20,000 are used annually in production.

   The price of £2.50 is considered to be competitive and the supplier has maintained good quality and service for a number of years. The production engineering department at Reynald Ltd has submitted a proposal to manufacture Alpha internally. Variable cost per unit produced is estimated at £1.20 and the additional annual fixed cost that would be incurred if Alpha were manufactured is estimated at £20,800.

   (i) Determine whether Reynald Ltd should continue to purchase Alpha, or manufacture it, showing computations. Indicate the level of production required that would make Reynald decide in favour of manufacturing Alpha itself.

   (ii) What other financial, production and marketing factors would need to be considered before a decision is made?

(c) Explain what is meant by the 'limiting key factor'. Discuss the practical problems which are likely to arise with the limiting key factor approach to planning for maximum profit.

No answer provided   *(ICSA)*

14 Investment appraisal

AIMS OF CHAPTER

- to introduce the concept of investment appraisal;
- to explain the calculation of the weighted average cost of capital;
- to explain the concept of the time value of money;
- to examine the different techniques for evaluating the viability of proposed capital projects;
- to construct spreadsheet models to perform investment appraisal using the various techniques.

SPREADSHEET SKILLS ACQUIRED

- @NPV;
- @IRR;
- @AVG;
- @SLN.

Introduction

In addition to planning and controlling the ongoing day-to-day operations of the company, management also has to look to the future to consider whether major investment in long-term projects will be profitable. The cost of long-term projects is referred to as *capital* expenditure. These projects may relate to the development of a new product; expansion of existing production facilities; improvement of existing processes; or choosing among different options in any one of the above. It is critical that care is taken in the evaluation of proposed projects since these are likely to involve substantial cost and, once started, it may not be possible to abort them without incurring substantial additional costs.

There are several methods for the evaluation of the various available investment opportunities; these are generally referred to as *investment appraisal* methods. They vary in their degree of sophistication from the relatively crude *payback* method which calculates how quickly the capital cost will be recovered from future cash inflows, to the *discounted cash flow* methods which take account of the time value of money. However, each method attempts to measure the estimated returns from an investment against the initial capital cost. With this information management can then either compare different investment possibilities or decide whether to proceed with a single investment opportunity based on preset criteria.

In the case of the payback method the criterion will be in the form of a maximum number of years over which the capital cost of a project must be recovered; a project which fails to meet this cut-off point should not be undertaken.

For most investment appraisal methods, such preset criteria may be in the form of a required rate of return on investment; if a proposed investment fails to produce at least this level of return the company should not proceed with it.

The cost of capital

The required rate of return should be at least equal to the cost of the company's capital since it is this capital that will be financing the project. Generally companies will be financed from two main sources, debt and equity. *Debt* refers to the finance provided by third-party lenders such as debenture or loan stock-holders. *Equity* refers to the investment in the company by its owners, in the form of share capital and retained profits.

Each type of finance may contain different tranches with varying costs; for example, a company may have more than one class of loan stock, each with a different coupon rate of interest.

The ratio of debt to equity is known as the *gearing ratio*. A highly geared company has proportionately more of its finance provided in the form of loans than a low-geared company.

When calculating the rate of return required of new projects, account must be taken not only of the rates of return to be paid on the different sources of finance but also of their relative proportions. This is the calculation of the *weighted average cost of capital*.

Cost of debt capital

The cost of debt capital is calculated as follows:

$$\frac{\text{Nominal rate of interest}}{\text{Market value of debt}}$$

Note that the denominator is the *market* value, not the nominal value. This will reflect (inversely) current market rates of interest which would be relevant if the company had to go to the market to raise more of such funds.

One refinement which needs to be made is to reduce the cost of debt by the applicable corporation tax rate since the interest payable is an allowable expense for tax purposes. In other words, the company is not bearing the full cost of the interest: the tax authorities share the burden.

Cost of equity

The cost of equity (both ordinary share capital and retained profits) is given by:

$$\frac{\text{Current net dividend}}{\text{Current market price}} \text{ (of the shares)}$$

Example 14.1

Chanjoy Ltd has a mixture of debt and equity in its capital structure. It has £1,000,000 in £1 ordinary shares, £500,000 in retained profits and £500,000 in 15% loan stock. The current net dividend is 25p per ordinary share. The market value of the shares is £2.50 and the loan stock is quoted at £1.50. The current rate of corporation tax is 35%.

The weighted average cost of capital calculation is as follows:

$$\text{Ordinary shares} \qquad \frac{25\text{p}}{£2.50} = 10\%$$

$$\text{Loan stock} \qquad \frac{15\text{p}}{£1.50} = 10\%$$

Loan stock interest net of tax allowance:

$$10\% \times (1 - 0.35) = 6.5\%$$

Weighting the different types of capital:

$$\frac{\text{Equity value}}{\text{Total value}} \qquad \frac{2.5\text{m}}{2.5\text{m}+0.75\text{m}} \times 10\% = 7.69\%$$

$$\frac{\text{Loan value}}{\text{Total value}} \qquad \frac{0.75\text{m}}{2.5\text{m}+0.75\text{m}} \times 6.5\% = 1.50\%$$

Weighted average cost of capital = 9.19%, say 9%

To be acceptable proposed projects will have to produce rates of return in excess of this cut-off rate of return.

This basic calculation can be further developed so as to take into account expected future rates of growth in dividends but it is not considered here.

The time value of money

The time value of money is an important concept in finance. It stems from the fact that cash received later is worth less than cash received earlier because of the interest forgone.

Compounding

Consider whether you would prefer to receive £100 now or £100 in two years' time. Setting aside the prospect of immediate consumption, it is obvious that an amount receivable now is worth more than the same amount at some point in the future. Cash received now can be invested to earn interest which itself could be reinvested to earn interest.

How much extra would you need to be given to compensate for having to wait to get your hands on the money? Would an additional £10 be sufficient? Your decision would depend on prevailing interest rates. At 6% the interest on £100 invested for one year will be £6. If this interest is reinvested, also at 6%, the interest at the end of the second year will be £6.36, (£106 × 6%), giving a total of £112.36. So you would be better off if you chose the £100 receivable immediately (and invested it for two years) rather than £110 in two years' time.

Note that this has nothing at all to do with the effects of inflation. Even assuming no rise in general prices, as a rational investor you would not be indifferent to the timing of the receipt of cash. What is true for you as an individual is also true for businesses.

The process of earning interest on interest is known as *compounding*. The amount by which £1 can increase due to compound interest is given by:

$$(1 + r)^n$$

where r is the appropriate rate of interest, and n is the number of years of the investment.

Discounting

The reverse of compounding (discussed above) is *discounting*. The net present value approach takes the time value of money into account by discounting future cash flows to their present value using an appropriate interest rate. For businesses the appropriate rate would be the weighted average cost of capital. Businesses have to earn at least this amount if their net asset value and market value are to be maintained.

The discounting factor is given by:

$$\frac{1}{(1 + r)^n}$$

where r is again the appropriate rate of interest, and n is the number of years from now. Thus if the present rate of interest is 6%, the present value of £110 to be received in two years' time is:

$$\frac{£110}{(1 + 6\%)^2} = £97.90$$

Again this shows that you would be better off taking £100 now. Whereas if you had to choose between receiving £110 in two years' time and £97.90 now, you would be indifferent; the two are worth the same. Looking at it the other way, £97.90 invested now and earning 6% interest would grow over two years to £110.

Discounted cash flow methods

There are two basic types of investment appraisal technique which take into account the time value of money. These are the net present value and the internal rate of return methods.

Net present value

The net present value method of investment appraisal discounts the value of a project's cash flows using the company's cost of capital as the discount rate to arrive at a *net present value* (NPV).

If the NPV is positive then the project is acceptable: the project will cover its own costs, the cost of the initial investment and the interest which could have been earned on the capital. If the result is a negative NPV, the project is unacceptable.

Example 14.2

A company is looking at the possible purchase of a new machine which will improve operating efficiency by reducing running costs. There are two machines on the market which will do the job. Both machines cost £30,000, but they will have different patterns of cost savings.

Machine A is easy to set up but after the first year of running will require increasing amounts of maintenance which will reduce the total cost savings in later years. Machine B takes longer to set up to run efficiently but after a couple of years will be able to run with relatively little maintenance, so the bulk of its cost savings will occur in the later years. Both machines have an expected life of 5 years, after which time they will have to be scrapped. Their scrap value will only be sufficient to cover the cost of dismantling.

The company has estimated the cost savings after deduction of the additional maintenance charges for each machine as follows:

Year	Machine A	Machine B
1	16,000	2,500
2	10,000	2,500
3	6,000	10,000
4	4,000	15,000
5	2,000	15,000

Table 14.1 *Calculation of net present value for two alternative purchases*

Year	Machine A			Machine B		
	Cost Savings	Discount Factor	NPV	Cost Savings	Discount Factor	NPV
0	(30,000)	1.00	(30,000)	(30,000)	1.00	(30,000)
1	16,000	0.917	14,672	2,500	0.917	2,293
2	10,000	0.842	8,420	2,500	0.842	2,105
3	6,000	0.772	4,632	10,000	0.772	7,720
4	4,000	0.708	2,832	15,000	0.708	10,620
5	2,000	0.650	1,300	15,000	0.650	9,750
			1,856			2,488

The task is now to calculate the NPV of each alternative by discounting the associated cash flows at the company's weighted average cost of capital. This is done in Table 14.1.

Internal rate of return

The internal rate of return of a project is the discount rate required to produce a zero NPV, that is, the rate at which future cash inflows have to be discounted in order to equal the initial cash outflow. If the project yields an IRR in excess of the company's weighted average cost of capital it is acceptable. If the IRR is below the cost of capital then the project should be rejected.

The manual calculation of the IRR for a project can only be performed through a process of trial and error, using different interest rates to discount the cash flows until the correct one (the one which produces a zero NPV) is found. An indication of the internal rate of return can be obtained from the NPV calculations; if a positive NPV was obtained discounting the cash flows at the company's cost of capital then it follows that to reach a zero NPV the discount rate must be higher than that used in the NPV calculations.

Other appraisal methods

While the discounted cash flow techniques described above are considered superior to other, less sophisticated methods of investment appraisal, research has shown that these latter methods are popular with managers in practice.

The accounting rate of return

The accounting rate of return expresses the average annual accounting profit (or savings, in our case) as a percentage of the average cost of the project. Note that it is accounting profit *not* cash inflow which is the numerator. Any difference between cash inflow and accounting profit will arise from the application of the accruals concept, whereby revenues are matched against the expenses incurred in generating the revenues regardless of whether cash inflows or outflows occur in the period.

Thus to calculate the average annual accounting profit, the average annual cash inflow will have to be adjusted for any non-cash expenses such as depreciation. For project A the average annual cash inflow is £7600 (£38,000/5). The average annual depreciation charge (calculated by whatever method) is £6000 (£30,000/5). The average accounting profit is therefore £1600 (£7600 − £6000).

The next step is to calculate the average book value of the investment. Mathematically this could not be simpler; it is just the sum of the opening and closing book values divided by 2. In our case:

$$\frac{£30,000 + £0}{2} = £15,000$$

However, some students are confused by the addition of the final value (the scrap value); it would seem more natural to deduct this from the initial cost. But the point to remember is that the average book value of the project is that at its mid-life, that is, the value in the middle of the two extremes, the beginning and end values.

The accounting rate of return is then:

	Project A		Project B	
Accounting profit	£1600	= 10.7%	£3000	= 20%
Average investment	£15,000		£15,000	

Payback

This method of evaluating capital projects measures the length of time required for cash inflows to equal the initial capital outflow. For the cautious manager, with uncertainty increasing the further one looks to the future, the sooner the capital cost is covered the better. The payback method assumes that cash flows for a given year arise evenly over the course of that year.

In our example, project A's capital cost is covered by cash inflows after 2 years and 8 months (£16,000 + £10,000 + £6000 × 2/3); for project B payback occurs at the end of year 4 (£2500 + £2500 + £10,000 + £15,000).

The theoretical objections to this method are that no account is taken of the subsequent cash inflows once payback has been reached, and that there is no measure of the absolute benefits accruing to the company.

Nevertheless it is a popular method with practitioners, perhaps because it offers a 'quick and dirty' solution to dealing with uncertainty.

The spreadsheet solution

The control section for this example is given in Spreadsheet Solution 14.1. The input section of the spreadsheet should be set out so that the cash flows for the two projects are presented in columnar format. Additional data which will be needed to construct our model are the scrap value (currently zero) and the cost of capital (see Spreadsheet Solution 14.2).

Output sections 1 and 2, shown as Spreadsheet Solutions 14.3 to 14.6, concern the discounted cash flow techniques, NPV and IRR. You will be relieved to learn that, using a standard spreadsheet package, there is nothing easier than the calculation of NPV and IRR. Both are achieved using @ functions, @NPV and @IRR.

The @NPV function must be followed (in brackets), first by the discount rate to be used, then by the range of cash flows to be discounted. Since the initial outflow is assumed to take place at the present time, it is already expressed in present-value terms. It should not be discounted and so should be excluded from the range in brackets.

The initial cost should be deducted from the discounted cash inflows. The whole calculation can be performed in one formula, keyed into cell I40:

⟨ +E24+@NPV($E$35,AFLOW)⟩

The range name 'AFLOW' refers to the cash inflows for project A in the input section excluding the initial investment which is an outflow shown in cell E24. 'BFLOW' is the range name for project B's cash flows.

In output section 2, the @IRR function is used to calculate the IRR of each project.

Spreadsheet solution 14.1   Control section

	A	B	C
1	Spreadsheet Solution 14-1: Control Section		
2			
3	Example 14-2		
4			
5	A company has to choose between two mutually exclusive projects		
6	A and B. Both require the purchase of plant and machinery		
7	currently estimated to cost £30,000. Both projects will last		
8	for 5 years after which the plant and machinery will be worthless.		
9	The company's cost of capital is 9%.		
10			
11	SECTIONS	RANGE NAMES	
12	---	------------------------	
13	INPUT	INPUT	
14	OUTPUT:		
15	NPV	OUTPUT1	
16	IRR	OUTPUT2	
17	WHAT IF? NPV	OUTPUT3	
18	WHAT IF? IRR	OUTPUT4	
19	ACCOUNTING RATE OF RETURN	OUTPUT5	
20	PAYBACK	OUTPUT6	

Spreadsheet solution 14.2   Input section

		D	E	F
21	Spreadsheet Solution 14-2: Input Section			
22				
23	Year		Project A	Project B
24		0	(30,000)	(30,000)
25		1	16,000	2,500
26		2	10,000	2,500
27		3	6,000	10,000
28		4	4,000	15,000
29		5	2,000	15,000
30				
31	Life of Project		5	5
32				
33	End scrap value		0	0
34				
35	Cost of Capital		9%	

Spreadsheet solution 14.3   Output section 1

	G	H	I	J
36	Spreadsheet Solution 14-3: Output Section 1			
37				
38			Project A	Project B
39				
40	Net Present Value		1,862	2,495

Spreadsheet solution 14.4   Output section 1

	G	H	I	J
36	Spreadsheet Solution 14-4: Output Section 1			
37				
38			Project A	Project B
39				
40	Net Present Value		+E24+@NPV($E$35,AFLOW)	+F24+@NPV($E$35,BFLO\

Spreadsheet solution 14.5   Output section 2

	K	L	M	N	O
42	Spreadsheet Solution 14-5: Output Section 2				
43					
44				Project A	Project B
45					
46	Internal Rate of Return			12.4%	11.4%

Spreadsheet solution 14.6   Output section 2

	K	L	M	N	O
42	Spreadsheet Solution 14-6: Output Section 2				
43					
44				Project A	Project B
45					
46	Internal Rate of Return			@IRR($E$35,E24..E29)	@IRR($E$35,F24..F29)

The spreadsheet, of course, is much faster at performing the necessary calculations to find from a range of discount rates the one that produces a zero NPV; however, it first requires an estimate of the discount rate since IRR calculations can in some cases produce more than one solution. This estimate may only need to be a rough one. In our example, perhaps the current cost of capital would be a good guess. Furthermore the first amount in the range of cash flows must be negative. So for project A in our example the relevant formula, shown in cell N46, is:

⟨@IRR($E$35,E24..E29)⟩

Cell E35 contains the current cost of capital which we are using as a guess for IRR.

Sensitivity analysis

As stressed in previous chapters, the flexibility of the spreadsheet allows variables in a model to be changed and the impact of the changes to be immediately observed. One particular technique for which the spreadsheet is ideally suited is the solution of 'what if?' questions, where one variable is changed over a range of values. Output sections 3 and 4 illustrate this technique (see Spreadsheet Solutions 14.7 and 14.8).

The spreadsheet technique used for the solution of such questions is the data table. To construct the table we first need to produce a range of substitute values (P52..P62), which are the values assumed by the variable we are going to change. In output section 3 we are going to see the effect on the NPV calculations of using different discount rates. The column we create will represent the discount rates 5–15%. The quickest way to create this column is to use the ⟨/Data, Fill⟩ command.

The next step is to enter the cell references of the NPV calculations one column to the right of the substitute discount rates in the row above this column.

Now type the command: ⟨/Data, Table⟩. Select the 1-variable option (we will

Spreadsheet solution 14.7   Output range 3

	P	Q	R	S	T
48	Spreadsheet Solution 14-7: Output Range 3				
49					
50			Project A	Project B	
51			+I40	+J40	
52	5%		4,349	7,380	
53	6%		3,695	6,070	
54	7%		3,063	4,821	
55	8%		2,452	3,631	
56	9%		1,862	2,495	
57	10%		1,292	1,411	
58	11%		740	376	
59	12%		205	(613)	
60	13%		(312)	(1,558)	
61	14%		(813)	(2,462)	
62	15%		(1,299)	(3,327)	

Spreadsheet solution 14.8   Output range 4

	T	U	V	W	X
63	Spreadsheet Solution 14-8: Output Range 4				
64					
65			Project A		
66			+N46		
67		(5,000)	282.2%		
68		(10,000)	121.8%		
69		(15,000)	67.9%		
70		(20,000)	40.5%		
71		(25,000)	23.8%		
72		(30,000)	12.4%		
73		(35,000)	4.0%		
74		(40,000)	-2.4%		
75		(45,000)	-7.5%		
76		(50,000)	-11.7%		
77		(55,000)	-15.3%		

change only the discount rate). Now specify the block you want the table to fill, the row containing the formulae and the column containing the discount rates ⟨P51...S62⟩. Finally specify the input cell, E35, whose value will be substituted individually by the values in the column of discount rates. The table is created showing the NPV for the two projects under discount rates of 5−15%.

The same approach is used in output section 4 to see the effect on the IRR for project A of changes in the initial cost. The original estimate of the capital cost was £30,000, which becomes the input cell E24. If we vary this while keeping the subsequent inflows at the original values we can see how (as might be expected) the IRR declines as the initial outflow increases from £5000 to £55,000. The same sensitivity analysis can be performed for project B, but this will require a separate data table since, unlike the NPV data table of output section 4, the input cell is not common to both project A and B.

The fifth output section, shown in Spreadsheet Solutions 14.9 and 14.10, is designed to calculate the accounting rate of return. This requires us to estimate the average annual accounting profit. To do this we have to calculate the average annual cash inflows. This can be done using the @AVG function, with the range of inflows specified in brackets, in cells AA81 and AB81. From the average annual cash inflow we need to deduct the depreciation charge since this is a non-cash expense which is nevertheless taken into account when arriving at accounting profit.

We can easily calculate the annual depreciation charge using the @SLN function. In the brackets which follow @SLN we need to insert the cell references for the capital cost, the scrap value and the length of the life of the project. Note that each term within the brackets needs to be separated by a comma. Thus for project A, the formula in cell AA83 is ⟨@SLN(E24,E33,E31)⟩.

Note that most spreadsheets also include functions to calculate the depreciation charge using 'accelerated' depreciation methods. These commonly include the double declining balance:

Spreadsheet solution 14.9 Output range 5

	X	Y	Z	AA	AB
				Project A	Project B
78	Spreadsheet Solution 14-9: Output Range 5				
79					
80				Project A	Project B
81	Av. Annual Cash Flow			7,600	9,000
82					
83	Annual Depreciation			(6,000)	(6,000)
84				---------------	---------------------
85	Av. Annual Accounting Profit			1,600	3,000
86					
87	Average Investment			15,000	15,000
88					
89	Accounting Rate of Return			10.67%	20.00%

Spreadsheet solution 14.10 Output range 5

	X	Y	Z	AA	AB
78	Spreadsheet Solution 14-10: Output Range 5				
79					
80				Project A	Project B
81	Av. Annual Cash Flow			@AVG(AFLOW)	@AVG(BFLOW)
82					
83	Annual Depreciation			@SLN(E24,E33,E31)	@SLN(F24,F33,F31)
84				--	--
85	Av. Annual Accounting Profit			+AA81+AA83	+AB81+AB83
86					
87	Average Investment			(-E24+E33)/2	(-F24+F33)/2
88					
89	Accounting Rate of Return			+AA85/AA87	+AB85/AB87

> **@DDB(Cost, Scrap, Life, Year of charge)**

and the sum of the years' digits

> **@SYD(Cost, Scrap, Life, Year of charge)**

Nevertheless, whatever method is used, the *average* annual charge will be the same and it is this that we are interested in.

Having calculated the average annual accounting profit by deducting depreciation from the average cash inflow (cells AA85 and AB85), the average investment (the average net book value) can be found. This is simply the sum of the opening and closing book values divided by 2. Using cell references the formula is:

⟨(−E24+E33)/2⟩

This is repeated for project B.

The accounting rate of return can now be calculated by dividing the average accounting profit by the average investment, again using cell references. So for project

Spreadsheet solution 14.11 Output range 6

	AC	AD	AE	AF	AG	AH	AI
90	Spreadsheet Solution 14-11: Output Range 6						
91							
92		A			B		
93		NCF	Cum.		NCF	Cum.	
94	Year			Year			
95	0	(30,000)	(30,000)	0	(30,000)	(30,000)	
96	1	16,000	(14,000)	1	2,500	(27,500)	
97	2	10,000	(4,000)	2	2,500	(25,000)	
98	3	6,000	2,000	3	10,000	(15,000)	
99	4	4,000	6,000	4	15,000	0	
100	5	2,000	8,000	5	15,000	15,000	
101							
102	Payback Period is:		3	years		4	years

A this is shown in cell AA89:

⟨ +AA85/AA87⟩

The cells containing the rates of return are formatted to display the answer as a percentage.

The final output section 6 (Spreadsheet Solution 14.11) deals with what is conceptually the simplest investment appraisal technique, the payback method. Unfortunately, when it comes to modelling this technique on a spreadsheet the process is much less straightforward, perhaps providing proof if any were needed that there are limitations to the application of spreadsheet technology.

The approach used in output section 6 begins with the creation of a column for the cumulative cashflows — payback occurs when inflows equal outflows. Thus for a project which begins with an initial outflow payback will occur when the cumulative cash flows change from negative to positive.

While it is clear, from the column of cumulative cash flows, when the payback period is reached, to design a formula that gives the answer itself involves a rather complex procedure. This takes the form of a series of conditional statements along the lines of: if condition X is true, the answer is Y, if not the answer is Z. In our example we have to determine in which year the cumulative cash flow becomes positive. Thus the conditional statement will be: if the cumulative cash flow equals or exceeds 0, the answer is the number of that year, if not then the answer depends on whether the next year's cash flow equals or exceeds 0. In fact what we have to construct is a series of conditional statements, each dependent on the outcome of the previous statement.

The spreadsheet function used is **@IF** followed, in brackets, by the conditional statement. In our example for project A we need a series of these conditional statements referred to as *embedded* or *nested* **@IF** statements starting in cell AE102:

⟨ @IF(AE96⟩ =0,AC96,@IF(AE97⟩ =0,AC97,@IF(AE98⟩ =0,AC98,
@IF(AE99⟩ =0,AC99,@IF(AE100⟩ =0,AC100,0))))) ⟩

What this means is that if the cumulative cash flow in cell AE96 is greater than or equals 0, the answer (payback) is the number of the year in cell AC96, if not then if the cumulative cash flow in cell AE97 is greater than or equals 0, then the answer is the number of the year in cell AC97, if not then if the cumulative cash flow in cell AE98 is greater than or equal to 0, ... The formula ends with a zero since if the cumulative cash flow does not equal or exceed 0 by the final year, payback will not have been reached.

Another limitation of the spreadsheet application to solving the payback appraisal method is that the answer can only be found in integers (whole years, not fractions of years). Partial years can be obtained, but this requires even more sophisticated formulae.

'What if?' questions

Calculate the effect of the following changes to the model:

1. The cash inflow for both project A and project B is increased by £10,000 in year 2.

2. The capital cost of project B is £35,000.

3. For project B £10,000 of cash inflow is switched from year 4 to year 3.

4. The cash inflow for year 1 for both projects is increased by £10,000.

'What if?' solutions

		NPV	IRR	ARR	Payback
1.	Project A	£10,279	27.16%	24.00%	2 years
	Project B	£10,912	19.77%	33.33%	4 years
2.	Project B	£(2,505)	6.85%	11.43%	5 years
3.	Project B	£3,133	12.16%	20.00%	4 years
4.	Project A	£11,037	31.61%	24.00%	2 years
	Project B	£11,669	21.65%	33.33%	4 years

Conclusion

The evaluation of capital projects or investment appraisal is an important area of management control. The management accountant in practice plays a valuable role in providing information on which management bases its decisions regarding capital expenditure.

In this chapter we have reviewed the different methods of investment appraisal, their advantages and limitations. We have also seen how spreadsheet applications can make light work of the accountant's task in providing answers to specific questions, as well as providing data based on a variety of assumptions (the 'what if?' tables).

Unfortunately, not all of the investment appraisal techniques can be transferred comfortably to a spreadsheet. The payback method provides one example of the situation where the effort required to construct a spreadsheet model may exceed the benefits to be derived from the running of the model. Nevertheless, the rather complex part of the model constructed to solve the payback question provides additional exposure to the @IF function, a potentially invaluable tool for the spreadsheet modeller.

Exercises

Question 14.1

A company is facing the prospect of having to invest in new machinery to replace that used in one of its divisions. It uses 18% as its cost of capital. There are three options, only one of which needs to be chosen. The three possibilities have the following details:

	Machinery		
	1	2	3
Initial cost (£)	200,000	300,000	100,000
Expected life (years)	4	5	3
Scrap value (£)	10,000	15,000	4,000

The cash generated from the sale of the output from the machinery has been estimated for each of the options as follows:

	1	2	3
Year 1	80,000	200,000	30,000
2	70,000	150,000	35,000
3	65,000	100,000	50,000
4	60,000	100,000	—
5	—	100,000	—

You are required to calculate, for each alternative, the following:

(a) the net present value;

(b) the accounting rate of return;

(c) the payback period for each alternative.

No answer provided

Question 14.2

The following information relates to two possible capital projects of which you have to select one to invest in. Both projects have an initial capital cost of £200,000 and only one can be taken.

	X	Y
Expected profits		
Year 1	80,000	30,000
2	80,000	50,000
3	40,000	90,000
4	20,000	120,000
Estimated resale value at end of year 4	40,000	40,000

Notes:

(i) Profit is calculated after deducting straight-line depreciation.
(ii) The cost of capital is 16%.

(a) For both projects calculate the following:

  (i) the net present value;
  (ii) the accounting rate of return on average investment;
  (iii) the payback period.

(b) Advise the board which project in your opinion should be undertaken, giving reasons for your decision.

(c) The board has looked at your proposal and you have been asked to clarify a number of issues:

  (i) What is meant by the term 'cost of capital' and why is it important in coming to an investment decision?
  (ii) State two ways in which risk can be taken into account when making a capital investment decision.

Answer on page 304   (ACCA)

Question 14.3

To the model constructed in the chapter, create an additional output range for a 'what if?' table for project B which plots the IRR given changes in capital cost from £5000 to £55,000.

No answer provided

Question 14.4

Modify the input and output ranges of the model to cater for a third project, project C, with initial cost of £30,000 and inflows of £8000 per year for 5 years.

No answer provided

Question 14.5

In the model modified under Question 14.3 above, extend the cash inflows for the three projects for another 2 years with the cash inflow for year 5 being repeated in years 6 and 7.

No answer provided

Answers to exercises

The spreadsheet answers to the numerical parts of the end-of-chapter exercises are provided in the following section. For the sake of brevity, the spreadsheet models presented include control sections only where necessary. Sufficient material is presented in the text to make it unnecessary to provide answers to the written parts of the questions.

Answer 6.1

	A	B	C	D
1	Answer 6-1: Input Section			
2				
3	Note that the Input Section has been			
4	sorted into ascending order of hours.			
5				
6				
7				
8		Machine	Labour	Total
9		Hours	Hours	Costs
10	January	25	1,040	500
11	February	26	1,080	500
12	August	30	1,340	620
13	March	31	1,040	530
14	December	32	1,090	530
15	September	34	1,300	620
16	July	34	1,390	640
17	April	35	1,100	550
18	October	39	1,270	590
19	November	42	1,100	500
20	May	43	1,300	580
21	June	48	1,590	680

	E	F	G	H
22	Answer 6-1: Output Section 1			
23				
24	High Low Method (Machine Hours and Total Cost)			
25				
26	Maximum Value	48	Associated Cost	680
27	Minimum Value	25	Associated Cost	500
28		---------------		---------------------------
29		23		180
30				
31	b =	7.83		
32	a =	304.35		

	E	F	G
22	Answer 6-1: Output Section 1 (formulae)		
23			
24	High Low Method (Machine Hours and Total Cost)		
25			
26	Maximum Value	@MAX($MACHINE)	Associated Cost
27	Minimum Value	@MIN($MACHINE)	Associated Cost
28		--------------------------------	
29		+F26-F27	
30			
31	b =	+H29/F29	
32	a =	+H26-($F$31*F26)	

Answer 6.1 (*cont.*)

	I	J	K	L
34	Answer 6-1: Output Section 2			
35				
36	Linear Regression			
37				
38	(Machine Hours and Total Cost)			
39				
40		Regression Output:		
41	Constant			416.1058
42	Std Err of Y Est			55.2146
43	R Squared			0.252781
44	No. of Observations			12
45	Degrees of Freedom			10
46				
47	X Coefficient(s)	4.407471		
48	Std Err of Coef.	2.396297		

	M	N	O	P
50	Answer 6-1: Output Section 3			
51				
52	High Low Method			
53				
54	(Labour Hours and Total Cost)			
55				
56	Maximum Value	1590	Associated Cost	680
57	Minimum Value	1040	Associated Cost	500
58		---------------		---------------
59		550		180
60				
61	b =	0.33		
62	a =	159.64		

	M	N	O	P
50	Answer 6-1: Output Section 3 (formulae)			
51				
52	High Low Method			
53				
54	(Labour Hours and Total Cost)			
55				
56	Maximum Value	@MAX(LABOUR)	Associated Cost	@VLOOKUP(+N56,NALL,+1)
57	Minimum Value	@MIN(LABOUR)	Associated Cost	@VLOOKUP(+N57,NALL,+1)
58		---------------------------		--
59		+N56-N57		+P56-P57
60				
61	b =	+P59/N59		
62	a =	+P56-(N61*N56)		

Answer 6.1 (*cont.*)

	Q	R	S	T	U
65	Answer 6-1: Output Section 4				
66					
67	Linear Regression				
68					
69	(Machine Hours and Total Cost)				
70					
71		Regression Output:			
72	Constant			157.8378	
73	Std Err of Y Est			19.07312	
74	R Squared			0.910837	
75	No. of Observations			12	
76	Degrees of Freedom			10	
77					
78	X Coefficient(s)	0.337838			
79	Std Err of Coef.	0.033426			

Answer 7.1

	A	B	C
1	Answer 7-1: Input Section		
2			
3	Job No.	1234	
4	--	---------------	
5	Labour:	Hours	Rates
6			£
7	Dept. X	250	2.50
8			
9	Dept. Y	175	4.25
10			
11	Dept. Z	325	5.25
12		---------------	
13	Total	750	
14			
15	Materials:		£
16			
17	Dept. X		5,000
18			
19	Dept. Y		1,500
20			
21	Dept. Z		1,000
22			
23	Fixed Production Overhead		4.00
24			
25	Fixed Admin. Overhead		75%
26			
27	Profit Margin		25%
28			

Answer 7.1 (*cont.*)

		D	E	F
29	Answer 7-1: Output Section 1			
30				
31	Job No.		1234	
32	---------------------------------		-----------------	
33	Labour:			
34				
35	Dept. X		625	
36				
37	Dept. Y		744	
38				
39	Dept. Z		1,706	
40			-----------------	3,075
41	Materials:			
42				
43	Dept. X		5,000	
44				
45	Dept. Y		1,500	
46				
47	Dept. Z		1,000	
48			-----------------	7,500
49				
50	Fixed Production Overheads			3,000
51				----------------
52	Total Production Cost			13,575
53				
54	Fixed Admin. Overheads			10,181
55				
56				----------------
57	Total Cost			23,756
58				
59	Profit			7,919
60				----------------
61	Selling Price			31,675
62				=====

Answer 7.1 *(cont.)*

	D	E	F
29	Answer 7-1: Output Section 1 (formulae)		
30			
31	Job No.	1234	
32	--	-----------------	
33	Labour:		
34			
35	Dept. X	+B7*C7	
36			
37	Dept. Y	+B9*C9	
38			
39	Dept. Z	+B11*C11	
40		----------------	@SUM(E35..E39)
41	Materials:		
42			
43	Dept. X	+C17	
44			
45	Dept. Y	+C19	
46			
47	Dept. Z	+C21	
48		----------------	@SUM(E43..E47)
49			
50	Fixed Production Overheads		+B13*C23
51			-------------------------------------
52	Total Production Cost		@SUM(F40..F50)
53			
54	Fixed Admin. Overheads		+F52*C25
55			
56			-------------------------------------
57	Total Cost		@SUM(F52..F54)
58			
59	Profit		+F57*C27/(1-C27)
60			-------------------------------------
61	Selling Price		@SUM(F57..F59)
62			=============

Answer 7.2

A	B	C
1 Answer 7-2: Input Section		
2		
3	Product A	Product B
4	-----------------	-----------------
5 Units Produced:	10,000	30,000
6		
7 Units in Inventory		
8		
9 Sales Value per unit	5.60	6.00
10		
11 Joint Production costs:		
12		
13 Materials	83,600	
14		
15 Conversion costs	58,000	
16	-----------------	
17 Total cost	141,600	
18		
19 Further costs of processing (per kilo)	1.80	
20		
21 Yield on further processing	90%	

D	E	F
22 Answer 7-2: Output Section 1		
23		
24 Physical Quantity Basis		
25		
26 Joint cost per unit	3.54	
27		
28	Product A	Product B
29	-----------------	-----------------
30 Sales Revenue	50,400	180,000
31		
32 Cost of joint production	35,400	106,200
33		
34 Further processing	18,000	
35		
36	-----------------	-----------------
37 Net profit	(3,000)	73,800
38		
39 Profit per kilo	(0.33)	2.46

Answer 7.2 (*cont.*)

	D	E	F
22	Answer 7-2: Output Section 1 (formulae)		
23			
24	Physical Quantity Basis		
25			
26	Joint cost per unit	+B17/(B5+C5)	
27			
28		Product A	Product B
29		------------------------------	------------------------------
30	Sales Revenue	+B5*B21*B9	+C5*C9
31			
32	Cost of joint production	+B5*$E$26	+C5*$E$26
33			
34	Further processing	+B5*B19	
35			
36		------------------------------	------------------------------
37	Net profit	+E30-@SUM(E32..E34)	+F30-@SUM(F32..F34)
38			
39	Profit per kilo	+E37/(B5*B21)	+F37/C5
40			

	G	H	I
41	Answer 7-2: Output Section 2		
42	Market Value Basis		
43		Product A	Product B
44		-----------------	-----------------
45	Sales Revenue	50,400	180,000
46			
47	Further processing	(18,000)	0
48		-----------------	-----------------
49		32,400	180,000
50			
51	Joint costs	21,600	120,000
52		-----------------	-----------------
53	Net profit	10,800	60,000
54			
55	Profit per kilo	1.20	2.00

	G	H	I
41	Answer 7-2: Output Section 2 (formulae)		
42	Market Value Basis		
43		Product A	Product B
44		------------------------------	------------------------------
45	Sales Revenue	+E30	+F30
46			
47	Further processing	-E34	+F27*$E$26
48		------------------------------	------------------------------
49		@SUM(H45..H47)	@SUM(I45..I47)
50			
51	Joint costs	+H49/(H49+I49)*$B17	+I49/(H49+I49)*$B17
52		------------------------------	------------------------------
53	Net profit	+H49-H51	+I49-I51
54			
55	Profit per kilo	+H53/(B5*B21)	+I53/C5

Answer 8.1

	A	B	C	D
1	Answer 8-1: Control Section			
2				
3	XYZ Company			
4				
5	This spreadsheet presents a fully integrated budgeting model			
6	based on a manufacturing company producing three products X, Y & Z.			
7				
8	Each product requires direct labour, raw materials and needs to			
9	pass through one production process.			
10				
11	Location Table		Range Name	
12	--		-------------------	
13	Input Section		INPUT	
14	Sales Budget		OUTPUT1	
15	Production Budget		OUTPUT2	
16	Materials Usage Budget		OUTPUT3	
17	Direct Labour Budget		OUTPUT4	
18	Factory Overhead Budget		OUTPUT5	
19	Materials Purchasing Budget		OUTPUT6	
20	Production Cost Budget		OUTPUT7	

	E	F	G	H	I
22	Answer 8-1: Input Section				
23			X	Y	Z
24	Sales Forecasts (units)		2,000	4,000	3,000
25	Selling Price (£)		100	130	150
26					
27	Finished Goods:				
28	Closing Stock (units)		600	1000	800
29	Opening Stock (units)		500	800	700
30	Unit Cost of opening stock (£)		0	0	
31					
32	Standard hours per unit		4	6	8
33					
34	Standard hourly rate £		3	3	3
35	Stand hourly rate variable o/h £		2	2	2
36					
37	Standard Usage of Raw Materials				
38					
39	RM11		5	3	2
40	RM22		2	2	1
41	RM33		0	2	3
42					
43	Raw Materials:		RM11	RM22	RM33
44	Closing Stock (kilos)		18,000	9,000	12,000
45	Opening Stock (kilos)		21,000	10,000	16,000
46	Cost of Raw Materials (£)		5	3	4
47					
48	Factory Overhead:		292,000		
49					

	J	K	L	M
50	Answer 8-1: Output Section 1: Sales Budget			
51				
52		Demand	Price	Value
53		units	£	£
54	X	2,000	100	200,000
55	Y	4,000	130	520,000
56	Z	3,000	150	450,000
57				---------------------------
58				1,170,000

Answer 8.1 *(cont.)*

	J	K	L	M
50	Answer 8-1: Output Section 1: Sales Budget			
51	(formulae)			
52		Demand	Price	Value
53		units	£	£
54	X	+G24	+G25	+L54*K54
55	Y	+H24	+H25	+L55*K55
56	Z	+I24	+I25	+L56*K56
57				--------------------------
58				@SUM(M54..M56)

	N	O	P	Q
59	Answer 8-1: Output Section 2: Production Budget			
60				
61		X	Y	Z
62	Sales	2,000	4,000	3,000
63	Add Closing Stock	600	1,000	800
64	Less Opening Stock	(500)	(800)	(700)
65		----------	------------	------------------
66		2,100	4,200	3,100

	N	O	P	Q
59	Answer 8-1: Output Section 2: Production Budget			
60	(formulae)			
61		X	Y	Z
62	Sales	+G24	+H24	+I24
63	Add Closing Stock	+G28	+H28	+I28
64	Less Opening Stock	-G29	-H29	-I29
65		---------------------	----------------------	--------------------------
66		@SUM(O62..O64)	@SUM(P62..P64)	@SUM(Q62..Q64)

	R	S	T	U
67	Answer 8-1: Output Section 3: Materials Usage			
68				
69		RM11	RM22	RM33
70	X	10,500	4,200	0
71	Y	12,600	8,400	8,400
72	Z	6,200	3,100	9,300
73		---------------------	------------------	---------------
74		29,300	15,700	17,700
75	Cost/Unit	5.00	3.00	4.00
76				
77	Cost of Materials Use	146,500	47,100	193,600

	S	T	U	V
67	Answer 8-1: Output Section 3: Materials Usage			
68	(formulae)			
69		RM11	RM22	RM33
70	X	+$O$66*G39	+$O$66*G40	+$O$66*G41
71	Y	+$P$66*H39	+$P$66*H40	+$P$66*H41
72	Z	+$Q$66*I39	+$Q$66*I40	+$Q$66*I41
73		------------------------	------------------------	-------------------------
74		@SUM(S70..S72)	@SUM(T70..T72)	@SUM(U70..U72)
75	Cost/Unit	+G46	+H46	+I46
76				
77	Cost of Materials Used	+S74*S75	+T74*T75	+T77+S77

Answer 8.1 (cont.)

	V	W	X	Y
78	Answer 8-1: Output Section 4			
79				
80	Direct Labour Budget			
81				
82		Units	Hours	Total hrs
83	X	2,100	4	8,400
84	Y	4,200	6	25,200
85	Z	3,100	8	24,800
86				---------------
87				58,400

	V	W	X	Y
78	Answer 8-1: Output Section 4			
79	(formulae)			
80	Direct Labour Budget			
81				
82		Units	Hours	Total hrs
83	X	+O66	+G32	+X83*W83
84	Y	+P66	+H32	+X84*W84
85	Z	+Q66	+I32	+X85*W85
86				--------------------------
87				@SUM(Y83..Y85)

	Z	AA
88	Answer 8-1: Output Section 5	
89		
90	Factory Overhead Budget	
91		
92		
93		£
94	Allocated & Apportioned	292,000
95		
96	Labour Hours	58,400
97		
98	Absorption Rate per hour	5.00

	Z	AA
88	Answer 8-1: Output Section 5 (formulae)	
89		
90	Factory Overhead Budget	
91		
92		
93		£
94	Allocated & Apportioned	+G48
95		
96	Labour Hours	+Y87
97		
98	Absorption Rate per hour	+AA94/AA96

Answer 8.1 *(cont.)*

	AB	AC	AD	AE
99	Answer 8-1: Output Section 6			
100				
101	Raw Materials Purchasing Budget			
102				
103		RM11	RM22	RM33
104	Closing Stock	18,000	9,000	12,000
105	Production Requirements	29,300	15,700	17,700
106	Less Opening Stock	(21,000)	(10,000)	(16,000)
107		--------------	--------------	--------------
108	Purchase Requirements	26,300	14,700	13,700
109				
110	Cost per unit (£)	5.00	3.00	4.00
111				
112	Purchase Costs	131,500	44,100	54,800

	AB	AC	AD	AE
99	Answer 8-1: Output Section 6 (formulae)			
100				
101	Raw Materials Purchasing Budget			
102				
103		RM11	RM22	RM33
104	Closing Stock	+G44	+H44	+I44
105	Production Requirements	+S74	+T74	+U74
106	Less Opening Stock	-G45	-H45	-I45
107		-------------------------------	-------------------------------	-------------------------------
108	Purchase Requirements	@SUM(AC104..AC106)	@SUM(AD104..AD106)	@SUM(AE104..AE106)
109				
110	Cost per unit (£)	+G46	+H46	+I46
111				
112	Purchase Costs	+AC108*AC110	+AD108*AD110	+AE108*AE110

	AF	AG	AH	AI	AJ
113	Answer 8-1: Output Section 7				
114					
115	Production Cost Budget				
116		X	Y	Z	
117	RM11	25.00	15.00	10.00	
118	RM22	6.00	6.00	3.00	
119	RM33	0.00	8.00	12.00	
120	Direct Labour	12.00	18.00	24.00	
121	Variable Overhead	8.00	12.00	16.00	
122		--------------	--------------	--------------	
123	Total Variable Cost	51.00	59.00	65.00	
124	Fixed Overhead	20.00	30.00	40.00	
125		--------------	--------------	--------------	
126	Total Production Cost per unit	71.00	89.00	105.00	
127	Production Units	149,100	373,800	325,500	848,400

Answer 8.1 *(cont.)*

AF	AG	AH	AI	AJ
113 Answer 8-1: Output Section 7 (formulae)				
114				
115 Production Cost Budget				
116	X	Y	Z	
117 RM11	+G46*G39	+G46*H39	+G46*I39	
118 RM22	+H46*G40	+H46*H40	+H46*I40	
119 RM33	+I46*G41	+I46*H41	+I46*I41	
120 Direct Labour	+G32*G34	+H32*H34	+I32*I34	
121 Variable Overhead	+G35*G32	+H35*H32	+I35*I32	
122				
123 Total Variable Cost	@SUM(AG117..AG121)	@SUM(AH117..AH121)	@SUM(AI117..AI121)	
124 Fixed Overhead	+G32*$AA$98	+H32*$AA$98	+I32*$AA$98	
125				
126 Total Production Cost per unit	+AG124+AG123	+AH124+AH123	+AI124+AI123	
127 Production Units	+AG126*O66	+AH126*P66	+AI126*Q66	@SUM(AG127..AI127)

Answer 8.6

	A	B	C
1	Answer 8-6: Input Section		
2			
3			
4	Opening Stock	40,000	
5			
6	Closing Stock Increase	50%	
7			
8	Stock Turnover		6 times
9			
10	Gross Profit to Sales	40%	
11			
12	Production Costs:	£ per unit	
13	Raw Materials	0.16	
14	Direct Labour	0.20	
15	Fixed Production Overhead	0.18	
16			
17			
18	Selling and Administration		
19			
20	Variable Expenses		4% of sales
21		£	
22	Fixed Expenses	81,000	
23			
24			
25	Opening Stock Raw Materials	20,000	
26			
27	Depreciation Element	20,000	
28			
29	Asset Age		2 years
30			
31	Depreciation Rate		10% per annum
32			
33			
34	Opening Creditors	16,000	
35			
36	Opening Debtors	20,000	
37			
38	Debtors Collection Period		30 days
39			
40	Days in year		360 days
41			
42	Opening Overdraft	(18,000)	

Answer 8.6 *(cont.)*

	D	E
43	Answer 8-6: Output Section 1	
44		
45	Sales Level (units)	
46		
47	Opening Stock	40,000
48		
49	Closing Stock	60,000
50		
51	Average Stock	50,000
52		
53	Sales Units	300,000
54		

	D	E
43	Answer 8-6: Output Section 1	
44	(formulae)	
45	Sales Level (units)	
46		
47	Opening Stock	+B4
48		
49	Closing Stock	+B4*(1+B6)
50		
51	Average Stock	@AVG(E47..E49)
52		
53	Sales Units	+E51*B8

	F	G
55	Answer 8-6: Output Section 2	
56		
57	Selling Price	£
58		
59	Production Cost Per Unit	0.54
60		
61	Selling Price	0.90

	F	G
55	Answer 8-6: Output Section 2 (formulae)	
56		
57	Selling Price	£
58		
59	Production Cost Per Unit	@SUM(B13..B15)
60		
61	Selling Price	+G59/(1-B10)

Answer 8.6 (*cont.*)

	H	I	J
64	Answer 8-6: Output Section 3		
65			
66	Budgeted Profit and Loss Account		
67			
68		£	£
69	Sales		270,000
70			
71	Cost of Sales		162,000
72			----------------
73	Gross Profit		108,000
74			
75	Selling and Administration:		
76	Variable Expenses	10,800	
77	Fixed Expenses	81,000	
78		----------------	91,800
79			----------------
80	Net Profit		16,200
81			=====

	H	I	J
64	Answer 8-6: Output Section 3 (formulae)		
65			
66	Budgeted Profit and Loss Account		
67			
68		£	£
69	Sales		+G61*E53
70			
71	Cost of Sales		+J69*(1-B10)
72			-------------------------
73	Gross Profit		+J69-J71
74			
75	Selling and Administration:		
76	Variable Expenses	+B20*J69	
77	Fixed Expenses	+B22	
78		----------------	+I77+I76
79			-------------------------
80	Net Profit		+J73-J78
81			========

Answer 8.6 (*cont.*)

	L	M	N
		£	£
82	Answer 8-6: Output Section 4		
83			
84	Bank Balance		
85		£	£
86	Opening Balance		(18,000)
87			
88	Net Profit	16,200	
89			
90	Depreciation	20,000	
91		---------------	36,200
92			---------------
93			18,200
94			
95	Increase in Debtors		(2,500)
96			
97	Increase in Stock		(10,800)
98			---------------
99	Closing Bank Balance		4,900
100			=====

	L	M	N
82	Answer 8-6: Output Section 4 (formulae)		
83			
84	Bank Balance		
85		£	£
86	Opening Balance	+B42	
87			
88	Net Profit	+J80	
89			
90	Depreciation	+B27	
91		---------------	+M90+M88
92			---
93			+N91+N86
94			
95	Increase in Debtors		+B36-(+B38/B40*J69)
96			
97	Increase in Stock		(-B6*@SUM(B13..B15))*B4
98			---
99	Closing Bank Balance		@SUM(N93..N97)
100			================

Answer 8.6 (*cont.*)

	O	P	Q
101	Answer 8-6: Output Section 5		
102			
103	Opening Capital		
104			
105			£
106			
107	Fixed Assets (Cost)		200,000
108	Depreciation		20,000
109			---------------
110	NBV		180,000
111			
112	Stocks: Goods	21,600	
113	Stocks: Materials	20,000	
114	Debtors	20,000	
115	Bank	(18,000)	
116		---------------	43,600
117	Creditors		(16,000)
118			---------------
119	Opening Capital Balance		207,600
120			=====

	O	P	Q
101	Answer 8-6: Output Section 5 (formulae)		
102			
103	Opening Capital		
104			
105			£
106			
107	Fixed Assets (Cost)		+B27/B31
108	Depreciation		+B27
109			------------------------------
110	NBV		+Q107-Q108
111			
112	Stocks: Goods	+B4*@SUM(B13..B15)	
113	Stocks: Materials	+B25	
114	Debtors	+B36	
115	Bank	+B42	
116		------------------------------	@SUM(P112..P115)
117	Creditors		-B34
118			------------------------------
119	Opening Capital Balance		@SUM(Q110..Q117
120			==========

Answer 8.6 (*cont.*)

	R	S	T
121	Answer 8-6: Output Section 6		
122			
123	Balance Sheet		
124		£	£
125	Fixed Assets at Cost		200,000
126	Depreciation		40,000
127			---------------
128	NBV		160,000
129			
130	Stocks: Goods	32,400	
131	Stocks: Materials	20,000	
132	Debtors	22,500	
133	Bank	4,900	
134		---------------	79,800
135			
136	Creditors		(16,000)
137			---------------
138	Net Current Assets		223,800
139			=====
140			
141	Opening Capital Balance		207,600
142			
143	Net Profit		16,200
144			---------------
145			223,800
146			=====

	R	S	T
121	Answer 8-6: Output Section 6 (formulae)		
122			
123	Balance Sheet		
124		£	£
125	Fixed Assets at Cost		+Q107
126	Depreciation		+B29*B27
127			------------------------------------
128	NBV		+T125-T126
129			
130	Stocks: Goods	+E49*@SUM(B13..B15)	
131	Stocks: Materials	+B25	
132	Debtors	+J69*B38/B40	
133	Bank	+N99	
134		------------------------------------	@SUM(S130..S133)
135			
136	Creditors .		-B34
137			------------------------------------
138	Net Current Assets		@SUM(T128..T136)
139			============
140			
141	Opening Capital Balance		+Q119
142			
143	Net Profit		+J80
144			------------------------------------
145			+T141+T143
146			============
147			

Answer 8.7

	A	B	C	D
1	Answer 8-7: Input Section			
2				
3	Level	Preliminary	Intermediate	Final
4				
5	No: of Students	400	300	250
6				
7	Fee per Student £	2,000	3,000	4,000
8				
9	Class Size	20	20	10
10				
11	No. of classes	20	15	25
12				
13				
14	Tuition per year	30	weeks	
15				
16	Level	Preliminary	Intermediate	Final
17				
18	Hours per week	16	20	22
19				
20	Tuition £ per hour	20	22	24
21				
22				
23	Other Costs	£		
24				
25	Rental of college	500,000		
26	Administration Salaries	132,000		
27	Administration Costs	800,000		
28	Welfare Expenses	400,000		
29	Examination Fees	100,000		
30		--------------------		
31		1,932,000		
32				
33	Bad Debts	2%		
34				
35	Depreciation	5%	of administration costs	

	E	F	G	H	I
36	Answer 8-7: Output Section 1				
37					
38					
39	Cash Budget				
40					
41		Preliminary	Intermediate	Final	Total
42					
43	Receipts	784,000	882,000	980,000	2,646,000
44					
45	Tuition Costs	192,000	198,000	396,000	786,000
46					
47	Cash Contribution	592,000	684,000	584,000	
48					
49	Other Costs				1,892,000
50					------------------
51					2,678,000
52					
53	Surplus/(Deficit)				(32,000)

Answer 8.7 (*cont.*)

	E	F	G	H	I
36	Answer 8-7: Output Section 1 (formulae)				
37					
38					
39	Cash Budget				
40					
41		Preliminary	Intermediate	Final	Total
42					
43	Receipts	(+B5*B7)*(1-$B$33)	(+C5*C7)*(1-$B$33)	(+D5*D7)*(1-$B$33)	@SUM(F43..H43)
44					
45	Tuition Costs	+$B$14*B18*B20*B11	+$B$14*C18*C20*C11	+$B$14*D18*D20*D11	@SUM(F45..H45)
46					
47	Cash Contribution	+F43-F45	+G43-G45	+H43-H45	
48					
49	Other Costs				+B31-(+B35*B27)
50					-------------------------------
51					+I45+I49
52					
53	Surplus/(Deficit)				+I43-I51

Answer 9.4

	A	B	C
	Answer 9-4: Input Section		

STANDARD COSTS (per unit of output)

	Quantity (units)	Price £
Material A (kilos)	12	9.00
Labour (hours)	10	4.00

ACTUAL COSTS

Quantities & Costs of Actual Production

Actual Production (units)	290	
	Quantity (units)	Total Cost £
Material A	3,770	35,815
Labour	2,755	11,571

Answer 9.4 (cont.)

Answer 9-4: Output Section

	D	E Total Standard Cost SQ x SP [1]	F Total Actual Cost AQ x AP [2]	G Actual Input at Standard AQ x SP [3]	H Total Variance [1]-[2]	I Usage/ Efficiency Variance [SQxSP]-[AQxSP] [1]-[3]	J Price/ Rate Variance [AQxSP]-[AQxAP] [3]-[2]
						Variances	
26							
27							
28							
29							
30							
31							
32							
33							
34							
35 Material A		31,320	35,815	33,930	(4,495)	(2,610)	(1,885)
36							
37 Labour		11,600	11,571	11,020	29	580	(551)
38							
39 Total		42,920	47,386	44,950	(4,466)	(2,030)	(2,436)

Answer 9-4: Output Section (formulae)

	D	E Total Standard Cost SQ x SP [1]	F Total Actual Cost AQ x AP [2]	G Actual Input at Standard AQ x SP [3]	H Total Variance [1]-[2]	I Usage/ Efficiency Variance [SQxSP]-[AQxSP] [1]-[3]	J Price/ Rate Variance [AQxSP]-[AQxAP] [3]-[2]
						Variances	
26							
27							
28							
29							
30							
31							
32							
33							
34							
35 Material A		+$B$17*(B7*C7)	+C22	+B22*C7	+E35-F35	+E35-G35	+G35-F35
36							
37 Labour		+$B$17*(B9*C9)	+C24	+B24*C9	+E37-F37	+E37-G37	+G37-F37
38							
39 Total		@SUM(E35..E37)	@SUM(F35..F37)	@SUM(G35..G37)	+E39-F39	+E39-G39	+G39-F39

Answer 9.5

	A	B	C	D
1	Answer 9-5: Input Section			
2				
3				
4		Budget	Actual	
5				
6	Production (units)	1,200	1,300	
7				
8	Selling Price per unit	100	100	
9				
10	Fixed Overheads	19,200		
11				
12	Standard Cost per unit			
13				
14		Quantity	Price	Total
15			£	£
16	Variable Costs:			
17				
18	Raw Materials	5	4.00	20.00
19				
20	Labour	4	6.00	24.00
21				
22	Fixed Overheads		4.00	16.00
23	- per Labour hour			
24				
25				---------------
26	Total per unit			60.00
27				
28				
29	Actual Data:			
30		Quantity	Total Cost	
31		(units)	£	
32				
33	Material	6,600	25,080	
34				
35	Labour	5,330	32,513	
36				
37	Fixed Overheads		22,000	

	E	F	G	H	I	J	K	L	M
40	Answer 9-5: Output Section 1								
41									
42		Budget	Flexed	Actual	Actual	Total	Quantity	Price	Volume-
43			Budget		at Std	Variance	Variance	Variance	Related
44									
45	Sales	120,000	130,000	130,000	130,000	4,000		0	4,000
46									
47	Less:								
48									
49	Materials	24,000	26,000	25,080	26,400	920	(400)	1,320	
50									
51	Labour	28,800	31,200	32,513	31,980	(1,313)	(780)	(533)	
52									
53	Fixed Costs	19,200	20,800	22,000	21,320	(1,200)	(520)	(2,800)	2,120
54									
55	Under\over Recovery		(1,600)						
56		---------------	---------------	---------------	---------------	-----------	-----------------------	----------------	-------------------
57	Net Profit	48,000	52,000	50,407		2,407	(1,593)	(2,013)	10,120
58									
59									

Answer 9.5 (cont.)

Answer 9-5: Output Section 1 (formulae)

	E	F	G	H	I	J	K	L	M
		Budget	Flexed Budget	Actual	Actual at Std	Total Variance	Quantity Variance	Price Variance	Volume-Related
45	Sales	+B6*B8	+C6*B8	+C6*C8	+C6*B8	+M45+L45		+H45-I45	(C6-B6)*(B8-D26)
47	Less:								
49	Materials	+B$6*B18*C18	+C$6*B18*C18	+C33	+B33*C18	+G49-H49	+G49-I49	+I49-H49	
51	Labour	+B$6*B20*C20	+C$6*B20*C20	+C35	+B35*C20	+G51-H51	+G51-I51	+I51-H51	
53	Fixed Costs	+B10	+C$6*D22	+C37	+B35*C22	@SUM(K53..M53)	+G53-I53	+F53-H53	+I53-F53
55	Under/over Recovery		+F53-G53						
57	Net Profit	+F45-@SUM(F49..F53)	+G45-@SUM(G49..G53)	+H45-@SUM(H49..H53)		+J45-@SUM(J49..J53)	+K45+@SUM(K49..M53)	+L45+@SUM(L49..L53)	+M45+@SUM(M44..M53)

Answer 9.5 (*cont.*)

	N	O	P	Q
60	Answer 9-5: Output Section 2			
61				
62	Reconciliation of Budgeted and Actual Net Profit			
63			£	
64	Budgeted Profit		52,000	
65				
66	Less Variances:			
67				
68	Materials	920		
69				
70	Labour	(1,313)		
71				
72	Fixed Overheads	(1,200)		
73		--------------	(1,593)	
74				
75			-------------	
76	Actual Net Profit		50,407	
77			= = = =	

	N	O	P	Q
60	Answer 9-5: Output Section 2 (formulae)			
61				
62	Reconciliation of Budgeted and Actual Net Profit			
63			£	
64	Budgeted Profit		+G57	
65				
66	Less Variances:			
67				
68	Materials	+J49		
69				
70	Labour	+J51		
71				
72	Fixed Overheads	+J53		
73		--------------	@SUM(O68..O72)	
74				
75			----------------------------	
76	Actual Net Profit		@SUM(P64..P73)	
77			= = = = = = = = = =	

Answer 11.1

	A	B	C
1	Answer 11-1: Input Section		
2			
3	Estimated Sales	20,000	
4			
5	Average Unit Cost	£	% Increase
6			
7	Direct Material	30	20%
8	Direct Labour	10	5%
9	Variable Overhead	10	5%
10	Fixed Overhead	10	25%
11		---------------	
12		60	
13		=====	
14			
15	Cheaper Material	31.25	
16			
17	Rejection Rate	5%	
18			
19	Inspection Process	40,000	
20	Allocated Overhead	10,000	
21			
22	Selling Price Mark-up	50%	
23			
24	Forecast Accuracy	100%	
25			
26		Price	Demand
27		80	25000
28		84	23000
29		88	21000
30		90	20000
31		92	19000
32		96	17000
33		100	15000

Answer 11.1 (*cont.*)

	D	E	F
34	Answer 11-1: Output Section 1		
35			
36	Variable Cost		
37			
38		Regular	Cheaper
39		Material	Material
40		£	£
41	Direct Material	36.00	31.25
42	Direct Labour	10.50	10.50
43	Variable Overhead	10.50	10.50
44		---------------	---------------
45		57.00	52.25
46			
47	Cost of Rejects	0.00	2.75
48		---------------	---------------
49	Variable Cost	57.00	55.00
50		=====	=====

	D	E	F
34	Answer 11-1: Output Section 1 (formulae)		
35			
36	Variable Cost		
37			
38		Regular	Cheaper
39		Material	Material
40		£	£
41	Direct Material	+B7*(1+C7)	+B15
42	Direct Labour	+$B$8*(1+$C$8)	+$B$8*(1+$C$8)
43	Variable Overhead	+$B$9*(1+$C$9)	+$B$9*(1+$C$9)
44		---------------------------	-----------------------------------
45		@SUM(E41..E43)	@SUM(F41..F43)
46			
47	Cost of Rejects	0	+F45*(B17/(1-B17))
48		---------------------------	-----------------------------------
49	Variable Cost	+E47+E45	+F47+F45
50		==========	============

Answer 11.1 (*cont.*)

	G	H	I	J	K
51	Answer 11-1: Output Section 2				
52					
53	Contribution of each grade of material				
54					
55			REGULAR		CHEAPER
56	Price	Contibution	Total	Contibution	Total
57		Per Unit	Contibution	Per Unit	Contibution
58					
59	80	23	575,000	25	595,000
60	84	27	621,000	29	637,000
61	88	31	651,000	33	663,000
62	90	33	660,000	35	670,000
63	92	35	665,000	37	673,000
64	96	39	663,000	41	667,000
65	100	43	645,000	45	645,000

	G	H	I	J	K
51	Answer 11-1: Output Section 2 (formulae)				
52					
53	Contribution of each grade of material				
54					
55			REGULAR		CHEAPER
56	Price	Contibution	Total	Contibution	Total
57		Per Unit	Contibution	Per Unit	Contibution
58					
59	+A27	+G59-$E$49	+H59*B27	+G59-$F$49	(+J59*B27)-$B$19+$B20
60	+A28	+G60-$E$49	+H60*B28	+G60-$F$49	(+J60*B28)-$B$19+$B20
61	+A29	+G61-$E$49	+H61*B29	+G61-$F$49	(+J61*B29)-$B$19+$B20
62	+A30	+G62-$E$49	+H62*B30	+G62-$F$49	(+J62*B30)-$B$19+$B20
63	+A31	+G63-$E$49	+H63*B31	+G63-$F$49	(+J63*B31)-$B$19+$B20
64	+A32	+G64-$E$49	+H64*B32	+G64-$F$49	(+J64*B32)-$B$19+$B20
65	+A33	+G65-$E$49	+H65*B33	+G65-$F$49	(+J65*B33)-$B$19+$B20

	L	M
66	Answer 11-1: Output Section 3	
67		
68	Profit Maximization	
69		£
70	Regular	665,000
71	Cheaper	673,000
72		
73		£
74	Cheaper	673,000
75	Fixed Overhead	250,000
76		------------------
77	Profit Maximization	423,000
78		======

Answer 11.1 (*cont.*)

	L	M
66	Answer 11-1: Output Section 3 (formulae)	
67		
68	Profit Maximization	
69		£
70	Regular	@MAX(I59..I65)
71	Cheaper	@MAX(K59..K65)
72		
73		£
74	@IF(M71>M70,"Cheaper","Regular")	@MAX(M70..M71)
75	Fixed Overhead	+B10*B3*(1+C10)
76		------------------------------
77	Profit Maximization	+M74-M75
78		==========

	N	O	P	Q	R	S	T	U
79	Answer 11-1: Output Section 4							
80								
81	Sensitivity Analysis							
82								
83		Forecast				Reject		
84		Demand				Rate		
85		+M77		+L74		+M77		+L74
86	100%	423000	100%	Cheaper	5%	423000	5%	Cheaper
87	99%	415970	99%	Cheaper	6%	415000	6%	Regular
88	98%	408940	98%	Cheaper	7%	415000	7%	Regular
89	97%	401910	97%	Cheaper	8%	415000	8%	Regular
90	96%	394880	96%	Cheaper	9%	415000	9%	Regular
91	95%	387850	95%	Cheaper	10%	415000	10%	Regular
92	94%	380820	94%	Cheaper	11%	415000	11%	Regular
93	93%	373790	93%	Cheaper	12%	415000	12%	Regular
94	92%	366760	92%	Cheaper	13%	415000	13%	Regular
95	91%	359730	91%	Cheaper	14%	415000	14%	Regular

Answer 11.1 (cont.)

	V	W	X	Y	Z	AA	AB	AC
96	Answer 11-1: Output Section 5							
97								
98	Break-even Graph							
99				Regular			Cheaper	
100	Price	Sales	VC	FC	TC	VC	FC	TC
101	100	1,500,000	855,000	250,000	1,105,000	825,000	280,000	1,105,000
102	96	1,632,000	969,000	250,000	1,219,000	935,000	280,000	1,215,000
103	92	1,748,000	1,083,000	250,000	1,333,000	1,045,000	280,000	1,325,000
104	90	1,800,000	1,140,000	250,000	1,390,000	1,100,000	280,000	1,380,000
105	88	1,848,000	1,197,000	250,000	1,447,000	1,155,000	280,000	1,435,000
106	84	1,932,000	1,311,000	250,000	1,561,000	1,265,000	280,000	1,545,000
107	80	2,000,000	1,425,000	250,000	1,675,000	1,375,000	280,000	1,655,000

	V	W	X	Y	Z	AA	AB	AC
96	Answer 11-1: Output Section 5 (formulae)							
97								
98	Break-even Graph							
99				Regular			Cheaper	
100	Price	Sales	VC	FC	TC	VC	FC	TC
101	+A27	+B27*V101	+$E$49*B27	+$M$75	+X101+Y101	+$F$49*B27	+$M$75+$B$19-$B$20	+AA101+AB101
102	+A28	+B28*V102	+$E$49*B28	+$M$75	+X102+Y102	+$F$49*B28	+$M$75+$B$19-$B$20	+AA102+AB102
103	+A29	+B29*V103	+$E$49*B29	+$M$75	+X103+Y103	+$F$49*B29	+$M$75+$B$19-$B$20	+AA103+AB103
104	+A30	+B30*V104	+$E$49*B30	+$M$75	+X104+Y104	+$F$49*B30	+$M$75+$B$19-$B$20	+AA104+AB104
105	+A31	+B31*V105	+$E$49*B31	+$M$75	+X105+Y105	+$F$49*B31	+$M$75+$B$19-$B$20	+AA105+AB105
106	+A32	+B32*V106	+$E$49*B32	+$M$75	+X106+Y106	+$F$49*B32	+$M$75+$B$19-$B$20	+AA106+AB106
107	+A33	+B33*V107	+$E$49*B33	+$M$75	+X107+Y107	+$F$49*B33	+$M$75+$B$19-$B$20	+AA107+AB107

Answer 11.1 *(cont.)*

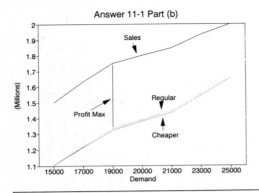

Answer 11-1 Part (b)

Answer 11.2

	A	B	C
1	Answer 11-2: Input Section		
2			
3	Variable Cost	16.00	
4			
5	Maximum Capacity	2,000	per annum
6			
7	Price	Sales	
8		20	2,000
9		30	1,600
10		40	1,200
11		50	1,100
12		60	1,000
13		70	700
14		80	400
15			
16	Year 2 Price	40.00	
17			
18	Demand Option	1,000	units
19			

Answer 11.2 (cont.)

Answer 11-2: Output Section 1

Demand at 3,600 units

	D	E	F	G	H	I	J	K	L	M	N	O
	Price	Sales	Revenue	Production	Total Costs	Net Income	Closing Stock	Production	Sales	Revenue	Net Income	Total
		31/7/X1	31/7/X1	31/7/X1	31/7/X1	31/7/X1		31/7/X2	31/7/X2	31/7/X2	31/7/X2	
26	20	2,000	40,000	2,000	32,000	8,000	0	2,000	2,000	80,000	48,000	56,000
27	30	1,600	48,000	2,000	32,000	16,000	400	2,000	2,400	96,000	64,000	80,000
28	40	1,200	48,000	2,000	32,000	16,000	800	2,000	2,800	112,000	80,000	96,000
29	50	1,100	55,000	2,000	32,000	23,000	900	2,000	2,900	116,000	84,000	107,000
30	60	1,000	60,000	2,000	32,000	28,000	1,000	2,000	3,000	120,000	88,000	116,000
31	70	700	49,000	2,000	32,000	17,000	1,300	2,000	3,300	132,000	100,000	117,000
32	80	400	32,000	2,000	32,000	0	1,600	2,000	3,600	144,000	112,000	112,000

Answer 11-2: Output Section 1 (formulae)

Demand at 3,600 units

	D	E	F	G	H	I	J	K	L	M	N	O
	Price	Sales	Revenue	Production	Total Costs	Net Income	Closing Stock	Production	Sales	Revenue	Net Income	Total
		31/7/X1	31/7/X1	31/7/X1	31/7/X1	31/7/X1		31/7/X2	31/7/X2	31/7/X2	31/7/X2	
26	+A8	+B8	+D26*E26	+$B$5	+G26*$B$3	+F26-H26	+G26-E26	+$B$5	+J26+K2	+L26*$B$16	+M26-H26	+N26+I26
27	+A9	+B9	+D27*E27	+$B$5	+G27*$B$3	+F27-H27	+G27-E27	+$B$5	+J27+K2	+L27*$B$16	+M27-H27	+N27+I27
28	+A10	+B10	+D28*E28	+$B$5	+G28*$B$3	+F28-H28	+G28-E28	+$B$5	+J28+K2	+L28*$B$16	+M28-H28	+N28+I28
29	+A11	+B11	+D29*E29	+$B$5	+G29*$B$3	+F29-H29	+G29-E29	+$B$5	+J29+K2	+L29*$B$16	+M29-H29	+N29+I29
30	+A12	+B12	+D30*E30	+$B$5	+G30*$B$3	+F30-H30	+G30-E30	+$B$5	+J30+K3	+L30*$B$16	+M30-H30	+N30+I30
31	+A13	+B13	+D31*E31	+$B$5	+G31*$B$3	+F31-H31	+G31-E31	+$B$5	+J31+K3	+L31*$B$16	+M31-H31	+N31+I31
32	+A14	+B14	+D32*E32	+$B$5	+G32*$B$3	+F32-H32	+G32-E32	+$B$5	+J32+K3	+L32*$B$16	+M32-H32	+N32+I32

Answer 11.2 (cont.)

Answer 11-2: Output Section 2

Demand at 1,000 units

	P	Q	R	S	T	U	V	W	X	Y	Z	AA
	Price	Sales 31/7/X1	Revenue 31/7/X1	Production 31/7/X1	Total Costs 31/7/X1	Net Income 31/7/X1	Closing Stock	Production 31/7/X2	Sales 31/7/X2	Revenue 31/7/X2	Net Income 31/7/X2	Total
37												
38												
39	20	2,000	40,000	2,000	32,000	8,000	0	1,000	1,000	40,000	24,000	32,000
40	30	1,600	48,000	2,000	32,000	16,000	400	600	1,000	40,000	30,400	46,400
41	40	1,200	48,000	2,000	32,000	16,000	800	200	1,000	40,000	36,800	52,800
42	50	1,100	55,000	2,000	32,000	23,000	900	100	1,000	40,000	38,400	61,400
43	60	1,000	60,000	2,000	32,000	28,000	1,000	0	1,000	40,000	40,000	68,000
44	70	700	49,000	2,000	32,000	17,000	1,300	0	1,000	40,000	40,000	57,000
45	80	400	32,000	2,000	32,000	0	1,600	0	1,000	40,000	40,000	40,000

Answer 11-2: Output Section 2 (formulae)

Demand at 1,000 units

	P	Q	R	S	T	U	V	W	X	Y	Z	AA
	Price	Sales 31/7/X1	Revenue 31/7/X1	Production 31/7/X1	Total Costs 31/7/X1	Net Income 31/7/X1	Closing Stock	Production 31/7/X2	Sales 31/7/X2	Revenue 31/7/X2	Net Income 31/7/X2	Total
37												
38												
39	+A8	+B8	+P39*Q39	+$B$5	+S39*$B$3	+R39-T39	+S39-Q39	@IF($B$18-V39>0,$B$18-V39,0)	+$B$18	+X39*$B$8	+Y39-(W39*$B$3)	+Z39+U39
40	+A9	+B9	+P40*Q40	+$B$5	+S40*$B$3	+R40-T40	+S40-Q40	@IF($B$18-V40>0,$B$18-V40,0)	+$B$18	+X40*$B$8	+Y40-(W40*$B$3)	+Z40+U40
41	+A10	+B10	+P41*Q41	+$B$5	+S41*$B$3	+R41-T41	+S41-Q41	@IF($B$18-V41>0,$B$18-V41,0)	+$B$18	+X41*$B$8	+Y41-(W41*$B$3)	+Z41+U41
42	+A11	+B11	+P42*Q42	+$B$5	+S42*$B$3	+R42-T42	+S42-Q42	@IF($B$18-V42>0,$B$18-V42,0)	+$B$18	+X42*$B$8	+Y42-(W42*$B$3)	+Z42+U42
43	+A12	+B12	+P43*Q43	+$B$5	+S43*$B$3	+R43-T43	+S43-Q43	@IF($B$18-V43>0,$B$18-V43,0)	+$B$18	+X43*$B$8	+Y43-(W43*$B$3)	+Z43+U43
44	+A13	+B13	+P44*Q44	+$B$5	+S44*$B$3	+R44-T44	+S44-Q44	@IF($B$18-V44>0,$B$18-V44,0)	+$B$18	+X44*$B$8	+Y44-(W44*$B$3)	+Z44+U44
45	+A14	+B14	+P45*Q45	+$B$5	+S45*$B$3	+R45-T45	+S45-Q45	@IF($B$18-V45>0,$B$18-V45,0)	+$B$18	+X45*$B$8	+Y45-(W45*$B$3)	+Z45+U45

Answer 11.2 (cont.)

	AB	AC	AD	AE
46	Answer 11-2: Output Section 3			
47				
48	Minimum Price for Unsold Stock			
49				
50	Price	Stock	Profit Change	Sale Price
51	20	0	0	0.00
52	30	0	0	0.00
53	40	0	0	0.00
54	50	0	0	0.00
55	60	0	0	0.00
56	70	300	11,000	36.67
57	80	600	28,000	46.67

	AB	AC	AD	AE
46	Answer 11-2: Output Section 3 (formuale)			
47				
48	Minimum Price for Unsold Stock			
49				
50	Price	Stock	Profit Change	Sale Price
51	+A8	@IF(+V39-$B$18<0,0,+V39-$B$18)	@IF(+AC51=0,0,@MAX($AA$39..$AA$45)-AA39)	@IF(@ISERR(+AD51/AC51),@FALSE,+AD51/AC51)
52	+A9	@IF(+V40-$B$18<0,0,+V40-$B$18)	@IF(+AC52=0,0,@MAX($AA$39..$AA$45)-AA40)	@IF(@ISERR(+AD52/AC52),@FALSE,+AD52/AC52)
53	+A10	@IF(+V41-$B$18<0,0,+V41-$B$18)	@IF(+AC53=0,0,@MAX($AA$39..$AA$45)-AA41)	@IF(@ISERR(+AD53/AC53),@FALSE,+AD53/AC53)
54	+A11	@IF(+V42-$B$18<0,0,+V42-$B$18)	@IF(+AC54=0,0,@MAX($AA$39..$AA$45)-AA42)	@IF(@ISERR(+AD54/AC54),@FALSE,+AD54/AC54)
55	+A12	@IF(+V43-$B$18<0,0,+V43-$B$18)	@IF(+AC55=0,0,@MAX($AA$39..$AA$45)-AA43)	@IF(@ISERR(+AD55/AC55),@FALSE,+AD55/AC55)
56	+A13	@IF(+V44-$B$18<0,0,+V44-$B$18)	@IF(+AC56=0,0,@MAX($AA$39..$AA$45)-AA44)	@IF(@ISERR(+AD56/AC56),@FALSE,+AD56/AC56)
57	+A14	@IF(+V45-$B$18<0,0,+V45-$B$18)	@IF(+AC57=0,0,@MAX($AA$39..$AA$45)-AA45)	@IF(@ISERR(+AD57/AC57),@FALSE,+AD57/AC57)

Answer 12.1

	A	B	C
1	Answer 12-1: Input Section		
2			
3	Barque Ltd		
4			
5	Selling Price per unit £	5.00	
6			
7	Specified Sales (units)	250,000	
8			
9		Method 1	Method 2
10		-----------------------	-----------------------
11	Variable Cost per unit	0.50	1.00
12			
13	Fixed Costs	420,000	370,000
14			
15	Investment	3,000,000	1,000,000
16			
17	Life of Plant	10	10
18			
19	Depreciation	300,000	100,000
20			
21	Advertising	135,000 *	
22			
23	* This value is changed to 0 to answer part (b)		

	D	E	F
26	Answer 12-1: Output Section		
27			
28	Advertising = 0		
29			
30	Break-even Point Calculations		
31			
32		Method 1	Method 2
33		-----------------------	-----------------
34	Contribution Per Unit	4.50	4.00
35			
36	Fixed Costs	720,000	470,000
37			
38	Break-even (Units)	160,000	117,500
39			
40	Break-even (£ 's)	800,000	587,500
41			
42	Maximum Profit	405,000	530,000

Answer 12.1 (*cont.*)

	D	E	F
26	Answer 12-1: Output Section		
27			
28	Advertising = £135,000		
29			
30	Break-even Point Calculations		
31			
32		Method 1	Method 2
33		-------------------------	------------------
34	Contribution Per Unit	4.50	4.00
35			
36	Fixed Costs	855,000	605,000
37			
38	Break-even (Units)	190,000	151,250
39			
40	Break-even (£ 's)	950,000	756,250
41			
42	Maximum Profit	270,000	395,000

	D	E	F
26	Answer 12-1: Output Section		
27			
28	The formula remains unchanged for part (a) and (b)		
29			
30	Break-even Point Calculations		
31			
32		Method 1	Method 2
33		-------------------------	-------------------------
34	Contribution Per Unit	+B5-B11	+B5-C11
35			
36	Fixed Costs	+B13+B19+B21	+C13+C19+B21
37			
38	Break-even (Units)	+E36/E34	+F36/F34
39			
40	Break-even (£ 's)	+E38*B5	+F38*B5
41			
42	Maximum Profit	+B7*E34-E36	+B7*F34-F36

Answer 12.2

	A	B	C	D	E
1	Answer 12-2: Input Section				
2					
3		Reading	Newbury	Basingstoke	Total
4		(000's)	(000's)	(000's)	(000's)
5	Budgeted ticket receipts	1,600	1,200	800	3,600
6					
7	Costs				
8					
9	Film hire	500	400	390	1,290
10					
11	Wages and Salaries	300	250	160	710
12					
13	Overheads	500	400	350	1,250
14					
15	Fixed Costs Apportioned	320	240	160	720
16					
17	Ticket prices	4.00			
18					
19	Basingstoke factor	100% *			
20					
21	* To answer part (a) (i) this cell should be set at 100%				
22	* To answer part (a) (ii) this cell should be set at 0%				
23	* To answer part (e) this cell should be set at 150%				
24					
25	Advertising	0 **			
26					
27	** To answer part (e) this cell should be set at 40				

Answer 12.2 (*cont.*)

	F	G	H	I	J
30	Answer 12-2: Output Section 1				
31					
32	Part (e)				
33					
34	Break-even Point Calculations				
35					
36		Readin	Newbury	Basingstoke	Total
37		(000's)	(000's)	(000's)	(000's)
38	Budgeted ticket receipts	1,600	1,200	1,200	4,000
39					
40	Costs				
41					
42	Film hire	500	400	585	1,485
43					
44	Wages and Salaries	300	250	240	790
45					
46	Variable Overheads	180	160	285	625
47					
48	Contribution	620	390	90	1,100
49					
50	Fixed Costs				760
51					
52	Net profit				340
53					
54	Break-even point				2,764
55					
56	Margin of Safety				30.91%

Answer 12.2 (*cont.*)

	F	G	H	I	J
30	Answer 12-2: Output Section 1				
31					
32	Part (a)(i)				
33					
34	Break-even Point Calculations				
35					
36		Readin	Newbury	Basingstoke	Total
37		(000's)	(000's)	(000's)	(000's)
38	Budgeted ticket receipts	1,600	1,200	800	3,600
39					
40	Costs				
41					
42	Film hire	500	400	390	1,290
43					
44	Wages and Salaries	300	250	160	710
45					
46	Variable Overheads	180	160	190	530
47					
48	Contribution	620	390	60	1,070
49					
50	Fixed Costs				720
51					
52	Net profit				350
53					
54	Break-even point				2,422
55					
56	Margin of Safety				32.71%

Answer 12.2 (*cont.*)

	F	G	H	I	J
30	Answer 12-2: Output Section 1				
31					
32	Part (a)(ii)				
33					
34	Break-even Point Calculations				
35					
36		Readin	Newbury	Basingstoke	Total
37		(000's)	(000's)	(000's)	(000's)
38	Budgeted ticket receipts	1,600	1,200	0	2,800
39					
40	Costs				
41					
42	Film hire	500	400	0	900
43					
44	Wages and Salaries	300	250	0	550
45					
46	Variable Overheads	180	160	0	340
47					
48	Contribution ·	620	390	0	1,010
49					
50	Fixed Costs				720
51					
52	Net profit				290
53					
54	Break-even point				1,996
55					
56	Margin of Safety				28.71%

	F	G	H	I	J
30	Answer 12-2: Output Section 1 (formulae)				
31					
32	The formulae remain unchanged for parts (a) and (e).				
33					
34	Break-even Point Calculations				
35					
36		Reading	Newbury	Basingstoke	Total
37		(000's)	(000's)	(000's)	(000's)
38	Budgeted ticket receipts	+B5	+C5	+D5*$B$19	@SUM(G38..I38)
39					
40	Costs				
41					
42	Film hire	+B9	+C9	+D9*$B$19	@SUM(G42..I42)
43					
44	Wages and Salaries	+B11	+C11	+D11*$B$19	@SUM(G44..I44)
45					
46	Variable Overheads	+B13-B15	+C13-C15	(+D13-D15)*B19	@SUM(G46..I46)
47					
48	Contribution	+G38-@SUM(G42..G46)	+H38-@SUM(H42..H46)	+I38-@SUM(I42..I46)	+J38-@SUM(J42..
49					
50	Fixed Costs				+E15+B25
51					
52	Net profit				+J48-J50
53					
54	Break-even point				+J50/(J48/J38)
55					
56	Margin of Safety				(J38-J54)/J38

Answer 12.2 *(cont.)*

	K	L	M	N	O
58	Answer 12-2: Output Section 2				
59					
60	Part (c) Contribution per ticket				
61					
62		Reading	Newbury	Basingstoke	Total
63		(000's)	(000's)	(000's)	(000's)
64					
65	Budgeted ticket receipts	1,600	1,200	800	3,600
66					
67	Volume of sales	400	300	200	900
68					
69	Contribution per ticket	1.55	1.30	0.30	

	K	L	M	N	O
58	Answer 12-2: Output Section 2 (formulae)				
59					
60	Part (c) Contribution per ticket				
61					
62		Reading	Newbury	Basingstoke	Total
63		(000's)	(000's)	(000's)	(000's)
64					
65	Budgeted ticket receipts	+B5	+C5	+D5	+E5
66					
67	Volume of sales	+L65/$B$17	+M65/$B$17	+N65/$B$17	+O65/$B$17
68					
69	Contribution per ticket	+G48/L67	+H48/M67	+I48/N67	

Answer 13.4

	A	B	C	D
1	Answer 13-4 (a) Input Section			
2				
3		£	£	
4	Selling Price		50	
5	Variable Costs:			
6	Production	30		
7	Selling	5		
8		----------------	35	
9			----------------	
10	Contribution per medal		15	
11				
12	Fixed Costs:			
13	Production	5		
14	Selling	1		
15		----------------	6	
16			----------------	
17	Profit per medal		9	
18			=====	
19				
20	Current Output Level		20,000	medals
21				
22	Proposed Output Level		40,000	medals
23				
24	Additional Rent		210,000	

	E	F	G
25	Answer 13-4 (a) Output Section (formulae)		
26			
27	Breakeven Points		
28			
29		Current	Proposed
30			
31	Fixed Costs	+C15*C20	(+C15*C20)+C24
32			
33	Contribution per medal	+$C$10	+$C$10
34			
35	Break-even output	+F31/F33	+G31/G33
36			
37	Margin of Safety (medals)	+C20-F35	+C22-G35
38			
39	Margin of Safety % target	+F37/C20	+G37/C22

Answer 13.4 (*cont.*)

	E	F	G
25	Answer 13-4 (a) Output Section (formulae)		
26			
27	Break-even Points		
28			
29		Current	Proposed
30			
31	Fixed Costs	+C15*C20	(+C15*C20)+C24
32			
33	Contribution per medal	+$C$10	+$C$10
34			
35	Break-even output	+F31/F33	+G31/G33
36			
37	Margin of Safety (medals)	+C20-F35	+C22-G35
38			
39	Margin of Safety. % target	+F37/C20	+G37/C22

	A	B	C	D
1	Answer 13-4 (b) Input Section			
2				
3				
4			Able	Baker
5				
6	Direct Materials per unit £		10.00	30.00
7				
8	Direct Labour	Rate per hour £	Hours	Hours
9	Grinding	5.00	7	5
10	Finishing	7.50	15	9
11				
12	Selling price per unit £		206.50	168.00
13				
14	Budgeted production (units)		1,200	600
15				
16	Maximum sales for the period (units)		1,500	800

	E	F	G	H	I	J
17	Answer 13-4 (b) Output Section 1					
18						
19	Contribution Statement					
20						
21						
22			Able		Baker	
23	Selling price		206.50		168.00	
24						
25	Direct Materials	10.00		30.00		
26						
27	Direct Labour					
28	Grinding	35.00		25.00		
29	Finishing	112.50		67.50		
30		---------------	157.50	---------------	122.50	
31			----------------		----------------	
32	Contribution per unit		49.00		45.50	
33	Budgeted production		1,200		600	
34			----------------		----------------	
35	Total Contribution		58,800		27,300	86,100
36			=====		=====	=====

Answer 13.4 *(cont.)*

	E	F	G	H	I	J
17	Answer 13-4 (b) Output Section 1 (formulae)					
18						
19	Contribution Statement					
20						
21						
22			Able		Baker	
23	Selling price	+C12		+D12		
24						
25	Direct Materials	+C6		+D6		
26						
27	Direct Labour					
28	Grinding	+C9*$B$9		+D9*$B$9		
29	Finishing	+C10*$B$10		+D10*$B$10		
30		-------------------	@SUM(F25..F29)	-------------------	@SUM(H25..H29)	
31		-----------------------------		-----------------------------		
32	Contribution per unit	+G23-G30		+I23-I30		
33	Budgeted production	+C14		+D14		
34		-----------------------------		-----------------------------		
35	Total Contribution	+G32*G33		+I32*I33	+G35+I35	
36		==========		==========	======	

	K	L	M	N
37	Answer 13-4 (b) Output Section 2			
38				
39	Contribution for scarce resource			
40				
41		Able	Baker	
42				
43	Contribution per unit	49.00	45.50	
44				
45	Grinding Labour Hours	7.00	5.00	
46				
47	Contribution per hour	7.00	9.10	
48				
49	Maximum Sales	1,500	800	
50				
51	Potential Hours	10,500	4,000	
52				
53	Budgeted Maximum	11,400	11,400	
54				
55	Contribution from Best Usage	0.00	9.10	
56				
57	Contribution from Second Best Usa	7.00	0.00	
58				
59	Maximum Best Usage	0	36,400	
60				
61	Remaining Hours	7,400	0	
62				
63	Remaining Usage	51,800	0	
64		---------------	---------------	
65	Contribution maximum	51,800	36,400	88,200
66		=====	=====	=====

Answer 13.4 (*cont.*)

	K	L	M	N
37	Answer 13-4 (b) Output Section 2 (formulae)			
38				
39	Contribution for scarce resource			
40				
41		Able	Baker	
42				
43	Contribution per unit	+G32	+I32	
44				
45	Grinding Labour Hours	+C9	+D9	
46				
47	Contribution per hour	+L43/L45	+M43/M45	
48				
49	Maximum Sales	+C16	+D16	
50				
51	Potential Hours	+L49*L45	+M49*M45	
52				
53	Budgeted Maximum	(+$C$14*$C$9)+(+$D$14*$D$9)	(+$C$14*$C$9)+(+$D$14*$D$9)	
54				
55	Contribution from Best Usage	@IF(L47>M47,L47,0)	@IF(M47>L47,M47,0)	
56				
57	Contribution from Second Best Usag	@IF(L55=0,L47,0)	@IF(M55=0,M47,0)	
58				
59	Maximum Best Usage	(+L49*L45)*L55	(+M49*M45)*M55	
60				
61	Remaining Hours	@IF(L55=0,L53-M51,0)	@IF(M55=0,M53-L51,0)	
62				
63	Remaining Usage	+L61*L57	+M61*M57	
64		----------------------------------	----------------------------------	
65	Contribution maximum	+L59+L63	+M59+M63	+L65+M65
66		====================	====================	=======

Answer 14.2

	A	B	C
1	Answer 14-2: Input Section		
2			
3	Year	Project A	Project B
4	0	(200,000)	(200,000)
5	1	120,000	70,000
6	2	120,000	90,000
7	3	80,000	130,000
8	4	100,000	200,000
9			
10	Life of Project	4	4
11			
12	End Scrap Value	40,000	40,000
13			
14	Cost of Capital	16%	

Answer 14.2 (*cont.*)

	D	E	F	G
15	Answer 14-2: Output Section 1			
16				
17			Project A	Project B
18				
19	Net Present Value		99,110	120,973

	D	E	F	G
15	Answer 14-2: Output Section 1 (formulae)			
16				
17			Project A	Project B
18				
19	Net Present Value		+B4+@NPV($B$14,AFLOW)	+C4+@NPV($B$14,BFLOW)

	H	I	J	K	L
20	Answer 14-2: Output Section 2				
21					
22				Project A	Project B
23	Av. Annual Cash Flow			95,000	112,500
24					
25	Annual Depreciation			40,000	40,000
26				--------------------	--------------------
27	Av. Annual Accounting Profit			55,000	72,500
28					
29	Average Investment			120,000	120,000
30					
31	Accounting Rate of Return			45.83%	60.42%

	H	I	J	K	L
20	Answer 14-2: Output Section 2 (formulae)				
21					
22				Project A	Project B
23	Av. Annual Cash Flow			@AVG(AFLOW)-(B12/B10)	@AVG(BFLOW)-(C12/C10)
24					
25	Annual Depreciation			@SLN(-B4,B12,B10)	@SLN(-C4,C12,C10)
26				-------------------------------------	-------------------------------------
27	Av. Annual Accounting Profit			+K23-K25	+L23-L25
28					
29	Average Investment			(-B4+B12)/2	(-C4+C12)/2
30					
31	Accounting Rate of Return			+K27/K29	+L27/L29

Answer 14.2 (*cont.*)

	M	N	O	P	Q	R	S
32	Answer 14-2: Output Section 3						
33							
34		A			B		
35		NCF	Cum.		NCF	Cum.	
36	Year			Year			
37	0	(200,000)	(200,000)	0	(200,000)	(200,000)	
38	1	120,000	(80,000)	1	70,000	(130,000)	
39	2	120,000	40,000	2	90,000	(40,000)	
40	3	80,000	120,000	3	130,000	90,000	
41	4	100,000	220,000	4	200,000	290,000	
42							
43	Payback Period is:			2 years		3 years	

	M	N	O	P	Q	R	S
32	Answer 14-2: Output Section 3 (formulae)						
33							
34		A			B		
35		NCF	Cum.		NCF	Cum.	
36	Year			Year			
37	0	+B4	+N37	0	+C4	+Q37	
38	1	+B5	+N38+O37	1	+C5	+Q38+R37	
39	2	+B6	+N39+O38	2	+C6	+Q39+R38	
40	3	+B7	+N40+O39	3	+C7	+Q40+R39	
41	4	+B8	+N41+O40	4	+C8	+Q41+R40	
42							
43	Payback Period is:			2 years		3 years	
44							
45	N.B. Please refer to Chapter 14 for the payback formulae.						

Index